Investing Psychology

Investing Psychology

The Effects of Behavioral Finance on Investment Choice and Bias

TIM RICHARDS

Creator of the Psy-Fi Blog
(www.psyfitec.com)

WILEY

Published by John Wiley & Sons, Inc., Hoboken, New Jersey.
Published simultaneously in Canada.

For general information on our other products and services or for technical support, please contact our Customer Care Department within the United States at (800) 762-2974, outside the United States at (317) 572-3993 or fax (317) 572-4002.

Wiley publishes in a variety of print and electronic formats and by print-on-demand. Some material included with standard print versions of this book may not be included in e-books or in print-on-demand. If this book refers to media such as a CD or DVD that is not included in the version you purchased, you may download this material at http://booksupport.wiley.com. For more information about Wiley products, visit www.wiley.com.

Library of Congress Cataloging-in-Publication Data:

Richards, Tim, 1961-
   Investing psychology : the effects of behavioral finance on investment choice and bias / Tim Richards.
      pages cm.—(Wiley finance series)
   Includes bibliographical references and index.
   ISBN 978-1-118-72219-0 (cloth)
   1. Investments—Psychological aspects. 2. Finance—Psychological aspects. I. Title.
   HG4515.15.R53 2014
   332.601'9--dc23

                                                                2013050096

Printed in the United States of America

10 9 8 7 6 5 4 3 2 1

To Skyla, Alexa, and Hallie;
for being there always,
as I will always be here for you.

Contents

Preface

As we move forward through the twenty-first century, it's more and more important for investors to understand the unconscious drivers that affect the way they make decisions about money because increasingly we're being left to fend for ourselves. It wasn't so long ago that retirees could look forward to a comfortable old age supported by employee sponsored, defined benefit pension plans and a generous social security system. Those days have gone, and more often than not we're being left to make our own investing decisions using 401(k) plans and other individually managed accounts.

At the same time, a vast expansion of the financial services industry has put us in charge of many more financial decisions—no longer are we limited in how much we can borrow by a wise old bank manager, but we are left to decide how much we can repay—and we must take the consequences when these decisions go wrong. This is especially so as a huge industry has grown up to exploit our biases, in order to part us from our money. The securities industry is a gigantic machine for extracting money from ordinary investors, and does so in a way that makes it all seem perfectly reasonable.

All this is happening as lifespans are lengthening due to improvements in medical care and a better understanding of healthy living. So the decisions we make about our money will determine whether our lengthening old ages are played out in comfort or misery. Learning how, and why, we make these decisions, and how we can improve them, should be a priority for all of us.

Although we've been given greater freedom of choice than ever before, we've not been granted any greater wisdom, or given any training about how to proceed. That's what this book is about, how to use the opportunity we've been given, how to avoid the traps set by our own minds and by those people who want to exploit them. It's a fascinating journey and one, I believe, that will leave you with a permanent advantage over those who don't choose to join us.

Although this is a book with a serious purpose, and is full of carefully chosen academic research to illustrate the points that I want to make, it is not, I hope, a seriously difficult read. Writing an important book that no one reads because it's too difficult and clever would be missing the point: unless this material is accessible to investors and their advisers, it can't help them.

Equally, though, I'd urge you not to be fooled by the often light-hearted tone—this is a book with a very serious purpose—to help us figure out how to overcome the enemy within, our own brains. Because if we can't, then we will end up being seriously impoverished.

The book is divided into nine chapters, the first four of which deal with particular aspects of the behavioral flaws that drive us to throw our money at people who are already rich. This is a whistle-stop tour of dozens of different types of behavioral biases, which intends to kick away any illusions you have about yourself and your investing abilities and trample them into the dust.

We start by looking at how our senses often fool us into thinking that there are things going on out there, when they're actually only going on in our heads. Our brains are attuned to the world around us, and they function in a way that gives us the best chance of survival; but these behaviors are often not appropriate when we're investing. Believing that we can influence or even predict markets in a desperate attempt to keep our brains happy is a one-way ticket to penury.

The second chapter looks at how our feelings of self-image and self-worth impact our investing behavior. Far from being careful, emotionless analyzers of financial data, most of us are as concerned about whether it looks like we're good investors as whether we actually are. Above all, we're horribly overoptimistic about our investing talents, and we go to great care to avoid proving that we're wrong: none of which is designed to improve our finances.

We then move onto the tricky subject of situation—the nasty fact that how we invest depends not on rock-solid objective facts but is dependent on the situation we find ourselves in. Sometimes this situation is environmental, sometimes it's other people, but if we're not on our guard it will always influence our investing approach, and usually not in a good way.

The fourth chapter delves into the complex area of social interaction, and the ways that different forms of group behavior can change our investing decisions. It's possible to get people to change their minds simply by modifying the way we ask a question, and this is exploited by a wide range of different influencers, from politicians to corporate managements. We're social animals, and we're very susceptible to social pressures, even though we don't always realize it.

You might think that the various professionals in the securities industry would be better able to resist these different types of behavioral pressure but, as Chapter 5 discusses, the truth is somewhat different. Although many professionals are more capable of managing their biases than private investors, they're exposed to a range of different incentives—and incentives can change behavior, often in ways that aren't in our interests. By all means use a professional money manager, but make sure you know how to manage them.

Although the study of behavioral finance is over 40 years old, in many ways it's still in its infancy and, although increasingly we know what to look for, the techniques for dealing with the problems are lagging behind. In the next chapter we look at some investing methods and how they relate to behavioral bias and discuss some techniques that can be used to help debias our investing decision making. Perhaps the biggest takeaway is that bias will always be with us—it's when we think we've got it cracked that we're most at risk.

In Chapter 7 we develop these ideas around investing methods and debiasing techniques into a method, or rather a methodology, to affect cognitive repairs—in essence, to shore up our dodgy defenses with a method that forces us step-by-step to consider the main issues. Above all, though, this approach is one that emphasizes change rather than stasis—what works today may not work tomorrow and learning to deal with that is a major component in dealing with behavioral issues.

Many of our biases are actually justified by what I describe as myths—ideas that have taken hold of our minds and have become accepted truths. In Chapter 8 I identify a bunch of these and show why we need to question everything. All too often what we believe to be true is not, and refusing to accept any idea unquestioningly is a habit we need to get into if we're going to improve our investing decision making.

Finally, in the last chapter, I round all of this up into seven key takeaways—but I'd urge you not to jump to the end. In this case the journey is every bit as important as the destination, because if you don't know why you need to behave in a certain way you'll never understand what you need to do when the situation you're in changes. And, in investing, the situation changes all the time.

So, let's get started. Let's go meet the enemy: our own brains.

CHAPTER 1

Sensory Finance

Wandering around inside the average investor's mind is very much like taking a tourist bus around Wonderland with the White Rabbit as a guide. Much that we think is obviously true turns out to be false and much self-evident nonsense is rather closer to reality than we could ever have thought.

We're going to start our tour in a place where everyone can "definitely" tell the difference between truth and falsehood, by looking at the way our senses interact with the world around us. Our ability to interact with the world and to learn from it allows us to extrapolate into the future, to make predictions and then to act on those predictions.

Unfortunately, the skills that serve us so well in everyday life combine to betray us in the topsy-turvy world of investing and finance. Our sensory system may keep us alive, but that's no guarantee it's going to make us rich.

BEATING THE BIAS BLIND SPOT

Although it's quite easy to convince people that we're biased in the way we perceive the world, it's very hard to persuade individuals that they are personally just as biased as everyone else. This is pretty irrational—how likely is it that you're the only unbiased person around? Yet there's an underlying reason for this belief and it says that we think we're better judges of the world around us than everyone else. Unfortunately, we're wrong and you are just as biased as me, and I'm just as biased as everyone else. Or I would be, if I hadn't spent a lot of time figuring out how to reduce my biases.

To demonstrate this we can start with a simple visual illusion, such as the one in Figure 1.1, where the two parallel lines are actually the same length, but don't look it. Don't take my word for it; get out a ruler and measure the lines. Remember: don't trust anyone until they've proven they deserve your trust. This trick is known as the Müller-Lyer illusion, and the unsubtle point I'm trying to make is that you can't entirely trust what your

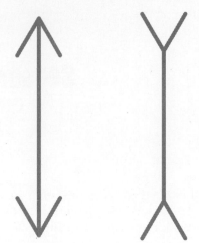

FIGURE 1.1   The Müller-Lyer Illusion

brain is telling you about what you see, which then leads to the idea that you can't always trust it about what you think. What the research shows is that it's virtually impossible to make people behave less irrationally until they can be made to accept this. The good news is that once the message gets home there are a lot of things we can do to improve matters. The less good news is that this is hard to achieve; people don't like to think they're biased, even if they're perfectly happy to believe everyone else is.

In fact, the Müller-Lyer illusion has a bit more to tell us about why we're not very good at financial decision making than it first appears. Many of the behavioral biases we meet arise for very good reasons. They're adaptations of our brain's limited processing power, designed to meet the needs of our ancestors, who were generally more concerned about not being flattened by woolly mammoths or mauled by saber-toothed tigers than they were about being fooled by financial advisers. These days, unfortunately, the predators are far harder to spot, although usually they're less hairy and toothy.

Currently, the best theory about why the Müller-Lyer illusion occurs is that it's accidentally triggering our brain's 3D mapping processes, which are tuned to "see" perspective, so we automatically "adjust" the lengths to suit this hypothesis: as Figure 1.2 shows, a real-world interpretation of the illusion suggests we're looking at the corners of a room or a box. In the real world, looking at a 3D scene like this is a far, far more common experience than someone randomly wandering up to us and showing us pictures of lines with arrowheads stuck on the end of them. For this reason, we need to be quite careful about the conclusions we draw from research in this field,

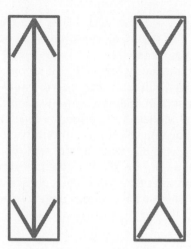

FIGURE 1.2   The Müller-Lyer Illusion as a 3D Perception

because what happens in the laboratory sometimes doesn't match up with what happens in real life.

As the Müller-Lyer illusion suggests, you can't even trust what your eyes are telling you because what we see is actually in the brain, not out there in the world, and therefore subject to whatever kinds of interpretation the brain decides to make. In fact, your eyes can't even see everything in front of you. Look at the picture in Figure 1.3, close your right eye, and focus on the + sign, holding the book about 20 inches away from your face. Now move your head towards the book, continuing to focus on the + sign. At some point the dot will vanish.

This is the point at which the image of the dot is falling on the blind spot in your left eye, where the optic nerve enters the back of the eye. Notice that your brain doesn't insert a gap where the dot should be, there's just a continuous blank field—this is your brain automatically filling in the gap as best it can. But what you're seeing is not what is actually there, and we're all affected by this, all the time. What we "see" is constructed inside the brain, based on the evidence of our eyes—but seeing is not the same as believing.

People have a similar problem when it comes to the mental filling in that accompanies behavioral biases: what the psychologists Emily Pronin and Matthew Kugler have dubbed a *bias blind spot*.[1] You'll happily agree that other people are subject to all sorts of biases, but you'll then argue that

●   +

FIGURE 1.3   + Sign

you yourself are a better judge of what biases you are affected by—which generally means that you think you can overcome your brain's willingness to fill in the gaps in your knowledge by making wild guesses and hopeful inferences, while simultaneously believing that no one else can.

Well, I'm sorry, but you're not *that* special. None of us are. Just as we all have a visual blind spot in each eye, which we don't normally notice, and we're all caught by the Müller-Lyer illusion, we're all trapped by the behavioral instincts that guided our forebears so well. The trick is to accept this, and move on—but, believe me, that's harder said than done. This chapter, and the ones that follow it, are about trying to convince you, against all your instincts, that you can't trust your brain, particularly when it comes to financial matters. Our brains have serious money issues, which impoverish us unnecessarily.

LESSON 1

Don't think that you are immune to the behavioral biases in this book: that's an outcome of the *bias blind spot*. Everyone thinks that they can overcome this by introspection, but no one actually can, anymore than you can overcome your eyes' blind spot or the Müller-Lyer illusion.

ILLUSORY PATTERN RECOGNITION

We use simple processes to navigate our way through life. We look at what happens around us and extrapolate to the future—so most of the time cars drive on the right and people in hospitals wearing white coats are doctors. Unfortunately, this process of relying on personal observation doesn't always work: in Britain the cars drive on the left and doctors in hospitals don't wear white coats—what works at home is often a local rule, not a general one, and this is especially true in stock markets. Get this wrong and you'll get knocked down by a car coming the "wrong" way and struggle to find anyone to treat your injuries.

In particular, we can generate illusory patterns using personal investing experiences, which can cause us to make really stupid decisions because we start imagining we can see trends where none really exist. Visual illusions are a type of illusory pattern, so they're an easy way of showing us we can't entirely trust our instincts and they give us some clues about how our brains interpret information about the world. In Western cultures, one of the most common illusions is the Man in the Moon effect: the perception of a human face peering at us across the void of space. This is an example of a bias called pareidolia, the ability to see order in randomness. Pareidolia gives rise to all sorts of peculiar behaviors, many of which seem to involve images of religious figures appearing in bakery products.

All of this is vaguely amusing, but masks a serious issue. In general, we try to fit the facts to our own preconceptions, rather than theorizing on the basis of the data. We'll see patterns where none really exist, we'll extrapolate on the basis of these illusory patterns, and we'll then wonder why we've lost a ton of money. People who see images of Mother Teresa in a cinnamon bun are using their imagination and memories to "see" the picture. Someone who had no idea who Mother Teresa was would just slather on some butter and eat it.

Illusory pattern recognition is a dangerous behavioral trait where investing is concerned, because much of what investors do is exactly that: we look for patterns. You'll frequently find people commenting on how similar current market conditions are to those from some past period, or see them pouring over charts of various kinds, trying to use them to predict what's going to happen next. This is nearly all based on a perceptual fallacy because the future of investment markets isn't written in the past in ways that can be easily extracted from the data through any kind of simple pattern analysis.

Mostly, though, we don't even bother trying to analyze anything, because we didn't evolve in an environment where we had the benefit of reams of statistics and we had to operate on the basis of what researchers call "observed frequencies": essentially we looked at what was going on around us and extrapolated from that data. So, if we were unlucky enough to have a family member stomped on by an irate woolly mammoth then we'd conclude that hairy pachyderms were dangerous, and resolve to avoid them whenever possible, and we'd tell everyone we knew to do so too. In our local neighborhood, avoiding the local mad mammoth would probably have been a good decision, but it might have been that we were simply unlucky enough to live in an area populated by particularly bad tempered mammoths and a hundred miles down the coast we'd be more in danger from big cats with big teeth. In general, more people might have died in the jaws of tigers than at the feet of mammoths, but that wouldn't have changed our own local view of the world and we'd take special care to avoid mammoths because that was the data—the experience—that we had available to us.

For investors, what's especially interesting about this is that it appears that there's a link between illusory pattern recognition, lack of self-control, and poor investment returns. Some remarkable research published in *Science*, by management research experts Jennifer Whitson and Adam Galinsky,[2] showed that people made to feel like they were out of control were more likely to see nonexistent objects in fuzzy displays, to create conspiracy theories, and to think superstitious behavior was able to change future events. In particular, they demonstrated similar behavior among expert investors in stock markets, showing the creation of illusory patterns in uncertain, volatile, and unpredictable conditions. This suggests that these conditions will cause us to generate random connections between events which, to all intents and purposes, look like superstitions, the key to which is that they allow us to try and exert control over the uncontrollable: they turn the unpredictable markets we can't control into patterns that we think we can use to predict the future.

Only we can't: we can't control or predict anything that happens in the stock market, and thinking we can is a dangerous misstep. Our personal experiences are not a reliable guide to future investment decisions and thinking that they are will lead to losses. What's worse is that the very times we most need to keep our wits about us—when the markets are in the middle of one of their periodic manic-depressive phases—are the same as when we're most likely to feel out of control, to imagine illusory patterns, and make really bad decisions.

LESSON 2

Don't extrapolate from personal experiences to general stock market trends: this will lead to *pareidolia* or *illusory pattern recognition* based on *observed frequencies*. Making investment decisions based on these intuitions will lose you money more often than not.

SUPERSTITIOUS PIGEONS—AND INVESTORS

It's no surprise that those investors who detected illusory patterns developed behaviors that look a lot like superstitions, because people are surprisingly inclined to develop irrational habits to bring them luck. Most of the time this doesn't really matter, but when these superstitions start overriding sensible investment decisions they can lead us into serious money-losing territory. It's very easy to develop investment superstitions because these can be triggered by a simple trick known as reinforcement. Unfortunately, investment markets are full of opportunities for reinforcement and if people don't continually monitor themselves they'll almost certainly fall victim to such problems.

Reinforcement is the same mechanism that Pavlov used to train his famous dogs to salivate at the sound of a bell and, in another famous example, the psychologist B. F. Skinner did something similar with pigeons. He developed an experiment in which he placed hungry pigeons in cages and then delivered food to them at irregular, random intervals. The birds developed responses that, to all intents and purposes, appeared to be superstitions linked to whatever actions they happened to be performing at the time that food was first served: head bobbing, turning repeatedly in the same direction, and so on.[3] This is another form of illusory pattern recognition, connected to a very basic instinct to get some control over their environments, even in situations where it's not possible.

Skinner went on to show that intermittent reinforcement—sometimes providing food in response to a superstitious action and sometimes not— actually *increased* the persistence of the behavior. The fact that the miracle movements quite often didn't work didn't have the effect of making the birds wonder whether they'd come up with a false hypothesis but simply made them try harder. Pigeons whose superstitions were intermittently reinforced with food proved immensely resistant to giving up their pet theories about how to get fed—one repeated its hopping behavior over 10,000 times after reinforcement had stopped.

Of course, we're not pigeon-brained, but there's quite a lot of evidence that suggests that simple learning processes like these are the basis for some of the most basic rules of thumb—what psychologists call *heuristics*—that guide us through our lives. We learn, from a very early age, that cause and effect are related, and we're always on the lookout for such links because they're excellent mental shortcuts, and very important if we're in a hurry, or tired, or hungry, or distracted by the kids, or simply too lazy to be bothered to think.

To be frank, it's quite hard to think of an environment more likely to give someone intermittent reinforcement of their beliefs than financial markets. If you wait a while, pretty much everything that can happen will happen. So if someone develops a pet theory about how and when they're successful, which occasionally works and which they never test with real data, it's quite easy to see why they'll continue to persist in damaging strategies in the teeth of the evidence. Stock markets, and other investment markets, are terrible places for humans operating on these legacy heuristics because it's all too easy to learn the wrong lessons from a few samples.

Research into the way that American investors in 401(k) investment plans operate suggests that pigeon type behavior definitely isn't confined to the birds.[4] Investors whose plans make high returns invest more, and investors who suffer from high volatility—wild swings in the value of their plans—invest less, as compared to those who get the opposite results. Having looked at a number of other possible explanations and dismissed them, the researchers concluded that this looks like basic reinforcement learning in action, where people simply extrapolate from their personal experiences that what's worked in the past will continue to work in the future. In everyday life, as a general rule-of-thumb, that's a valid approach but sadly the future performance of investment plans isn't predicted by their pasts, so the lessons learned aren't much more useful than doing a funky head bobbing, side to side dance. It's fairly typical of how basically sound heuristics fail when it comes to managing our money.

It's very hard to avoid developing investment superstitions, because they're attractive shortcuts, which means we don't have to do any hard work thinking about our investments. The only way to manage this is to actually test your theories. That's easier said than done, but the trick is to keep track of your investments and returns properly. Don't rely on your gut feeling because you'll be wrong—often surprisingly wrong.

For example, when Markus Glaser and Martin Weber analyzed how inexperienced investors operated, they uncovered that most of them didn't have a clue whether they were making any money or not, which suggests that they're highly unlikely to be learning anything much at all from their experiences.[5] If you're not getting any feedback then you're not going to change any investing superstitions you might have acquired along the way, like taking tips from strangers on Internet bulletin boards, reacting to TV pundits, "buying on the dips," or any of the myriad other ways there are of losing money in stocks. It's a simple, but important rule: make sure you know what your returns are, and analyze why things go wrong. Otherwise, you'll likely keep on repeating the same mistakes, just like Skinner's pigeons.

LESSON 3

Be very careful that you don't develop investment *superstitions*, based on your own personal experiences. These will fail just as soon as you really need them to work, but will probably offer enough *intermittent reinforcement* to keep you trading for far longer than is wise: make sure you know your investment returns and make an effort to learn from them. Bird-brains are for the pigeons, we don't have to behave the same way.

THE SUPER BOWL EFFECT: IF IT LOOKS TOO GOOD TO BE TRUE, IT IS

All too often, spurious patterns and superstitious thinking accidentally produce the right results and then get dressed up as good investment advice. Smart investors need to hone their critical faculties to detect these fake tools, in just the same way they need to be wary of people who claim to have a perfect investing strategy. For example, take the Super Bowl effect.

The Super Bowl effect states that the conference of the winner of the Super Bowl predicts the direction of stock markets in the following year. If the NFC team wins the markets go up, if the AFC team wins they go down. This is a completely crazy idea, yet it worked 28 years out of 31 between 1967 and 1997. Despite being an impressive result, it's certainly a complete coincidence. Consider that it was equally possible to predict the winner of the Super Bowl from the direction of the stock market: do you believe that's likely?

Of course, no one does. The winner of the Super Bowl is determined on the field of play through the relative strengths of the teams. We can roughly conceive of the things that will make a difference—strategy, individual battles between players, snap decisions by coaches and the quarterbacks, and so on—and we recognize that there's an element of luck involved. But, by and large, we feel comfortable that we understand the range of probable outcomes and what will determine them. No sensible football fan really thinks that the whims of Wall Street's finest will decide who carries off the spoils.

The stock market is swayed by infinitely more complicated factors than the result of the Super Bowl: political decisions, economic factors, mass psychological trends, consumer confidence, changes in population demographics—a whole range of stuff that no one in their right mind thinks they can forecast with any real chance of success (the fact that there's a whole industry dedicated to trying to make such predictions doesn't make that last statement any less true). So why on Earth would anyone think that the result of the Super Bowl could possibly influence market returns?

Well, of course, it's about our need to try and predict the future on the basis of experience using whatever patterns we can detect. The fact that financial markets are so darned complicated that even the most clever people backed up by the most powerful computers in the world don't have more than the faintest clue what they're going to do next doesn't stop us from trying to do this, and we latch onto any random superstition that seems to help us.

So, we need to be suspicious of simple explanations and surefire investment plans. If it looks too good to be true, it undoubtedly is. No one with a basic understanding of investment could have possibly believed the returns that Bernie Madoff was making for years, yet many intelligent people happily gave him their life savings, having apparently taken leave of their critical senses. Hone your sensors to detect rubbish explanations because as soon as you start to trust them they'll fail on you, with disastrous financial consequences.

LESSON 4

Beware of simple explanations for complex market movements and surefire techniques for making money. Remember that the *Super Bowl effect* doesn't predict the movement of markets any more than markets predict the outcome of the Super Bowl. Learn to be skeptical in the face of investment theories.

YOUR FINANCIAL HOROSCOPE: FORECASTING AND THE BARNUM EFFECT

Unfortunately, there are lots of people around who will try to take advantage by using our biases against us. We're amazingly credulous about "expert" opinions, especially when they're designed to trigger our capacity to look for patterns and meanings where none exist. For example, take horoscopes.

Most sensible people don't really believe in horoscopes even if they occasionally glance at them for amusement. Yet when it comes to investing we're happy to rely on the financial industry's equivalents: newspaper articles, stock-tipping magazines, and investment reports. It's a bit of a shock to realize that these expensive and professionally produced pieces of stock analysis are about as reliable a way of forecasting the future as the mystic divining of astrologers, soothsayers, and necromancers. They all rely on a simple behavioral trick, known as the Barnum effect, using your brain's own preferences to fool you.

Consider the following horoscope, and think about how closely it fits your personal situation:

You have a great need for other people to like and admire you. You have a tendency to be critical of yourself. You have a great deal of unused capacity, which you have not turned to your advantage.

While you have some personality weaknesses you are generally able to compensate for them. Your sexual adjustment has presented problems for you. Disciplined and self-controlled on the outside, you tend to be worrisome and insecure on the inside. At times you have serious doubts as to whether you have made the right decision or done the right thing. You prefer a certain amount of change and variety and become dissatisfied when hemmed in by restrictions and limitations. You pride yourself as an independent thinker and do not accept others' statements without satisfactory proof. You have found it unwise to be too frank in revealing yourself to others. At times you are extroverted, affable, sociable, while at other times you are introverted, wary, and reserved. Some of your aspirations tend to be pretty unrealistic. Security is one of your major goals in life.

Could this be describing you?

In 1949, psychologist Bertram Forer[6] presented this to each of his students, telling them it had been individually customized for each of them, asking if the horoscope accurately represented them. Most of them agreed that it did, even though they were all presented with exactly the same statement. It's basic human nature to see insightful information in random rubbish: we read into information what we want to, based on our own experiences. This is the *Barnum effect*, named for the famous entertainer P. T. Barnum, who observed that "we've got something for everyone" even though it would have been truer to state that everyone had something for him—their money. As Forer noted of his students:

> *It was pointed out to them that the experiment had been performed as an object lesson to demonstrate the tendency to be overly impressed by vague statements and to endow the diagnostician with an unwarrantedly high degree of insight. Similarities between the demonstration and the activities of charlatans were pointed out.*

If you were to replace the word "charlatans" with "stock market forecasters" you'd be getting close to the truth in our investing world. In general, we look for evidence to support our hypotheses, not to reject them—so when we're presented with random information we look for things we recognize and then latch onto them. It's an advanced form of illusory pattern recognition, but a biased one: If the horoscope above had contained mainly negative statements do you think the students would have agreed that it described them? Would you?

LESSON 5

Be wary of anyone who confidently predicts market movements: at best they're trading on the *Barnum effect*, trying to deliberately exploit your tendency to think "experts" know more than you do. At worst they believe their own shtick. Remember that we always look for evidence to confirm our beliefs, so be careful when you hear or read something that makes you feel good about yourself or your investments.

UNCERTAINTY: THE UNKNOWN UNKNOWNS

You may have noticed a couple of themes so far in this chapter. The first, obviously, is about pattern recognition, why we rely on it and how it keeps on leading us into investment mistakes based on superstitions and plausible but unprovable theories. The other one is that markets are very unpredictable places, which is why our patterns don't always help us as investors. There's a technical term for this, known as "uncertainty," and understanding this is a key takeaway from this chapter.

Uncertainty is an odd concept, but for our purposes we can think of it as the stuff that happens in the world that we can't predict. Former U.S. Secretary of State Donald Rumsfeld called these the "unknown unknowns": the things that we don't know we don't know. The unknown unknowns of the world are always with us, but a lot of the time we ignore this uncertainty. Roughly, if you feel confident about the future, if you believe that your job is going well and the mortgage is going to be paid, you're pretty certain about things. On the other hand, if the direction of future events is cloudy and you're worried about what's going to happen next then your level of uncertainty is rising, because the unpredictability of the world—its unknown unknowns—are becoming more apparent. I'd stress the word "apparent": the unknown unknowns are *always* with us, it's just sometimes we don't realize it.

In general, we're quite good at assessing actual risks when we have real data and the time to think about it, and at judging what to do next based on the information we have on hand, but we're useless at coping under conditions of uncertainty where, by definition, no one has a clue what to do. As we saw earlier, in the section on Illusory Pattern Recognition, putting professional investors in conditions of uncertainty means they're more likely to develop conspiracy theories, see visual patterns in random static, and lose money in markets by following mistaken superstitions—and these are the people who are most familiar with these conditions.

Uncertain conditions are those that are most likely to cause us to generate the random connections between events that, to all intents and purposes, look like superstitions. The key to these superstitions is that they allow us to try and exert control over the uncontrollable: they turn the unknown unknowns we can't control into knowns that we can. As investors, this means we start thinking we can predict the future, when the truth is we haven't got a clue. What do you think happens when an investor starts making investment decisions on the basis of illusory patterns? Yep, they tend to lose a ton of money.

In fact, there's evidence that the longest serving investors on Wall Street are those who tend to sit on their hands during uncertain and volatile conditions.[7] This is perfectly sensible behavior for people who are generally good at predicting the movements of markets and stocks: Why take big risks when you don't know what's going to happen next?

LESSON 6

Remember that the movements of markets are not in your control and resist attempts to create imaginary methods of exerting it. Embrace *uncertainty*: it's always with us, it's just that we don't always realize it. Remember that the best investors tend to sit on their hands when uncertainty is especially high: sometimes doing nothing is just fine.

ILLUSION OF CONTROL

The superstitious links we create in uncertain times are all about trying to make ourselves feel as though we're in control, when really we aren't. This effect, known as the illusion of control, is a very powerful behavioral instinct. Unfortunately, it turns out that the more you are in thrall to the illusion of control the more likely you are to lose money.

There are lots of examples of how the illusion of control leads us into error. Take flying or driving for instance. You and I will probably both agree that we *feel* safer driving, but the statistical evidence is overwhelming that we're actually much safer flying on a commercial airline. It's now well established that in the wake of the 9/11 Twin Towers attack a further 1,600 people died on America's roads during the subsequent year as a result of switching from air travel to road transport.[8] A similar argument can be made around the decision about whether to invest actively, making your own stock choices, or passively, by investing in an index tracker. The former makes you feel like you have more control but actually exposes you to all sorts of new ways of losing money.

In fact there are probably good reasons for us to want to take control of our lives, because feeling we're not in control is bad for our health. In a rather scary study, psychologists Ellen Langer and Judith Rodin showed that giving old people in a retirement home even very small amounts of control—a plant to look after, or self-determination of when to watch a movie—didn't just improve their quality of life, but increased their life expectancy.[9] So, our quest for control, even when it's through foolish superstitions and irrational links, is actually entirely rational. Even the illusion of control may be health giving.

Famously, Ellen Langer has carried out a whole range of experiments that show that people will do all sorts of strange things in order to make themselves feel that they're in control of their environment, even when they blatantly aren't. For example, in a rigged coin tossing test participants were asked to predict the outcome of 30 coin spins and were given feedback as they went along.[10] Although everyone was given a 50 percent "correct" result overall, some people were told that their early guesses were right. These people, the ones who got early positive feedback, developed a belief that they had some skill at coin tossing, and promptly overestimated their overall success rate.

This type of pattern is quite common in investing careers—some people will get lucky early on and develop beliefs that they're "naturally" good at investing. It's not hard to see why this initial success can lead to unrealistic expectations about the amount of control and skill they're exhibiting. Unfortunately, when it comes to stock markets the evidence is that most of the time what happens is largely random; even though there's an entire industry devoted to doing nothing but analyzing the data in order to make predictions its record is not far short of disastrous, especially when it comes to the turning points of markets. These types of situations are simply full of unknown unknowns, and we'd expect this to offer up many examples of people forming illusory links between events and then acting on them in order to maintain an illusion of control.

Here's further proof—a study of professional traders[11] exposed to fairly normal looking, but actually completely random, conditions concluded that many of the participants demonstrated illusion of control problems. Notably, the individuals who were most inclined to illusions of control were also most likely to perform the worst: they were more likely to see their successes as evidence of their skill, and to take more risks because of this—they simply failed to recognize the limits of their own abilities. In essence, the more deluded the individual trader was about their own ability to influence outcomes, the poorer their investing results were.

Thinking we're in control when we're not is always a dangerous illusion. For investors it's a guaranteed way of losing money and the safest position to adopt is that in the short-term markets are always unpredictable. Many people find that almost impossible to accept: they shouldn't be allowed anywhere near stock markets.

LESSON 7

If you think you can predict stock markets in the short term you're wrong: this is just the illusion of control trying to make you feel better. If you feel especially confident, be careful that you're not overreaching: try imagining how you'd feel if all your investments went bust. And if your financial adviser makes short-term market predictions, ditch them: they're hazardous to your wealth.

STOCKS AREN'T SNAKES

Of course, when uncertainty really rears its ugly head in the form of major economic turmoil the fact that we don't really have any control becomes perfectly clear. In uncertain conditions our general pattern recognition rules of thumb for proceeding will tend to go wrong and we'll react to this. Our default reaction to situations involving high levels of uncertainty is carefully designed to keep us alive in the jungle, by fighting or running away, but is perfectly useless for investors who need to learn to keep calm when every nerve is screaming at them to panic. Investors should never make rushed decisions.

Some market panic or other will strike at least a couple of times a decade. Cheap stocks will get cheaper, the go-go-growth stocks we've learned to love will suddenly turn turtle, companies that produce improved earnings year after year will suddenly announce profit warnings, and buying on the dips will just increase our losses. You'll become unsure as to how to proceed. You'll feel fearful and nervous, and prone to try and react to remove these feelings.

Usually we feel like this in situations where we really need to react quickly, and our nervous systems are set up to make fast decisions in these conditions, based on whatever rough and ready rules we can quickly bring to mind. We're far better off reacting 99 times to a stick that we think is a snake and once to a snake that is a snake than we would be sitting around carefully considering whether that snake-like object is actually a stick—because it only takes one stick to be a snake for us never to have to worry about thinking about anything ever again.

Investment is different: we can get bitten frequently by poisonous investments and still do okay. So a rule of thumb that saves us in the tropical jungle is not going to work in our modern investment equivalent because it is almost never necessary to react quickly in stock markets—these are not time-critical decisions.

Putting people under time constraints to make difficult decisions is an old compliance trick used by sales people. They know that giving you a short window of time to make a decision puts you under pressure and is more likely to cause you to react irrationally. Of course, the fact that they feel they need to do this should immediately raise your suspicions and this applies doubly to investment decisions which, even in conditions of uncertainty, should be made calmly and in slow time: making them quickly accentuates a whole range of other bias related problems. Putting yourself under time pressure isn't just stupid, it's also likely to be very, very expensive.

When we make decisions quickly we engage the old parts of our brain that are set up to react quickly to keep us alive. By slowing down we give the newer forebrain, where logic and rational thought is generated, the chance to take charge and make rational choices. No matter how urgent that stock tip is, or how quickly your broker or adviser wants you to trade, you're always better off sitting back and thinking about it. Any financial decision that can't be slept on should be firmly ignored and any financial adviser that pressures you into making a quick decision should be fired.

LESSON 8

Mistaking a stick for a snake can save you from a potentially dangerous situation, but mistaking a stock for a snake is not as helpful. Don't make snap judgments about investments: time is your friend and investment decisions are almost never really *time-dependent*. Stocks aren't snakes, although they can bite you if you're unwary.

HERDING

Uncertainty has another, quite odd, effect on the way we behave. If you look at how stocks perform when we're deep in conditions of uncertainty you'll see that they tend to synchronize—everything tends to go up and down together. This is a sign of a very common investor behavioral trait known as herding, where we copy each other. Like so many other biases this behavior is programmed into us, is a sensible rule of thumb in everyday life, and is perfectly wrong for investors who are likely to follow the herd leaders right over the nearest investment cliff.

On the rare occasions when anyone is foolish enough to invite me to a vaguely up-market sit-down dinner I can never remember whether my bread roll is on my right or my left. So I do what everyone does, and wait for someone who can remember to eat their roll first, and then hope I'm not following the only person at the table who doesn't care or know about social conventions. We copy each other when we don't know what to do. So what do you think we do when no one knows what to do?

Well, when we're exposed to conditions of uncertainty, such as our bread roll conundrum, following what other, confident looking people are doing is often a very good heuristic. So, we adjust our investments based on what other people are doing, rather than through any fundamental analysis of our own.

This is what's happening in markets when stocks start synchronizing. As Research from the New England Complex Systems Institute has shown that as uncertainty increases so does the tendency for stocks to move together.[12] These synchronized moves are an outward sign of investment herding, as sentiment changes on a daily basis. The problem is that there will always be some people who are confident, even though they don't actually have a clue what's really going on, and if we follow them we're outsourcing our judgment to other people who have no better ideas than us, but either make a living pretending that they do, or simply don't know that they don't know.

The weight of evidence, built up over years of research, is that social effects such as herding are very powerful forces in investment markets. These apply to you and me, but also to professional investors, who are just as biased by their brains as everyone else. Studies of professional stock market analysts frequently demonstrate both herding and a lack of ability to forecast. When the economist Hersh Shefrin[13] analyzed the performance of the forecasters both before and after BP's *Deepwater Horizon* oilrig spectacularly collapsed, he found that herding in forecasts increased after the event, as the highly paid analysts huddled together in an acute state of uncertainty—and they still got their forecasts wrong, on the high side as usual. Obviously, none of us like to think that we're simply a steer in a herd of stampeding cattle, but in conditions of uncertainty this is often what we're reduced to if we're not careful, with no idea if our leaders are heading towards the high ground or the edge of a canyon.

Oddly, though, we don't just herd when we're uncertain of what to do next. Its exact opposite can cause this as well. Hands up—who threw money at dot-com stocks at the end of the last century? Many people invested in these for no better reason than everyone else was doing so, and the more people threw money at them the more they went up and the more people wanted to own them. Of course, feelings of uncertainty were very low at that point—everyone felt confident about the future of the Internet, so much so that they were prepared to pay any price to own a part of that future. Extreme certainty about the future is another sort of error: the unknown unknowns are always with us.

It's not true that herding is always bad for investors, but following other people and market sentiment without thinking about it is. Market trends eventually stop, and the only money we lose by following other people is our own.

LESSON 9

Be careful about following investment trends. *Herding* is not always bad, but you may eventually end up in a canyon, and blaming other people for your losses when you're upside down in a hole with a heifer on your head doesn't make them any less real.

Salience

Conditions of uncertainty also trigger another reaction: they get lots and lots of mass media attention. Let's face it, there's no story in nothing much happening in the world, but if something extreme is going on—like a major stock market crash—then that's newsworthy. We're social creatures, we're interested in what other people are doing. The mass media is the modern equivalent of us running around our friends telling them about the nasty accident with the mammoth. These stories, whether sensationalized or not, are what tend to stick in the mind—they're salient and they resonate with us, particularly when we have money at stake or we think our loved ones are at risk.

Salience is an important concept, because we're particularly driven by events that have meaning for us. You tend not to pay much attention to stories that don't affect you, but you'll be absolutely drawn to those that you have an interest in. Of course, news outlets know this, and they know the hot buttons to press—stories about child molesters, nuclear disasters or stock market crashes or celebrities to whose lives we aspire, and so on. As research has shown, the effect of these stories is to give people a disproportionate view of the risks involved. We worry more about the tiny chance of a nuclear disaster than we do about the radiation we get from X-ray machines—yet scientists rate the latter as much more dangerous in aggregate. Of course, this is linked to the uncertainty—the unknown unknowns—associated with nuclear power coupled with the potential for utter catastrophe. There's a term for this fear of extreme events—dread risk—and situations characterized by both dread and uncertainty seem to provoke extreme reactions.[14]

The impact of the salience of events combines with some of the other factors we've already discussed—in particular, our tendency to use observations from our own experience—to generate illusory patterns, which we then use to predict the future. Scare someone enough with a salient story about how child molesters are prowling our suburbs and you get people extrapolating to their kids, and a generation who aren't allowed outside without supervision.

Similarly, if you put someone in conditions of uncertainty and then bombard them with frightening information about the dread risk of stock market crashes then you're quite likely to get a reaction, as people either become paralyzed into inaction or, just as likely, start taking inappropriate countermeasures, selling stocks when they shouldn't and buying them at equally inappropriate moments.

The effects of salience can be quite odd. You probably have experienced bad service at some outlet or another, from time to time. Some people take such experiences and extrapolate them to an entire firm. Sometimes this may be valid, but often it isn't—developing a dislike of a company simply because one person got out of bed on the wrong side one day is just silly, but seems to be a quite common reaction. However, some companies can get away with bad service all the time, because they're so powerful—sometimes bad service is the sign of a good investment. Not often, though, and hopefully not for long.

The use of single anecdotes to justify major decisions is the stock-in-trade of politicians and other influencers who know that nothing sells a policy like a good human interest story. From our perspective, though, a single anecdote is just one data point—to make decisions we should be looking for hundreds, if not thousands, of similar anecdotes, and not rely on our own limited personal experiences.

LESSON 10

Be wary of sensationalized stories; they're written because they're salient for us, and they're not representative of the entire world. This is particularly true in situations evoking dread risk, such as the threat of the end of the known investment world destroying your life savings. Look for real data, not stories.

AVAILABILITY

Salience has one further impact, which is that it makes information easily available to our brains. Availability is, perhaps, the single most important behavioral bias we'll meet because it's implicated in so many different situations. Yet it's a very simple concept—availability is a key aspect of how we make decisions because we will tend to use information that is easily retrievable from memory—the information that is most available. When it comes to investing our recent experience is not a good guide to future performance, and investing on the basis of whatever we can easily bring to mind is a one-way ticket to the poorhouse.

Obviously, information that is very salient is also information that is very available—if you're considering whether or not to let your kids go play in the park you'll likely be drawing on your experiences of similar events and any stories about lurking threats from shadowy stalkers. This information is easily retrieved from memory. The statistic that the total of non-family related child abductions in the United States in a typical year was a total of 115 children and youths[15] is not, as it's not remotely sensational, rarely publicized, and hardly salient.

This, on a lesser scale, is the kind of logic that goes into many decisions. Again, remember the research that showed many more people dying on the roads after 9/11? This event is seared into people's memories, and it takes a considerable time before the memories recede sufficiently enough for the increase in traffic deaths to decline as people returned to flying. Similarly, many people who lived through the Wall Street Crash in 1929 never forgot the lesson to avoid stocks—even though investing in American stock markets from around 1933 through 1965 would have proved to be one of the best investing decisions anyone could ever have made.[16]

One of the greatest investors of all time was Ben Graham, often known as the "father of investing" and the mentor of Warren Buffett, billionaire chief executive of Berkshire Hathaway. Graham lost a fortune during the Wall Street Crash, although he made it back in the years following. His investment style from then on was intensely cautious, a style that worked extraordinarily well in the markets that followed the market collapses of 1929 and 1931. However, his experience was so salient that he retired from investing in 1956 because he thought markets were too high. They continued to rise for another decade and, despite all the trials and tribulations of the world since, have never fallen back to the levels at which he decided they were too risky. That's salience and availability in action, and it affects us all, even the very wisest of us.

The only way for investors to guard against the effects of availability is to have a strategy, which means you don't have to rely on salient information like this. To do this you'll need to understand a bit of history, about the returns from markets and different types of assets over longer periods, and you're going to have to learn to use wider sources of data than your own memory.

LESSON 11

We will preferentially access and use information that's easily available to us—this is often a poor strategy for investment decisions. Look for objective evidence, don't rely on subjective opinion.

ASSUMING THE SERIAL POSITION

Salience is not the only factor that affects the availability of information in your mind. Investors are particularly attracted to recent information and are also impacted by the order in which they receive information. It turns out that the order in which information is imparted changes the outcomes of our investing decisions, and often not for the better. Overcoming this requires more than simple knowledge of the problem, it means you need a system.

Here's a list—read it and memorize it quickly:

Paul
John
Michael
Roger
David
Richard
Simon
Stuart
Ian
Peter
Henry
Larry
Dan
Joe
William
Andrew

Now do the same with another list:

Ruth

Barbara

Cynthia

Joan

Amelia

Alice

Isabelle

Cathy

Susan

Deborah

Leanne

Charlotte

Kelly

Okay, now without looking back, write down as many names as you can—from the first list. (The second list was a decoy, to stop you refreshing the data from the first list in your head, not that that would help you very much.)

In general, people will preferentially remember the first name and the last name on the list. Recalling the first and the last names is known as the primacy effect and the recency effect—the first and most recent items on a list are more memorable than the others, all things being equal. This is the result of a more general bias known as the serial position effect, the finding that the order in which information is presented determines how well we can bring it to mind—how available it is. Remember the illusion of control task on coin tossing, where people who received early feedback about their "successes" began to believe they were demonstrating skill at what was an obviously random task? That was an example of how primacy can bias our judgment as we form early opinions, which we're then loathe to change in the face of new data.

Recency is particularly implicated in a range of investor misbehaviors, because we tend to overweight the importance of the most recent events and to downplay more distant ones. This can have some strange and counter-intuitive results, including the so-called gambler's fallacy. This occurs when people believe that a run of luck—such as black turning up on a roulette wheel multiple times—means that a reversion is more likely—so that red is predicted for the next spin. But the spin of a roulette wheel leads to random outcomes and the previous result doesn't predict the next one.

Mostly, markets are also random, so a few days of a stock going up or down is likely to have no cause whatsoever, but recency effects such as the gambler's fallacy seem to bias some people into expecting a change of direction. However, others will develop exactly the opposite hypothesis and assume that a particular sequence will carry on, presumably forever.

The rough rule here is that you shouldn't assume that recent events tell you anything about the longer-term trajectory of stocks or markets. Investment decisions should be based around a longer-term view of corporate prospects and an understanding of the risks involved. Because we find it difficult to overcome these problems, even if we recognize them, we're going to need to develop processes to ensure we give all information equal weight, not just the most recent or most salient pieces.

LESSON 12

We're heavily biased by recent information, by recency, but recent events are often not a good basis for making long-term investment decisions. We need to be aware of long-term investment trends and learn how to relate these to short-term market events, and to do this successfully we're going to need some simple tools.

HOT HANDS

Another effect of recency is the idea that stocks can demonstrate "hot streaks." This is related to the deeply ingrained belief that certain sportsmen can, at certain times, demonstrate a "hot streak," in which they defy all normal levels of skill to hit home runs, ride winners, or shoot baskets at will. This, the so-called hot-hands effect, is nothing more than the all-too-human tendency to see order in random patterns, plus the impact of recency, as we just look at the recent results and ignore the long-term trends. Extrapolating from recent market behavior to the future, or from a stock tippers' recent results to his or her next ones, is a dangerous tendency.

For example, take the following four sets of coin tossing results. Which one wasn't generated at random?

1. T H H H H T T T H H H H T T T H
2. H T T T T T T T H T H T H T H H
3. H T T T T T H T T H T T T H H H
4. T H H T T H T H T H T H T H H H T

The actual answer is number 4, which I made up to try and make it look roughly random, and without trying managed to end up with equal numbers of heads and tails, although most people would probably reckon that's the most likely candidate for a really random set. However, the other three sequences, all of which contain long runs of heads or tails, and unequal numbers of each, are completely random: in fact in a really big, really random set of coin tosses you'd find sequences of hundreds of successive heads or tails. In reality, you need about 200 coin tosses to be reliably able to tell the difference between a true random sequence and one that's generated by a human—but it's nearly always possible to tell, as long as you know what you're looking for.*

So, when we see a sportsperson on a hot streak what we're generally seeing is someone at one point in one of these sequences. This isn't to say that a good player won't get better results than a bad player, but it is saying that one good player won't get better results overall than another good player if you look at the complete data set, rather than just the most recent bit. Once again, what we're seeing here is the human brain looking at a small part of a random pattern and discerning order where none exists. It's a sort of pareidolia applied to data—we're seeing the Man in the Moon again.

In general, the world is a disorderly place, full of random events. We're attuned to look for cause and effect because where we find order we generally find human beings at work, turning the randomness of the world into something less perplexing. So, order is a sign of some kind of a directing mind, someone in control and, in the main, that someone is another human being. Of course, where there is apparent order, which couldn't have been created by humans—such as the so-called face of Mars—some people leap to the conclusion that we're looking at the work of alien intelligence, rather than reaching for the more prosaic explanation of pareidolia.

Hence, when we see something that looks like order we usually attribute it to human intelligence and skill. Unfortunately, recency means that we only tend to look at the most recent events in a long sequence, those which are available to our brains, which means we can be fooled into thinking we're

* In "The Impossibility of Faking Data," Theodore P. Hill recounts: "To demonstrate this to beginning students of probability, I often ask them to do the following homework assignment the first day. They are either to flip a coin 200 times and record the results, or merely pretend to flip a coin and fake the results. The next day I amaze them by glancing at each student's list and correctly separating nearly all the true from the faked data. The fact in this case is that in a truly random sequence of 200 tosses it is extremely likely that a run of six heads or six tails will occur (the exact probability is somewhat complicated to calculate), but the average person trying to fake such a sequence will rarely include runs of that length."

looking at the results of skill and intelligence when actually all we're seeing is a snapshot of a small sequence of the output of a coin tossing machine.

So here we have pareidolia, illusory pattern recognition, superstitious thinking, availability, and recency, all combining to create the hot-hands effect. It's the combination of these behavioral effects that make a compelling story for our brains. When you apply this kind of analysis to stock market investors you can suddenly see why markets can get on a roll for reasons that have nothing to do with the true valuation of the underlying securities. Most stock price changes, for instance, are nothing more than random jitters in the system for which no explanation is ever required—yet you can find people obsessing over every miniscule movement and explaining them in terms of some causal event. If a stock you own happens to start traveling in one direction for a number of days in a row this can provoke all sorts of explanatory storytelling, yet if you look at the long-term price movement in terms of actual earnings events you'll probably see nothing more than a random sequence.

These kinds of short-term effects, triggered by combinations of behavioral biases, almost seem to compel people to make investing decisions, yet they're irrelevant to the proper business of stock analysis and long-term strategy required to be successful in markets. In fact, the overreaction of people to recent information may offer up attractive opportunities for investors with longer investing horizons, while that very overreaction will damage investor returns through overtrading and excess fees.

LESSON 13

The hot-hands effect is caused by only looking at a small snapshot of a much longer sequence of data. It's an example of recency, where we are biased by the latest available information. Try to look at the bigger picture: don't expect an average slugger to keep on hitting home runs, and don't expect a biased investor to even make average returns.

FINANCIAL MEMORY SYNDROME

You've probably noticed that the ideas of salience and availability, along with the gambler's fallacy and the hot hands effect, are linked to our abilities to remember and recall information, but they're only a few of the memory-related problems that investors suffer from. In particular, we have a problem when we're bombarded with lots of information because in that kind of situation we tend to focus only on the most memorable stuff. Company managers and others know this and will tend to highlight the information they want us to see, and hide away information that they don't. Unsurprisingly, the hidden information is often the stuff we really need to read.

Usually, we treat memory as unproblematic, a sort of photographic repository of stuff that's happened to us. In fact, it's anything but photographic, because we recreate memories on-the-hoof as we need to. Recent events color past ones, and our memories are constructed out of the bits and pieces we can actively bring to mind: which means that if you can plant a story in someone's memory you can get them to "remember" things that never actually happened. This problem, known as *false memory syndrome*, was shown quite startlingly by the cognitive psychologists Elizabeth Loftus and Jacqueline Pickrell,[17] who were able to convince various people that they'd had experiences which were, in fact, entirely fictitious. Indeed, their research subjects then elaborated the stories with details of their own, and later found it hard to believe that the fake memories weren't real.

The practical applications of this finding are really important—uncorroborated witness statements aren't a safe basis upon which to make criminal convictions, and reports of child abuse by individual victims are suspect, especially when recalled out of the blue after therapy or if prompted by authority figures, and we simply can't always accurately remember the past performance of stocks and markets. It turns out that many of us think we actually had quite severe reservations about whether to invest in stocks in late 2007 or real estate in 2006—only we didn't of course, it's just that's what we think we remember.[18] Mostly, we were still investing like lemmings on a day-trip to the nearest cliff top.

These problems are associated with long-term memory, the stuff we think we recall, but there are a whole other set of problems with short-term memory, which is where we store information so we can work on it moment by moment. Remember the lists of boys and girls names we saw previously? Well, those lists were far too long to remember, because working memory, as short-term memory is called, can generally only hold about seven items of information.[19] If we try to hold more than seven we start to lose data, a phenomena known as *information overload*: initially, as we add more data our decision making improves, but this rapidly plateaus and then goes into decline as we hit the limits of our working memory. After a while, we stop taking notice of most of the information presented and availability effects start to predominate.

If you've tried to read a corporate report recently you'll know exactly how this works—huge amounts of information provided in order to meet regulatory requirements, most of which gets ignored in favor of reading a few choice bits. It turns out that the old saying "less is more" was never more applicable—we really only pay attention to the most salient and vivid pieces of information, especially if they're presented in an easy-to-consume form. Unsurprisingly, our limited abilities to attend to complex pieces of information will tend to get exploited, and there's evidence to suggest that company managers try to manipulate highly visible and easy to understand financial ratios like the earnings-per-share, and hide expenses and liabilities in less visible locations—exploiting both salience and availability.[20]

If this sounds like a minefield for the unwary investor then you're getting the idea. A whole industry has evolved to exploit our cognitive biases and use our own minds against us. Fortunately, because most people don't realize this it's quite easy for those of us who do to develop some defenses against this exploitation. Keeping an investment diary is a good start, making sure you record your decisions and reasoning, and frequently revisiting it to refresh your memory. Above all, you need to analyze your mistakes in light of subsequent experience—successful investing is mainly about avoiding big mistakes, not finding big winners.

LESSON 14

Beware of using your unaided memory to process comparisons and of situations in which you're being asked to process lots of information. These can lead to false memory syndrome and information overload problems. Keep a diary, and make sure you understand your mistakes. Everyone makes them, most people don't learn from their experiences.

ATTENTION!

The trick to making the information someone wants us to look at highly visible is actually exploiting another, quite simple, human limitation. If you've ever got stuck on a narrow sidewalk behind someone trying to walk and text at the same time you can testify that we find it difficult to attend to more than one thing at once, even when one of them is as automatic a function as walking. This behavior lies behind the research that shows that if we acquire too much information we actually *reduce* our rate of investing success: information overload again.

The problem of divided attention due to too much information is why various states and countries have banned the use of cellphones and other hard-to-use gadgets in cars, because they cause us to lose attention from the rather more important business of trying to drive in a straight line—and if we stop attending to the road for more than two seconds the probability of an accident increases dramatically. Having too much information available erodes our ability to focus on the salient points, and reduces our performance.

The evidence for information overload comes from multiple sources. The classic study involved horse handicappers and showed that increasing the data available to them beyond five items and up to 40 slightly *decreased* their success rate.[21] Similar results have been found for doctors, clinical psychologists, and, of course, investors. As the Internet makes ever more mountains of information available to us this problem is likely to get worse, unless we take steps to deliberately focus our attention on the things that really matter.

The problem, of course, is deciding what's important and what's not. Combating the problems of information overload and our limited attention capability means we need to develop techniques to help us because our memories simply aren't good enough to do this unaided. Even an investing diary isn't going to be much good if we don't develop a systematic way of analyzing the results. Probably the best way of doing this is to create a checklist.

Checklists are incredibly powerful—they help to turn difficult analytic problems into simple lists, to allow us to identify the key issues for any given investment. They also force us to look at "obvious" things that our biases will otherwise cause us to neglect. In general, every investment has its potential downsides so the important thing is to isolate them and then focus our attention on them. Checklists help to remove some of the subjectivity associated with investing decisions, although they're always going to be more effective if you develop your own.

The power of checklists is testified to by their use in safety critical industries, where missing important issues due to attentional weaknesses can result in disaster. When Captain Chesley Sullenberger and copilot Jeff Skiles successfully guided their crippled plane onto the Hudson River and to safety on January 15, 2009, they did so by rigorously following the checklists set out in front of them.

Skill matters, but if it's not accompanied by focused attention then it's not going to be of much use to you. And, frankly, if a checklist can help land an Airbus on a river it's probably good enough to help make you a better investor.

LESSON 15

Don't let yourself be distracted from important tasks like driving or investing: make sure your attention is focused. Build your own checklists ahead of time and apply them consistently.

THE PROBLEM WITH LINDA

This chapter has been all about how our senses and our memories can deceive us, particularly in uncertain times, and how the resulting mistakes can manifest themselves in investing errors—mistakes that the financial services industry is all too ready to exploit. We'll end this excursion into the peculiarities of perception with an example that superficially looks completely different, but which turns out to be one of the most important pieces of the puzzle that is behavioral finance. It's a famous piece of research known as the Linda problem:

> *Linda is 31 years old, single, outspoken, and very bright. She majored in philosophy. As a student, she was deeply concerned with issues of discrimination and social justice, and also participated in antinuclear demonstrations. Which of these two alternatives is more probable?*
>
> *a.   Linda is a bank teller.*
> *b.   Linda is a bank teller and is active in the feminist movement.*

Okay, so what do you think?

The Linda problem was created by a couple of young researchers, Amos Tversky and Daniel Kahneman, in 1974,[22] and was the start of a revolution in economics, what we now generally call "behavioral economics" or "behavioral finance." In 2002, Kahneman justly won a Nobel Prize for this and their later work, a prize Tversky would have shared had he not died in 1996. The answer that you probably gave—and that most people who haven't seen this before also give—is that Linda is a bank teller *and* a feminist. This is very, very wrong.

It's wrong firstly because of something called the conjunction fallacy. To understand this, consider which of the following is more likely?

a. Linda is a woman.
b. Linda is a woman and 31 years old.

Of course it's not more likely that Linda is a woman *and* 31 years old than it is she's just a woman. This is always true whenever one of the options has that "and" in it: the "conjunction" of the conjunction fallacy. So why do most people reckon Linda is a feminist *and* a bank teller?

It's because of the additional information provided in the question, which seems to suggest she's a bit of a do-gooder, with leanings towards social responsibility. This extra information *primes* our brains into thinking about the sort of people that would be inclined to this sort of behavior, so when the question suddenly includes "feminist" a bunch of easy to find positive matches go off in our heads because the priming has made them available to us. This is yet another aspect of availability.

Priming causes all sorts of surprising behavior. One of its effects is that you may have got the Linda problem right—because this book has by now, I hope, primed you to expect the unexpected. This is exactly the problem that many researchers face, and they have to find sneaky ways of overcoming this bias. One of the most clever was carried out by John Bargh and colleagues,[23] which showed exactly how powerful priming is.

Firstly, he got his participants to carry out a word-related test, unscrambling muddled up sentences. However, this wasn't the real experiment, which was to measure the speed with which the people exited the laboratory facility. What was being investigated was the effect of priming some of the participants with words related to being old—old, lonely, wise, knits, and so on. Those so primed were significantly slower to walk to the lab exit. Aside from priming, this is an example of the ideomotor effect, where suggestion or expectation unconsciously affects motor behavior, the processes behind physical movement. The ideomotor effect has been known about since 1852, when William Carpenter used it to provide a non paranormal explanation for various sorts of magical hocus pocus, like divining for water and magic pendulums. It's also the unconscious force behind the "success" of Ouija boards.

So, priming doesn't just change the way we think, but the way we physically act. This sort of thing is immensely revealing regarding the way our brain works, and it really makes perfect sense that various terms should preprepare us—or prime us—for related information or actions. It's just that it has some very odd side effects because priming makes the targeted ideas, concepts and words highly available and this makes us very suggestible—we can easily be manipulated into giving different answers to what is essentially the same question simply by phrasing it differently, a trick politicians exploit ruthlessly.

This matters a lot for investors. A study by Dalia Gilad and Doron Kilger[24] showed that it was possible to predict the riskiness of peoples' investment decisions by whether they first primed them with stories about risk taking or risk aversion. In fact, they also showed that professional investors were more affected by priming than nonprofessionals, and suggest that this is because the professionals were relying on their experience and intuition rather than hard research to make their decisions.

The power of priming is such that we need to be very, very careful about making investment decisions when in an emotional state. As the previous study suggests, the best antidote for this is proper research, and solely relying on any expertise you've gained along the way is a dangerous and risky business. This is true for everyone—experience, wisdom, and a track record are of limited use when you're investing.

LESSON 16

Priming will bias our decision making, and can be used to manipulate us into making wrong decisions. Don't invest purely on gut instinct or experience—no matter how convinced you are of the correctness of your judgment always back it up with hard research, and allow yourself time to think through a decision. And don't make investing decisions when in an emotional state.

REPRESENTATION

If we go back to the Linda problem, the normal answer—that Linda is a feminist *and* a bank teller—is wrong for a second reason, a simple short cut known as the representative heuristic. That's a long-winded and technical way of saying we make decisions by making comparisons with whatever we can bring to mind—yes, yet another application of availability—rather than by thinking through all the possible options. For investors, this can create some really nasty problems, because if we're relying on our limited range of experiences to make investing decisions, we're virtually bound to spend most of our time comparing new opportunities with ones we've already experienced, and it's quite likely that while these may be superficially similar they'll probably really be quite different.

Specifically, our normal answer to the Linda problem is wrong because of a problem known as base rate neglect. Remember that we tend to operate on observed frequencies based on our own limited experiences, so if we're primed to look for feminists by the question then they'll be high on the list of "observations" we can bring to mind and we'll tend to ignore all the non-feminists around, and also all the ones that are bank tellers to boot. Think of it like this: if we see someone run down by a woolly mammoth then that's going to be at the front of our minds, and we'll likely ignore the fact that we've just witnessed the only mammoth drive-by accident in the whole world this entire millennium and that the risks of this reoccurring to us are vanishingly small. However, if we got a video of it we'd probably be rich.

So, the base rate for Linda is the actual number of feminist bank tellers around compared to the total number of bank tellers, and that would probably be pretty low. So even if Linda does have a few vaguely feminist leanings, it's still very far from certain that she'd be a feminist. Normally, instead of considering base rates, people try to figure out whether the description of Linda is *representative* of a feminist and, finding that it does, they jump to conclusions: hence why this decision-making process is known as the representative heuristic, a shortcut for making decisions by comparing information that's easily available to our brains.

Of course, the fact we don't naturally make decisions by analyzing the data in detail shouldn't really be a surprise, but it does flag the fact that if we go around judging things by similarity in the investment world we're really rather asking for trouble. It's the numbers that matter and if we just skim the surface looking for simple comparisons we'll end up ignoring the details. Remember that every time you read an investment report or a statement of company earnings you'll find that you're being asked to make comparisons by people who have a vested interest in getting or keeping your money. Do we really think they'll be making comparisons based on proper base rates? Or might they preferentially make comparisons with something else that makes them look good?

If we want to see how well an investment is doing, we need to use our own data, not rely on comparisons that other people are priming us with. Hopefully, by now, you'll recognize this message: we need to create our own investment diaries, update our own investing checklists, and begin to hone our skills in specific areas. Removing our personal biases from our investing decision making is something we can learn to manage—but only if we recognize that it's a problem to start with. Fortunately, because the investing industry has such an easy time with gullible dupes we don't need to be particularly clever or skillful to avoid the obvious traps, just dogged and persistent.

For now, remember that stock markets are unpredictable and we'll try to exert control even where we can't, especially in conditions of uncertainty—so combining behavioral effects like availability, salience, herding, and pareidolia with intermittent reinforcement can lead us into making up our own random superstitions out of bits of available data and/or copying what everyone else is doing. And no one really has a clue what is going on.

In short, our brains have money problems, and they can lose us money.

LESSON 17

Priming and the representative heuristic will cause us to make comparisons with whatever we've been primed with, and you should recognize when you're being primed by stories to make comparisons with biased examples. Better still, avoid the problems of behavioral bias by developing your own tools for analyzing stocks.

THE SEVEN KEY TAKEAWAYS

This chapter has aimed to introduce you to the core concepts of behavioral biases in investing by relating them to the kinds of perception and memory issues you'll have experienced in everyday life. Many of the rules of thumb—the heuristics—we've discussed should already be familiar in other contexts. It's quite a scary thought that many of these natural traits are already being exploited by people and firms who want to part us from our money without us even being aware that we're being exploited but, fortunately, just becoming aware of the issues is an important first step to dealing with them.

To finish, let's draw together a few key ideas from this chapter before we move on. The main takeaways are:

1. We are all biased to some extent, you as much as me, but many biases are related to perception, memory processes, and heuristics, which are useful adaptations to help us get through our everyday lives.
2. These biases are almost wholly unconscious and virtually impossible to eradicate by willpower or training, although we can learn to develop techniques to manage them.
3. Our biases are exaggerated by conditions of uncertainty, such as those we regularly experience in stock markets.
4. Our biases don't just lead us into investing errors, but are often deliberately exploited by people who want to make money from us.
5. Experience is not sufficient to avoid these biases—in fact, relying on experience will almost certainly lead you into more errors by incorrectly extrapolating from local, personal examples to general trends.
6. Investing decisions—and many others—aren't time critical, and we shouldn't make them in a hurry, or in an emotional state.
7. Managing these biases requires a range of tools, such as carefully keeping track of your returns and developing a checklist of things to look at before investing. The best investors have a method, and don't simply rely on personal judgment, because they know this will be biased, however much they work at it.

That's enough for now. Don't worry about all of the details because we'll revisit and extend many of these ideas and techniques as we look at the next set of biases. These are problems that aren't based in our perception or memory processes but in our belief systems.

NOTES

1. Emily Pronin and Matthew B. Kugler, "Valuing Thoughts, Ignoring Behavior: The Introspection Illusion as a Source of the Bias Blind Spot," *Journal of Experimental Psychology* (2006).
2. Jennifer Whitson and Adam Galinsky, "Lacking Control Increases Illusory Pattern Perception," *Science* 322 (2008).
3. B. F. Skinner, "Superstition in the Pigeon," *Journal of Experimental Psychology* 38 (1948): 168–172.
4. James J. Choi, David Laibson, Brigitte C. Madrian, and Andrew Metrick, "Reinforcement Learning and Savings Behavior," *Journal of Finance* 64 (2009): 2525–2534.
5. Markus Glaser and Martin Weber, "Why Inexperienced Investors Do Not Learn: They Do Not Know Their Past Portfolio Performance," *Finance Research Letters* 4 (2007): 203–216.
6. B. R. Forer, "The Fallacy of Personal Validation: A Classroom Demonstration of Gullibility," *Journal of Abnormal and Social Psychology* 44 (1949): 118–123.
7. Steve Sapra, Laura E. Bevin, and Paul J. Zak, "A Combination of Dopamine Genes Predicts Success by Professional Wall Street Trader," *PLOS ONE* 7, no. 1 (2011): e30844. doi/10.1371/journal.pone.0030844.
8. Gerd Gigerenzer, "Out of the Frying Pan into the Fire: Behavioral Reactions to Terrorist Attacks," *Risk Analysis* 26, no. 2 (2006).
9. Judith Rodin and Ellen J. Langer, "Long-Term Effects of a Control-Relevant Intervention with the Institutionalized Aged," *Journal of Personality and Social Psychology* 35, no. 12 (1977): 897–902.
10. Ellen J. Langer and Jane Roth, "The Illusion of Control as a Function of the Sequence of Outcomes in a Purely Chance Task," *Journal of Personality and Social Psychology* 32, no. 6 (1975): 951–955.
11. Mark Fenton-O'Creevy, Nigel Nicholson, Emma Soane, and Paul Willman, "Trading on Illusions: Unrealistic Perceptions of Control and Trading," *Journal of Occupational and Organization Psychology* 76, no. 1(2003): 53–68.
12. D. Harmon, M. de Aguiar, D. Chinellato, D. Braha, I. Epstein, and Y. Bar-Yam, "Predicting Economic Market Crises Using Measures of Collective Panic" (February 13, 2011), arXiv:1102.2620v1.
13. Hersch Shefrin and Enrico Maria Cervellati, "BP's Failure to Debias: Underscoring the Importance of Behavioral Corporate Finance," *Quarterly Journal of Finance* 1, no. 1 (2011): 127–168.
14. Paul Slovic, "Perception of Risk," *Science* 236 (April 17, 1987): 280–285. Our views on risk are not the same as those of the experts, which is one reason why having experts reassure us when catastrophes happen often doesn't help calm anyone.
15. National Incidence Studies of Missing, Abducted, Runaway and Thrownaway Children, "Nonfamily Abducted Children: National Estimates and Characteristics," 2002. "Most children's nonfamily abduction episodes do not involve elements of the extremely alarming kind of crime that parents and reporters have

in mind (such as a child's being killed, abducted overnight, taken long distances, held for ransom or with the intent to keep the child) when they think about a kidnapping by a stranger."

16. Ulrike Malmendier and Stefan Nagel, "Depression Babies: Do Macroeconomic Experiences Effect Risk Taking?" *Quarterly Journal of Economics* 126, no. 1 (2011): 373–416. "We find that individuals who have experienced low stock-market returns throughout their lives so far report lower willingness to take financial risk, are less likely to participate in the stock market, invest a lower fraction of their liquid assets in stocks if they participate and are more pessimistic about stock returns."

17. Elizabeth Loftus and Jacqueline Pickrell, "The Formation of False Memories," *Psychiatric Annals* 25, no. 12 (1995): 720–725.

18. Joachim Klement, "The Flaws of Our Financial Memory," *CFA Institute Conference Proceedings Quarterly* 28, no. 3 (2011): 1–8.

19. George A. Miller, "The Magical Number Seven, Plus or Minus Two," *Psychological Review* 101, no. 2 (1956): 343–353.

20. Robert Bloomberg, "The 'Incomplete Revelation Hypothesis' and Financial Reporting," *Accounting Horizons* 16 (2002): 233–243.

21. Richards J. Heuer Jr., *Psychology of Intelligence Analysis*, (United States Government Printing, 1999, available at www.cia.gov/library/center-for-the-study-of-intelligence/csi-publications/books-and-monographs/psychology-of-intelligence-analysis/PsychofIntelNew.pdf.

22. Amos Tversky and Daniel Kahneman, "Judgement Under Uncertainty: Heuristics and Biases," *Science* 185, no. 4157 (1974): 1124–1131.

23. John A. Bargh, Mark Chen, and Lara Burrows, "Automaticity of Social Behaviour: Direct Effects of Trait Construct and Stereotype Activation on Action," *Journal of Personality and Social Psychology* 71, no. 2 (1996): 230–244. The paper also shows priming effects for rudeness and racial stereotyping, all completely unconscious behavior as far as the participants were concerned.

24. Dalia Gilad and Doron Kilger, "Priming the Risk Attitudes of Professionals in Financial Decision Making," *Review of Finance* 12, no. 3 (2008): 567–586.

CHAPTER 2

Self-Image and Self-Worth

O kay, so we now know that while we can trust our senses to help us determine the future trajectory of a ball we can't trust them to help us predict the future trajectory of stocks. But we can deal with that, because we're smart, right?

In fact, we know we're smarter than the average investor, so we can be pretty sure that we will make money on the markets. After all, if we didn't think we were going to make money on the markets we wouldn't be investing, would we?

It's time to start the tour bus again, because we've just strayed into the counterintuitive world of investors' beliefs about themselves. Only we'd better be careful, because the bus driver almost certainly thinks they're a better than average driver, along with over 90 percent of other Americans. We are woefully overconfident about our investing abilities, and we don't even know it.

THE INTROSPECTION ILLUSION

I have two left feet and a cloth ear, which makes me peculiarly unsuited for engaging in any activity that involves music, a sense of rhythm, or the ability to count a beat. Imagine a baby giraffe trying to dance in roller-skates. On ice.

Despite this sad lack of musical ability I don't hold it against myself, and my own sense of self-worth isn't particularly damaged by this gaping hole in my abilities. Like most reasonably well-adjusted people, I take a sensible approach to activities I'm not very good at—I avoid them if at all possible and make a joke of them when I can't. Whenever I have cause to think about my own abilities I do so in terms of the things I think I'm good at, rather than those I think I'm bad at and I certainly don't start a catalog of my attributes by considering my modern dance skills. And I don't doubt you do the same.

Go on, make a list of things you're bad at and then consider whether you care about them?

This is typical of everyone, because no even moderately self-aware adult is going to choose to spend a lot of time doing something that they know they're bad at, and which is going to provide an unremitting sequence of embarrassing experiences. We actively edit our own lives, and simple self-selection ensures that we'll spend most of our lives doing things we're at least average at and which provide a positive stream of feedback, which makes us feel good about ourselves. It's unsurprising, then, that when most of us think about ourselves we generally have a positive self-opinion—after all, most of us have mainly positive experiences to remember once we escape the clutches of our parents, who usually insist on us doing things they'd never consider for themselves. Like modern dance lessons. Not that I'm bitter or anything,

In its most extreme form this preference for favoring one's self is known as self-serving bias and, at "its" worst, it can lead to a complete failure of introspection. Sufferers will blame their failures on external influences that they couldn't control and insist that their successes are purely due to their own innate skill. This isn't an attractive quality at the best of times, but when applied to investing it's likely to be severely wealth limiting.

Of course, when we do think about ourselves we don't actually realize that our positive self-regard is generated by our careful selection of activities that make us feel good. We generally recall our triumphs and carefully avoid remembering our failures. This is known as the *introspection illusion*, and it's quite probably the reason that we don't recognize we're biased, even though we agree everyone else is, why we trade too much and lose a load of money by doing so, why we keep our very worst stocks and sell our best, and why we think we can predict the future, even though the evidence shows we couldn't predict the present and that mostly we can't even remember the past. For very good psychological reasons most of us are positive thinkers, especially about ourselves, but this has a terrible affect on our ability to manage our investments. It's good for our health, but rotten for our wealth.

LESSON 1

Positive thinking is not a positive thing for an investor. We have to deal with the way the world is, not the way we want it to be. Save positivity for other aspects of your life.

BLIND SPOT BIAS, REVISITED

The work of Emily Pronin and Matthew Kugler[1] I touched on in the previous chapter suggests that *blind spot bias*—our knack of thinking we're not biased but that everyone else is—is a side-effect of the introspection illusion. When we think of ourselves we think of someone who is above average—and, after all, we have a generally positive view of our experiences. So, we have inflated expectations of our own abilities and when asked to compare ourselves with other people we think that we're better than them, so we end up believing that we can rise above our brain's constant stream of trickery.

Famously, more than 50 percent of drivers think that they're above average—a clear statistical impossibility and an equally clear case of self-serving bias. Of course, many well-known "facts" are actually urban myths but this one isn't, and is actually backed up by some real research by Ola Svenson,[2] who showed that 93 percent of American drivers thought they were better than the other crazy bozos on the road. At least the other 7 percent were honest, although they're probably not people you want to nominate as your designated drivers on a night out.

However, the introspection illusion can lead to far worse problems than a skewed view of our driving abilities. This brings us to one of the most famous experiments in the history of psychology, Stanley Milgram's electrocution test.[3] It touches a nerve, in more ways than one.

The experimental setup had two participants who couldn't see each other, with one asking questions and the other answering. Every time a question was answered incorrectly the questioner applied an electric shock to the unseen responder, and the size of the shock was increased each time a question was answered incorrectly. After a while, the victim, understandably, started pleading to stop the experiment but a white coated researcher would then instruct the questioner to continue to turn up the electricity—and they nearly always did, applying shocks to a level that could have caused significant, long-lasting harm.

Or at least they would have, had the experiment been real. In fact, the "victim" was a stooge who was acting a role and the whole experiment was designed to test the willingness of the actual participants, the people doing the shocking, to defer to authority figures. In a whole series of experiments, under different circumstances, Milgram was consistently able to replicate these results: over and over again people would apply shocks to pleading, begging victims simply because they were instructed to do so. These results were, quite literally, shocking for what they revealed about our willingness to defer to authority figures.

These types of experiments aren't allowed anymore because of the psychological harm that they can cause to participants, but they're scarily reminiscent of real-world situations where people seem to collectively lose sight of the nature of morality: Milgram was working at a time when Nazi Germany was still prominent in many peoples' minds. This was just the start of a whole host of experiments suggesting that we have an instinctive tendency to defer to authority, even when those authority figures are false. How often do people suspend their critical judgment in order to follow some stock market guru or other?

When a follow-up study was carried out on the Milgram experiment, looking at what people *thought* they would do if placed in the same situation, the vast majority believed that they would find the inner strength to resist and stop the experiment.[4] You probably think the same thing—I certainly do. Unfortunately, we're both almost certainly wrong. This is blind-spot bias in action. It's frightening what we can be induced to do in general life, but applied to investing it's potentially disastrous.

LESSON 2

Blind-spot bias affects us all. It can't be avoided but it can be recognized. Good investors are humble in the face of the markets: that's a positive mental attitude to take into investing.

ROSE-COLORED INVESTING

So, the introspection illusion will cause us to be *overoptimistic* about our abilities to overcome our biases and our overoptimism will typically lead us into *overconfidence*. This turns out to be a particular problem when we engage in activities where we don't get timely and clear feedback, as we only remember our successes and tend to conveniently overlook our failures. Obviously, if you're so bad at dancing you fall over every time you shuffle onto the dance floor you won't persist unless you're oddly determined, exceptionally stupid, or possess an unusually forceful mother, but as long as you do reasonably well some of the time you're quite likely to persist in believing you're above average at the pasodoble and a dab hand at the tango.

Of course, doing reasonably well some of the time is a fair description of our results when we go investing. Even if we're the worst stock-picker in the history of the known universe we will, purely by chance, occasionally happen upon a successful investment—and, as we've seen already, many investors don't actually know how well their portfolios have been doing against the broader market—a clear case of base-rate neglect—so we'd expect them to tend to remember their successes, forget their failures, and generally be way too optimistic about their abilities to pick winners.

All of which is exactly what Brad Barber and Terrance Odean[5] found when they analyzed data from Internet traders. Barber and Odean's work is famous within the behavioral finance community because they've pulled some extraordinary findings out of data relating to the way people behave when they're given a computer, an Internet connection, and an online trading account. To summarize: we're not rational. But we knew that already. What we didn't know was how much it costs us.

One of their studies showed that most traders gave up money most times they transacted. By and large the stocks they sold proceeded to outperform while the ones they bought underperformed. On top of this, traders pay brokerage fees to make these trades, handing over tons of cash every year to the financial industry in the process. In fact, it's quite hard to get an exact handle on how much money is passed from active investors to financial institutions each year, but in aggregate it's in the *billions* of dollars. Come on, where did you think the finance industry makes its money? It's from us.

Clearly, people wouldn't be making these trades if they didn't think they would make more money by doing so but the evidence shows that they're misplacing their faith in their own abilities. Another study by Markus Glaser and Martin Weber[6] suggests that the more overconfident the investor the more they tend to trade, which is roughly equivalent to the worst drivers spending the most time behind the wheel. Overconfidence is a bane for investors, and it's a hard habit to kick, even for experienced traders, but we all need to take off the rose-colored trading spectacles and get real.

LESSON 3

Overconfidence is deadly for investing returns. It allows the financial industry to make a fortune and loses us one. Trade rarely and only when the evidence is overwhelming; otherwise you're better off doing nothing.

PAST AND PRESENT FAILURES

Overoptimism as a source of our monetary failings is hardly a new finding. As far back as 1915, a stockbroker using the pseudonym Dan Guyon[7] showed that people were able to lose money even while the stocks they were buying rose by 65 percent. Worse, they actually thought they were making money! They constantly mistimed their trades, buying after stocks had risen and selling after they'd fallen, thus missing out on the majority of the potential gains.

Then, in the 1930s and 1940s, an American economist named Alfred Cowles[8] started looking at tip sheets and other public forecasters. Rather than blindly believing the sweet-tongued blandishments of these snake charmers he did some real analysis and attempted to use their forecasts as a basis for making investment decisions. Analysis of these results revealed— surprise, surprise—that the forecasters had absolutely no forecasting ability and were permanently biased to an optimistic view, by a factor of 4 to 1. As the study remarked:

> *The persistent and unwarranted record of optimism can possibly be explained on the grounds that readers prefer good news to bad, and that a forecaster who presents a cheerful point of view thereby attracts a following without which he would probably be unable to remain long in the business of forecasting.*

Indeed, Cowles went on to remark, dryly, that the only way of using tip sheets to make money in the markets was to find the very worst ones and then do the exact opposite of what they recommended!

The inability of investors to capture positive market returns isn't just ancient history, either. Similar findings have been shown more recently—a Dalbar, Inc, study[9] showed that the difference between market returns and investor returns varied between 300 and 500 percent: in some years active investors made only a fifth of what they would have done had they simply stuck their cash in an index tracker and went on vacation all year. The problem, as the Barber and Odean study revealed, is that we just trade way too much, because we're relentlessly overoptimistic about our ability to pick winners, and don't track our successes and failures properly, because that would force us to address our introspection illusion head on. Unfortunately, we're not as good at investing as we think we are. Although, as it turns out, one way of possibly reducing the problem is to make yourself really, really miserable.

LESSON 4

Don't take any notice of unsubstantiated share tipping ideas. Do track your own returns carefully against the market, and make sure you analyze the results.

DEPRESSED BUT WEALTHY

There are indications, as the Cowles quote suggests, that we're designed to prefer good news to bad. It turns out that one way of improving your investment returns is to make yourself really, really depressed. I really, really don't recommend this, but the so-called depressive realism effect has been shown to remove our rose-colored investing spectacles and to cause us to face the world as it really is. Obviously, trading off our mental health in order to improve our investment returns is a bit of a bum deal, but the finding adds further weight to the idea that we're permanently biased towards good news and away from bad, and that this leads us into all sorts of financially unwise behavior.

Why we're so addicted to believing the best about the world is still a bit of a mystery, but one theory is that if we really faced up to the contingent uncertainty and general awfulness of existence then we would be unable to function properly. Another theory suggests that it's an unintended by-product of consciousness: self-awareness means we understand the limits of our own mortality and that, in turn, means that we need to be unrelentingly optimistic in the face of certain death. All of this is a bit depressing, especially if we want to be successful investors, although, ironically, believing this would probably improve our investment returns.

Our overconfidence and over optimism seem to be built on our natural need to bolster our self-esteem and feelings of self-worth, traits that may well be fundamental to our general well-being. So, once again we find that a behavior that is natural and healthy in the context of normal life will undermine our investments and, once again, we need to find ways of restraining this behavior in an investment context.

Overconfidence is, in fact, difficult to completely eradicate, but the research indicates that this is one area where experience does tend to help a bit. A behavioral finance study by Steffen Meyer, Maximilian Koestner, and Andreas Hackethal[10] shows that as we become more experienced investors we tend to churn our portfolios less, and this will tend to result in improved returns, exactly what the Barber and Odean research would suggest. This is the sort of result we ought to expect because any moderately self-aware person should eventually notice that the stocks they buy don't usually do very well and the ones they sell are successful: it's cause and effect, more or less, and realism will slowly seep in.

Obviously we would be better served learning this lesson early, and doing so by learning from the experiences of others before incurring our own losses. However, failing that, it's better that we learn through small losses rather than big ones. And a bit of realism always helps.

LESSON 5

Overconfidence is something that a bit of experience can overcome. The lesson here is not to risk too much too early on in your investing career. And, if you're an unrelenting optimist be very careful indeed, because you may end up very poor and depressed.

DISPOSED TO LOSE MONEY

Unfortunately, as the Koestner research identifies, experience doesn't eradicate all biases and one such issue seems to be a tendency that Barber and Odean also identified in their erratically overconfident Internet traders—our preference for selling our winners and keeping our losers, a behavior known as the disposition effect.

This finding is one of the oldest in behavioral finance, and again can be traced back to the work of Amos Tversky and Daniel Kahneman.[11] Roughly speaking, we can think of our disposition as our fundamental set of innate qualities—the behaviors we're born with, or at least those we demonstrate regularly and consistently. Disposition is to be contrasted with situation—the stuff that is dependent on the particular situation we find ourselves in. So, disposition is permanent, situation is temporary. Unfortunately, in the modern world, we often seem to get a bit confused about which is which, with some damaging consequences.

We discussed one example of the disposition effect earlier in the chapter, in the infamous Milgram experiment. Our innate disposition is to defer to authority, so we will tend to obey figures who exude a certain kind of confidence, regardless of their actual knowledge or abilities. This has led to a whole range of sad outcomes, everything from doctors chopping off the wrong leg to commercial airlines flying into mountains in perfect visibility and cavalrymen charging gun emplacements armed with the equivalent of small pointy sticks.

An experiment by Lee Ross, Teresa Amabile, and Julia Steinmetz[12] has even shown that people think that game show hosts are more intelligent than the contestants, because they know the answers to the questions. Somehow they manage to ignore the fact that the hosts have the answers in front of them! Another related behavior is known as the beauty effect, where we think that an attractive person is also likely to be intelligent. These problems are triggered by the misapplication of social cues and, as the evidence suggests, are very, very difficult to overcome.

This confusion between disposition and situation—not all men in white coats in hospitals are doctors—is a problem known as the fundamental attribution error. It's nastily tied up with the introspection illusion, blind spot bias, and deferral to authority and helps explain why we tend to listen to stock market gurus, celebrity CEOs, and other supposed experts. Sadly, they can't predict the future any better than we can, they're just reading off their cue cards.

LESSON 6

Experience can't solve all of our problems—sometimes it's better to figure out what works for others without making your own mistakes.

LOSS AVERSION

When the behavioral economists Hersh Shefrin and Meir Statman[13] looked at the disposition effect in investors they identified a particular type of irrational behavior—a tendency to sell winners too quickly and to hold losers too long, something they refered to as "an aversion to loss realization," which is obviously closely related to the finding that Internet investors tend to trade away their gains. These days, we typically refer to this, a little more simply, as loss aversion.

Loss aversion, as its name suggests, is a strong inclination to avoid losers, which in the stock market tends to mean avoiding taking a loss—that is, we will try and avoid selling a stock while we're losing money on it. Like all of the other biases we've met this isn't just an investing issue and can be found in many other areas of life. In fact, the strength of the effect was demonstrated in a neat study of professional golfers by Devin Pope and Maurice Schweitzer.[14] Each hole on a golf course has a "par" score, which is the number of strokes you're expected to take to get the ball in the hole. If you take more than the par number of strokes you make a "bogie" or, in investment language, you take a loss. On the other hand, if you take less than the par number of strokes you make a "birdie," or make a profit.

The researchers hypothesized that the players would suffer from loss aversion and be more worried about losses than gains. They analyzed the relative success of golfers when putting to avoid a bogie or achieve a birdie and found, as they suspected, the players were far more successful at avoiding losses than they were at making gains when making their final putts (which, for non golfers, is the part where you try to get the ball in the hole). Interestingly, on the final day of the tournament, when what really mattered were the golfers' positions relative to each other, as this determines their prize money, this effect disappeared.

The same par-bogie effect appears to apply to investors. Even professional investors demonstrate it, as Peter Locke and Steven Mann[15] showed. The experts hold losing investments longer than winning ones and their average position size—the number of stocks they hold—is larger for losers than winners. We all hate taking losses, and will grimly hang on to duff stocks in the hope that they'll rise to our buying price. Because we want to register gains we will also tend to sell our winners simply because they've gone up, regardless of whether or not they remain excellent homes for our money. This is madness, but it applies in all sorts of situations and seems to be a problem that investors find almost impossible to overcome. The net effect, as with so many other biases, is to reduce our potential gains significantly, as those studies from Cowles and Dalbar we looked at earlier show.

LESSON 7

Treat every golf shot with the same seriousness, and every investment decision on its own merits. Losses are arbitrary, value is usually not.

ANCHORED

One reason we're so reluctant to take a loss is related to our issues with self-esteem. As long as we can delay accepting a loss we can pretend it's not real and avoid challenging our beliefs about our innate investing ability. We also sell our winners for a similar reason, because it locks in the "win." Unfortunately, this rather ignores the fact that winners often keep on winning for good fundamental reasons. You know, things such as they're fine companies run by intelligent managers in industries where it's possible to prevent intense competition undercutting margins.

Loss aversion and the disposition effect reveal yet another fundamental human deviation from rationality. Technically, the price we happen to buy a stock at is no more meaningful than any other price the stock ever trades at. Even if we do our research with incredible care and diligence it's a slam dunk certainty that the share price of some of the companies we buy stakes in will decline after we buy them. In fact, I know that the majority of my investments do this (and this isn't an accident or even bad luck, as I'll explain later).

It's an old market mantra that you can never sell at the top or buy at the bottom, and it's one of the rare truisms associated with the markets that's true: you'll never time a trade perfectly other than by chance. So, if the price we buy at is, at some level, a random number, then rationally that price should be no more or less meaningful than any other price. What should matter is the underlying value of the corporation, not the price it's currently trading at.

But, of course, if that were true, loss aversion wouldn't occur, because a loss is only ever relative to the buying price. As it turns out this isn't true—humans exhibit yet another effect, known as anchoring, where we attach ourselves to the buying price and assess the success, or failure, of our investment relative to it. In this we're not helped by the prevalence of stock portfolio trackers, which kindly point out our relative successes and failures in graphic and colorful detail.

Anchoring is yet another powerful bias, and it occurs in all sorts of situations. Take real estate for instance, where people will often anchor on the high-water price of a similar property and then refuse to sell for less. This can have major economic impacts, as real estate markets can grind to a halt in the event of a downturn, as everyone refuses to sell, despite the fact that if you sell for less you can usually buy for less.

A similar problem can occur with stocks as well, where people shift their anchors from a buying price to a high-water price. When markets as a whole come off a boom whole swathes of investors may choose to sit on their hands, waiting for the previous highs to be breached before they sell. Unfortunately, market booms are usually associated with a disconnection between price and value, and corrections are about bridging that gap through price reductions—people who have anchored on peak prices in that situation may wait a lifetime to make back their "losses."

In a beautifully simple experiment that the behavioral economist Dan Ariely[16] has used to illustrate the concept of anchoring, simply getting people to write down the last two digits of their Social Security numbers affect the prices they subsequently bid for a range of different items. Roughly speaking, the higher the Social Security number the higher the bid. Yet, if the participants had truly been aware of the real value of the items on offer the arbitrary anchor of the Social Security number couldn't have worked—and this is a critical bit of information, because anchoring causes these problems in situations characterized by uncertainty, where it's difficult to accurately assess the true value of an item. So, this is a situation very similar to that which we might experience in stock markets in times of turbulence, or if we were novice investors, or if we simply weren't very good at valuing stocks or are tired or emotional or . . . well, the list goes on and on.

Why is anchoring so powerful in these situations? We've already seen the cause of this—it's salience and availability. A buying price, or a peak price, is an easily retrievable and very salient piece of information in an otherwise uncertain world. It's a lot easier to look at a simple number than it is to do the nasty grind of analyzing the true value of a stock. Yet that's the real information we need—does the current share price make the stock a bargain at the current price or not?

Fortunately for us, in a world dominated by biased investors who don't have any understanding of their problems and who are inherently disposed not to seek feedback to solve them, we don't need to have that much of an insight into the issues to give us a vital edge. Stock markets are a zero sum game—if we win someone else loses—so if we have a better idea of what we're doing than the competition we should do okay.

LESSON 8

A buying price is simply a random point on a chart, and shouldn't affect buying or selling decisions. Make sure you trade based on the current evidence, not on some historically irrelevant data point.

TWO STRANGERS

Applied to money, all of this foregoing behavior should, I hope, seem plainly irrational. We are, in effect, acting in a way designed to destroy our own returns. Economists generally operate on the basis that we won't do this and they have a point, because it's completely idiotic that we don't—But the fact remains that we don't, and a lot of the problems with the world's economy can be explained by this (along with a marked reluctance to believe economists about most things).

As we discussed earlier, we all have met people who express these general biases to an extreme extent. I'm sure you know someone who is never to blame for anything that goes wrong, yet who is always responsible when things go well. This self-serving bias is most strongly expressed by people who meet success and failure and regard them as complete opposites, rather than simply the normal expression of a normal life.

The research done by Ola Svenson into people's attitudes toward their own driving abilities shows the effect in operation when people are faced with a lack of insight into their own driving skills, an area where most of us get fairly regular feedback from other road users, often involving strange hand gestures. In investment we see the same effect replicated; people seem to form strong positive opinions about their investments and then behave accordingly.

For instance, Kent Daniel, David Hirshleifer, and Avanidhar Subrahmanyam[17] have shown that if new information is released that backs up an investor's beliefs, then their confidence in their decision grows, but if the information contradicts their beliefs then they tend to ignore it. There's an even more peculiar bias known as the backfire effect, where if you present people with evidence that their beliefs are wrong—that UFOs aren't real, that President Obama isn't an alien, or that Elvis isn't alive and well and selling yakburgers in Outer Mongolia—then they become even more convinced that they're right. Somehow, it's not the information that's relevant but the reinforcing effect of discussing it that seems to trigger the bias.

It was Rudyard Kipling who said that we should meet triumph and disaster and treat them the same, but mostly we can't. If you trace the path of our bias for feelings of positive self-worth through the introspection illusion and the blind spot bias to overconfidence, and from overconfidence to the disposition effect and anchoring, you'll find a clear case for finding that self-serving bias is critical to our notions of self-esteem. Unfortunately, our self-esteem is often wrapped up with our beliefs about our investing skills, and so behavior that is fine in everyday life may be something we need to put behind us when we turn to handling money and investing, if we want to achieve the best returns.

Oddly, we don't always want the best returns from our investing activities, but that's another story. For now, let's focus on another odd feature of this array of peculiar behaviors—just like drivers we constantly get feedback that should show us whether we're doing stupid things or not. So why don't we learn from it?

LESSON 9

We're not easily swayed from our prior opinions by new information, because our self-esteem and self-belief is wrapped up in those beliefs. Ideally we need to leave our egos behind when we start investing; there are plenty of other places to be self-serving, most of them far less expensive.

HINDSIGHT'S NOT SO WONDERFUL

Why don't we seem to learn from the lessons of the past? After all, if we keep on making mistakes based on the type of behavioral biases discussed here you'd think that eventually we'd notice that we're not particularly good at investing. The large hole in our bank accounts might be a giveaway, you'd think. Unfortunately, there's another bias at play, one that the CIA describes as ineradicable—hindsight bias.

Hindsight bias is the peculiar finding that we think we predicted the present in the past, when in fact we did no such thing, because what we actually do is modify our memories to make us think that way. It appears that we're utterly unable to divorce the actual experience of the present from our memories of what we thought was going to happen: the present colors our perception of history. What's even worse is that the past is, at best, a very imperfect guide to the future.

One of the world's experts on judgement and decision making, Baruch Fischhoff,[18] has performed a raft of interesting research around the topic of hindsight and has shown that people are largely unaware that their perceptions are changed by becoming aware of actual results—or, to put it more simply, our memories of what we predicted are biased by the knowledge of what actually happened. He also points out that knowing that this happens doesn't offer us any way of fixing the problem, which is why the CIA has such a problem, because they can't rely on even the best trained agents to give a true picture of prior events. It's not that they're lying, it's that they can't help interpreting events in the context of eventual outcomes.

This matters for the simple reason that if we project this issue forward it means that we're generally rather confident—overconfident in fact—about our ability to predict the future. After all, we successfully predicted the present so why should the future be any different? Only we didn't predict the present, we simply misremember this. The net result is, of course, overconfidence, and that overconfidence is the killer for our investment returns.

Goetzmann and Peles[19] conducted some research on investor recollection of their returns against actual performance. For reasons that escape me, their first group of subjects were architects, a profession not especially known for its investment expertise—although perhaps that was the point. Anyway, the research showed that in between designing carbuncles and flat-pack housing they recalled a performance that was over 6 percent higher than it actually was. Looking at people who thought they were actual investors produced a slightly better result—they only overestimated by over 5 percent.

As Fischhoff suggests, we simply cannot remember the past accurately—our memory systems aren't built for that purpose, but rather are designed to help us adapt to future challenges. Unsurprisingly then, hindsight bias is another issue that experience doesn't help resolve. But while this type of problem is something we can't eliminate we can drive ourselves closer to a safer approach to investing, by continually attempting to reconstruct our past decision-making processes in order to put in place systems to manage and reduce our errors.

This is another reason for keeping a diary of when and why we made trading decisions, what the outcomes were, and why those outcomes were achieved. It's absolutely critical to our investment management, as we attempt to drive ourselves toward behaviors that err on the side of caution. We can't improve without constantly exposing ourselves to the results of our own mistakes, no matter how little we like the experience.

LESSON 10

Hindsight bias is impossible to prevent, but we can at least find ways of limiting its impact.

DEFERRAL TO AUTHORITY

Oddly, all of this manipulation of our own self-image to make us feel good about ourselves exposes us to being gamed by charlatans. As Milgram's experiment showed, we're scarily inclined to defer to authority figures. Milgram's white-coated researchers were fakes, and as Alfred Cowles demonstrated, the investment world is full of experts with an equivalent level of knowledge and skill. Yet these experts are just as unhinged by behaviorally induced overconfidence as the rest of us.

The foremost research on the inability of experts to actually predict anything very well has been done by Philip Tetlock,[20] mainly in the study of political forecasts—although there's no reason to presume that his findings don't apply to the world of investment as well. To simplify a vast body of research, he found that most experts were slightly worse at forecasting results than the average man in the street, yet were profoundly unwilling to accept the fact—more evidence for blind-spot bias—with a whole heap of hindsight bias and overconfidence thrown in, alongside yet more examples of the conjunction fallacy.

In general, experts come up with one of three excuses. Firstly, there's the "I was right but it just hasn't happened yet" get-out clause. So that stock market crash is still just around the corner, and if you keep on forecasting it forever, you'll eventually be right. Many investment pundits have made a career out of this technique.

The second excuse is the "I was right but for something that happened that couldn't have been predicted." This, of course, ignores the fact that most events are contingent on other events and that life is essentially unpredictable. And if you don't accept that in real life there's plenty of evidence to show that it's true in stock markets.

Finally, experts come up with the "I wasn't wrong" excuse. This works a surprisingly large amount of the time. In fact, it turns out that most people don't actually analyze the track records of so-called experts but simply take their word regarding their expertise. Joseph Radzevick and Don Moore[21] investigated this finding and uncovered the scary fact that the pundits we prefer are not the ones that are most accurate but the ones that express the most confidence that they're right. Sadly, the ones we should trust are sometimes the less bullish, less confident, more diffident ones who at least recognize that the world is simply too complex to predict with any certainty.

So it shouldn't be a surprise that it's not just overconfidence that's the hallmark of the convincing but inept expert. It turns out to be a particular kind of overconfidence known as overprecision: "an excessive certainty about the accuracy of one's beliefs."[22]

The best pundits, and the worst forecasters, come up with extremely detailed and convincing arguments about what's going to happen and why, most of which never come true. They are as much victims of the introspection illusion as we all are but the gullibility of their public means they never need to improve.

LESSON 11

Most experts aren't any better than us. The ones that are may just be short-term lucky. Never, ever put all of your trust in one person who you don't even know very well.

EMOTION

By now it should be fairly obvious to you that we're not really very rational when it comes to money. In fact, most of the time we're downright emotional about it. And emotions are central to our money management issues.

One fascinating series of experiments, by psychologist Antonio Damasio,[23] was centered around people who have suffered a type of brain damage and don't feel emotions the way that most people do.

It ought to be reasonably clear that we have emotions for good reasons. If we drive around a sharp bend too quickly we get a quick shot of fear and next time we're more likely to take it easy. But someone who doesn't experience emotions isn't likely to learn that lesson. However, what in the real world may open us to danger is actually advantageous when it comes to investing, because in investing we need to learn to play the odds in a world that is essentially full of ambiguity and uncertainty.

So, where uninjured people will get all emotional over a loss or a gain and demonstrate the behavioral effects we've already discussed—loss aversion, the disposition effect, and so on—the brain-damaged individuals will keep on investing based on what appears to be a rational calculation of the odds. They're simply not swayed by the kinds of emotional considerations that most of us take for granted.

Which leads, you'd think, to the conclusion that unemotional investing is best, and also to the immediate problem of what we should do about it. After all, emotions are hard-wired into us for good reason. Well, as it turns out, it's a bit more complicated than you might expect.

In a famous experiment by Damasio known as the Iowa Gambling Task,[24] the researchers produced four decks of cards, two of which would consistently produce losses and two of which would consistently produce gains. What's interesting is that the way that the losses and gains are generated are different: so one of the losing decks consists of lots of losses while the other one consists of lots of gains and one whopping great big loss.

The history of the experiment is long and tortuous, but roughly it turns out that brain-damaged participants never learn to avoid the losing decks, while the uninjured participants do—and they do so surprisingly quickly. Although it takes them 50 card choices before they can consciously report a problem with the bad decks they actually start to preferentially avoid them after only 10. Somehow, emotion and logic are integrated to allow us to sense danger.

This, unfortunately, is exactly the wrong thing to do in the stock market, where a trend is probably simple random noise, and tends to ignore the problem of Black Swans, otherwise known as disaster myopia.

LESSON 12

The best investing is done unemotionally, but not randomly.

BLACK SWANS

Nassim Nicholas Taleb is rightly famous for his trenchant views about, well, almost everything. He's often very rude about investment managers, and other members of the financial community, and he often has a point. Perhaps the phrase most associated with him is that of the Black Swan—the idea that sudden, unexpected events can overturn our expectations.[25] All swans are white, until one day we meet a black one. This bolt from the blue overturns all of our expectations—and, really, just shows us that all of our expectations about the world are provisional: Black Swans are unpredictable and have huge consequences. The ground is solid until you experience an earthquake and markets can only go up until they collapse.

Well, there's a similar bias in human behavior. Typically we're myopic—short-sighted—about the world for the reasons we discussed in the previous chapter—it's a form of observer bias, where we draw wide-ranging conclusions about the world from our small sample of personal experience—and it's a form of hindsight bias, where we misinterpret our own history. In particular, we are very disinclined to see the world as random, and desperately try to make order out of chaos. As humanity's success shows, this isn't a bad model, and it works most of the time. However, occasionally disaster strikes and our models, and our lives, are overturned.

When some Taiwanese researchers re analyzed the results of the Iowa Gambling Task they noticed something strange that was hidden by the original experiment design.[26] Although it was correct that undamaged individuals did appreciate the risks inherent in the bad deck, where there were lots of poor results, it turns out that the most popular deck was the other bad one, the one in which there were lots of good outcomes and one hugely bad one. As Taleb would be quick to point out, this is pretty much analogous to the way that stock markets work—mostly they chug along, moving gently upward until one day the whole thing blows up. There's a natty little phrase for this: "picking pennies up in front of the steamroller." It's a great way of making money until you slip over.

That we're attracted to situations that give us lots of positive feedback, even if we're only making very small amounts of money, isn't surprising. We like to win, to make profits, and we don't like losing. Yet many of the great investors seem to do the opposite—they lose more often than they win, but they cut their losses quickly and they run their winners so that when they win they win big. It's been described as the Babe Ruth effect, after the great baseball hitter, because he struck out often but when he connected he hit a lot of home runs.

Our failure to recognize that a disaster is always possible is a bit more puzzling, but is associated with an issue known as disaster myopia. It seems that we're very quickly able to adjust to the new reality after a disaster, and as time goes on we rapidly discount the possibility of one happening again. And, of course, the more we discount the possibility the more likely a problem is to occur.

LESSON 13

A disaster is always just around the corner, be prepared.

DIRTY MONEY, MENTAL ACCOUNTING

It's impossible to disentangle the effects of emotion from the way we treat money. Here's an example. Jonathan Levav and Peter McGraw[27] showed that people associate money with emotional tags that are dependent on how they earned it. This so-called moral accounting means that money that people have earned by less than honest means tends to be laundered by purchasing virtuous stuff, like education, rather than on hedonistic pleasures, like alcohol or tobacco.

This is a form of mental accounting, where people assign money to different mental pots and then treat them separately. Mental accounting is a very odd thing, but we all do it. People "put aside" money for a rainy day, keep special accounts for holiday savings, and generally segregate their capital for different reasons. All of which is done for good reasons of self-control, in order to make sure that the future is paid for. Unfortunately, a virtuous behavior in normal life turns into a malicious one in investing.

Remember the idea of loss aversion, where we seek to avoid taking a loss if at all possible? Well, if you add mental accounting to this mix you suddenly find that people are able to segregate different parts of their capital and manage their profit and loss on each account separately. This can have pernicious consequences—how often have you heard about someone who sells half their stock when it doubles because they're now in the stock for free? This is rubbish, of course, because what matters is the total amount money, not the loss or profit on a single share.

People will take advantage of mental accounting to shift loss-making stocks about and to aggregate them with others, in order to minimize their feelings of regret. Regret is a yet another nasty bias, because we tend to regret actions we have taken more than ones we didn't—sins of commission matter more than sins of omission—and we often get tangled up with our feelings about past decisions. In some further Barber and Odean research, along with Michal Strahilevitz,[28] they showed that people buy back stocks they previously sold for a profit, but not ones they sold at a loss, but only if they've fallen in value.

Fiddling about with our mental accounts is a particularly effective way of indulging our preferences for avoiding losses in order to reduce any feelings of regret we have. This leaves us feeling happier, but is utterly hopeless behavior when it comes to maximizing our returns.

LESSON 14

Mental accounting is not something investors should do. Do not segregate your portfolio into different bits, it's all the same money at the end of the day.

A FAINT WHISPER OF EMOTION

Of course, "feeling happier" is exactly the point; it's all about our emotional responses to financial transactions. All of this odd fiddling around with money is intimately connected with the way we regard ourselves and the emotions that failure or success generates. In theory, when it comes to investing, whether or not we're successful should be an easy thing to assess—it's all in the numbers, after all. But even if we do measure these correctly, which we're inclined not to do, we still have a lot of ways of avoiding taking responsibility for our actions. Many of these are downright peculiar when we analyze them logically, but make perfect sense to anyone who spends their days studying how humans actually handle themselves in situations governed by risk and uncertainty—which is pretty much any situation you care to mention when it comes to stock market investing.

What psychologists have found is that we definitely don't rationally assess the risk and reward of any given situation but rather rely on a sense of goodness or badness in any given situation. Just as people will morally account and tag money as tainted under certain circumstances, we tag everyday events in the same way. This emotional tagging is often described as a "faint whisper of emotion" but is more accurately known as "affect." The affect heuristic is yet another one of those loose rules that we use to guide us through our lives, lying virtually unconscious below the surface of our minds, and is consciously accessible only with real effort.

While the affect heuristic is a darn useful technique for managing risk in everyday life it's certainly not without its problems. For instance, if we like something we judge it as less risky and if we don't like it we judge it as more. So, for example, take an example we've already seen, the fact that most people judge nuclear power as riskier than X-ray machines when the reverse is probably true. Exactly the same sort of behavior is seen with investors, both private and professional.

So when Yoav Ganzach[29] looked at how professional securities analysts judged the risk-return opportunity of specific stocks, he found that where the experts already knew the corporations in question then the actual risk and expected returns were correlated, but when they didn't they fell back on global attitudes rather than relying on their own. This looks like the affect heuristic in operation, rather than some careful assessment of real risk and reward. And one result of this is that stock market sectors with a buzz about them get rated more highly than those with bad karma—and this has nothing to do with real valuation, but is solely based on that whispering emoting voice at the back of our heads.

There's a correlate to this: sectors associated with bad news often outperform over three- and five-year periods. This is just the action of the invisible hand, as unreasonably depressed valuations are picked up by astute value-hunting investors.

LESSON 15

Don't buy stocks just because they're in a feel-good sector. Humans have emotions, stocks don't.

PSYCHOLOGICALLY NUMBED

The affect heuristic seems to have another impact on us as well, something that Paul Slovic,[30] who has led much of the research into risk perception, refers to as "psychophysical numbing." Remember that we're highly sensitive to personal observation in preference to statistical analysis of broad trends for the good reason that this is the environment we evolved in. You would expect people to respond to their own experiences rather than those of other people, even if their own experiences are atypical. Overcoming this is difficult.

Slovic goes beyond this and suggests that we're actually biased against the type of statistical analysis that is most beneficial to us as investors, and suggests that this is a side effect of the affect heuristic. He thinks that the affective system is designed to make us acutely sensitive to small changes in our local environment, but at the cost of making us insensitive to big changes. In essence, we can respond to anecdotes and stories because we can understand personal risks and empathize with the participants but we simply can't grasp the vastness of some of the numbers that modern life throws at us.

This isn't just about investing, of course. At the end of the twentieth century the United Kingdom found itself in the grip of a panic about the affect of the so-called triple jab—a single vaccination against measles, mumps, and rubella. An article published in *The Lancet* purported to find a link between the triple jab and the rise of autism in children. It was clear almost from the beginning that the risks associated with not having the jab were greater than the risks of having it, even if the research was correct, but it was also clear that there were grave concerns about the research itself, which was eventually thoroughly discredited.

The result, of course, was predictable. Faced with scary anecdotes of autistic children versus statistical evidence of a lack of a real correlation people abandoned the vaccination program in droves, driving down the level of vaccinations for that particular cohort of children to the point where group immunity was compromised. The consequence was inevitable, and has led to a rise in measles cases across the UK. Now, faced with more media-driven anecdotes of children suffering and potentially dying from a lack of immunity, parents are flocking to fix the problem. Stories are powerful, statistics are not.

In general, we need to be wary of anecdotal evidence. Statistics strip away the emotional whispers we like to rely on, and that's often a good thing in life. In investing it's essential.

LESSON 16

We prefer emotionally charged stories to complex numbers. Unfortunately, this is not a great way to invest and we need to work to understand the numbers properly.

MARTHA STEWART'S BIASES

For a real-world example of the problems that unsuspecting investors can run into with their biases we need look no further than celebrity chef, and one-time penitentiary inmate, Martha Stewart. During her trial for insider trading her portfolio was published as part of the evidence and this allowed

Meir Statman[31] to analyze it for behavioral bias. What he discovered is probably pretty typical of most private investor portfolios.

Ms. Stewart demonstrated loss aversion, through her unwillingness to sell stocks at a loss, and regret, because she was also unwilling to sell them at a profit—what would she feel like if the stock went up a lot the following day? She also demonstrated a peculiarly American bias, the December effect, where she was willing to sell stocks at a loss in December, but only to mitigate taxes before the end of the tax year, a clear case of mental accounting and a rare one where it's influenced by actual accounting.

She also showed a tendency to scapegoat her advisers—if the stock goes up it was the investor's decision, but if it goes down the adviser got it wrong: the fundamental attribution error, and evidence for the disposition effect. These biases are not fictions, and they have real effects on ordinary investors' personal wealth and life prospects. Advisers can perform their clients a real and ongoing service by educating them about these facts.

All of this odd, interconnected behavior is ultimately linked back to emotions and the way we regard ourselves. The obvious counter to this is to be more aware of why we're doing things, to ensure we're mindful in the face of all of the things that can cause our biases to trigger and lead us into temptation, and losses, and sometimes worse.

Mindfulness, and its opposite, mindlessness, is a subject Ellen Langer has studied carefully over a long period of time. This work comes out of her illusion of control problems we looked at in the previous chapter, and draws on the idea that we need to pay conscious attention to what we're doing in order to obtain the best possible outcomes. Unfortunately, paying this kind of attention to anything, let alone something as confusing as money, seems to actively deplete our mental resources: as Kathleen Vohs and colleagues[32] have shown, the more decisions we make the more likely we are to impair our self-control.

It's clear from most of the evidence in this chapter that our emotions, especially around our feelings of self-esteem, can drive us into some particularly poor decision making. Paying active and careful attention, in light of the knowledge of how we're biased, ought to improve this. However, the issue of resource depletion means that even with this level of self-knowledge we still really need to try and minimize the number of decisions we make, which, as Barber and Odean would observe, should lead to immediately better outcomes, for Martha Stewart and us all.

LESSON 17

Most investors are mindless. We need to be mindful.

RETROSPECTIVE

Let's pause briefly and look at the ground covered in this chapter. We can trace a set of fundamental problems from our over reliance on the introspection illusion. Because we're fundamentally biased towards a positive self-image, we're led into overconfidence. The same bias means we don't like facing up to evidence that we're wrong, which prevents us from adjusting our overconfident behavior. Our overconfidence leads us into overtrading and our failure to elicit feedback, which can damage our self-image; this means we preferentially sell successful investments, to lock in winners, and keep unsuccessful ones, to avoid taking losses—the disposition effect, which is an outcome of loss aversion. Loss aversion is conditioned by anchoring, and anchoring is an outcome of the more fundamental biases of salience and availability.

We also tend to defer to authority figures, such as investment experts and tipsters, particularly ones that specialize in overconfident and overly precise forecasts. Unfortunately, these people are generally no better than average at making such calls, are usually just as biased as the rest of us, but are heavily incentivized to avoid facing up to this—after all, if your career depends on being regarded as an expert you're not likely to go around admitting you're no such thing.

All of this is linked by the underlying, ever present whisper of emotion, our reliance on the affect heuristic in order to judge whether things are safe or not. And, as so often happens, this doesn't work in the stylized and complex environment of the stock market. So what can we do about this? What measures are available to us to protect ourselves from our lack of self-knowledge?

Even though it's a nasty minefield of self-deception, we're not completely defenseless in the face of our own egos. With a bit of conscious effort we can overcome many of these issues, and the ones we can't face head on we can avoid, if we know what we're doing.

ANNUAL RETURNS

Exactly how the disposition effect and overconfidence interact, as witnessed by overtrading, loss aversion, and anchoring, is hard to say. In fact, this is one of the weaknesses of behavioral finance because we still don't understand how the various biases interact, but it's still perfectly clear that these behaviors tend, on average, to drag down our investment returns. One possible reaction to this is to avoid inspecting our portfolios on a regular basis, because the more notice we take of what our stocks and investments are doing on a short-term basis the more likely we are to be panicked or otherwise persuaded into trading. The question then, of course, is how often we should take a peek at how our money is managing by itself.

The answer turns out to be not more than once a year. This unexpected finding was the result of research by Werner de Bondt and Richard Thaler and is, unsurprisingly, known as the de Bondt-Thaler hypothesis. Their empirical data suggested, just as the evidence above indicates, that the more often investors inspect their portfolios the more often they trade and the appropriate response to this, they argue, is to avoid the problem entirely.

The idea of self-control by abstinence is one that reoccurs throughout the research on behavioral finance; there's a persuasive line of thought that many of these underlying biases are simply so strong that most of us will be unable to overcome them by active means so we need to practice the investing equivalent of chastity. It's a miserable thought, but if our self-image is so strongly bound up in our relationship with money then, for many people, it may be the only way. We can trace the rise of passive index tracking funds that essentially take asset allocation control out of the hands of individual investors or fund managers to the recognition of this situation.

NUDGED

Richard Thaler, along with Cass Sunstein, has taken this idea a step further into the realm of so-called "nudge theory." The concept has been used in a wide variety of situations, but most famously in retirement savings. One of the big issues facing the Western world, with its aging populations, is that most of us don't save enough for our retirement years. Part of the problem is that we have to constantly make decisions about investing for our futures and, it turns out, we're actually not very good at delaying gratification and spending less now in order to have a more comfortable life later on.

Thaler and Sunstein[33] have come up with a Save More Tomorrow™ scheme, which means that savers only need to make one decision and the rest happens automatically—the amount they save automatically increases as the amount they earn goes up. This relies on people tending to fail to make difficult decisions and defaulting to the standard option—in this case the default option selected is to save more and most people never change this.

Default options are now being used in a wide variety of situations in order to coax people into doing what's best for them, from health care through to social policy, but they may well be most effective when used in financial situations, which seem to bring out the worst in us. Coming up with sets of rules and following them rigidly is one way of using the theory, but it takes a very strong-minded person to stick to such an approach when things go wrong; but the beauty of such methods is that they remove our issues of self-worth and self-esteem from the investment equation because if we don't take a personal interest in the stocks we invest in then we don't invest ourselves in them.

MINDFULNESS

The idea that we should be consciously aware of our own biases and pay attention to how they affect our investing is easy enough to state, but a lot harder to do. We have the problem of resource depletion—paying attention to things saps our ability to keep on paying attention—and have the issue of deciding what we want to focus on. There are so many things going on when we invest that it can be hard to decide what to pay attention to—which is one reason why a rules-based checklist is a good thing to have.

Catherine Weick and colleagues[34] came up with an interesting variation on this theme when they took a look at the problems of mindlessness in safety critical organizations—like nuclear power stations. Their checklist is a very useful starting point for logical investors:

- Be preoccupied with failure.
- Do not simplify interpretations.
- Be sensitive to odd events.
- Be resilient.
- Don't get too clever.

So, before we end this chapter, let's take a brief look at each of these in turn.

Be Preoccupied with Failure

An overt concern for getting things wrong, and a furious determination to get them right in the future is the hallmark of a safety first investor. In fact, because stock markets are far less predictable than, say, nuclear power stations, this is harder to do than you might think, but there are some quick wins.

Firstly, you have to identify your failures. There's no point engaging in mental accounting in order to spare your ego the humiliation of recognizing that you've got things wrong again. It's necessary to aggregate your accounts and carefully track your profits and losses.

Secondly, you need to analyze the data properly. What went wrong and why? Is this failure absolute—perhaps you made a mistake—or is it relative—maybe the market went up 200 percent while you only made 50 percent? It's easy to be pleased with a gain, but when it's a lot worse than the return on an index tracker then you're fooling yourself.

Finally, codify your actions: turn them into actionable rules that you can build into a checklist or some other form of guidance. Don't just assume you will remember what went wrong when you go investing again—hindsight bias will guarantee that you can't.

Do Not Simplify Interpretations

It's terribly easy to lapse into simple default behaviors, to do this time what you did last without thinking about it—the very definition of mindlessness. "Buying on the dips" worked right up until it didn't, but brainless investors carried on with this approach while the markets kept on falling. A checklist is a good starting point but it needs to be continually reviewed in the light of reality.

Moreover, the decision-making processes that sit behind what stocks we choose and when we choose to buy and sell them are not straightforward either. You will be amazed by the reasons we find for buying and selling shares. For instance, we will often buy back a stock that has fallen from our selling price but we won't if it has risen. And we positively hate buying stocks we sold at a loss when they've risen, regardless of the circumstances. We don't like being reminded of our tendency to regret things.

Availability and salience figure highly amongst the issues we face in stock selection. Yet they're awful ways of choosing stocks, which don't care about whether their brands are well known, their CEOs are in the news a lot, or our best friend tipped them. Understanding why we choose the shares we do, and why we choose when to buy and sell is essential, otherwise we'll all end up like Martha Stewart. Only not in jail, hopefully.

Be Sensitive to Odd Events

There's nothing quite like an exception to a rule for improving our models. We will tend to ignore such exceptions, because we prefer to ignore data that contradicts our prior opinions in favor of that which supports them. However, exceptions are interesting because the investing environment is ever fluid and changing. We regularly see market behavior change, and we should be on the outlook for such signs.

Learning to pay attention and to appreciate odd events is far harder than you might think, but yields invaluable lessons. Investors who happen to learn to invest in one particular type of market—the long bull market of the 1980s and 1990s, for instance—are apt to believe that the market behavior they experience is fixed and unchanging. They're wrong, as we saw when these markets faded into the bear market at the start of the twenty-first century.

It's important to recognize that not even the big picture remains constant. If we build our models and tools purely based on our own experiences, even of the wider world, we'll still have a problem when that world changes again.

Be Resilient

Things go wrong when we go investing. As we've seen, we often contribute marvelously to these things going wrong but it's important not to get overly fixated on this. All too often things will go wrong that we have little control over. In 2005, investors in the UK Internet retailer ASOS woke up to discover that its main warehouse had just gone up in flames because a nearby oil storage facility had exploded. Obviously this is the type of thing that can happen when you hang out around petrochemical plants, but investors could have been forgiven for not factoring this into their analyses.

A lot of stuff in markets is simply random, and we can't get every decision right, all of the time. It's important that we analyze what we do, and draw the appropriate lessons, but it's equally important that we stay resilient in the face of disaster. Sometimes we make good decisions and things still go wrong; that's the nature of very complicated environments like stock markets. Unfortunately, we're programmed to learn to avoid things which give us nasty negative shocks, but this is not the way of the logical investor.

Don't Get Too Clever

Yes, it's very, very easy to over complicate things and come up with huge lists of variables, which you can feed into computers for them to churn out results. This is, more or less, how we ended up with the subprime crash in 2008, when the risk managers convinced themselves that they could model the real risk of lending mortgages to people whose only asset was a tin bath and a sink.

In fact, too much data leads to a problem known as information overload, where our limited brains start to fizzle and fuse under the pressure of data. And, unsurprisingly, our ability to process it accurately also declines. So we really need to spend time simplifying our processes and our thinking—it's simply not enough to add more and more data points to our analysis tools, unless we can turn this data into information that we can use. And, as we'll see, this is definitely an approach worth considering.

THE SEVEN KEY TAKEAWAYS

This chapter has introduced our personal feelings in the investing equation, and shows that a natural bias in favor of ourselves—the so-called introspection illusion—can lead to a whole range of poor investing behaviors. These problems occur in everyone, not just private investors: so-called experts are just as prone to them as you and I, so you need to choose your advisers with care.

To finish, let's draw together a few key ideas from this chapter before we move on. The main takeaways are:

1. Most of us think that we're better than average at things that matter to us, so if we care about investing we're quite likely to be exaggerating our abilities: this, at least, should be our key starting assumption. So there is a definite bias in favor of overoptimism, and overoptimism leads us into overtrading, and overtrading forces us to make more decisions and, the evidence shows, we're more likely to make mistakes.
2. Overconfidence leads to loss aversion and the disposition effect, where we sell our winners and keep our losers in order to avoid taking a loss; this is silly behavior given that all too often losers go on losing and winners go on winning.
3. Many experts are no better than average at making predictions, but we're attracted to confident individuals, a feature known as deferral to authority, and, as usual, we ignore the data—make sure you can test your expert's abilities.
4. Some biases, such as hindsight bias, cannot be entirely removed but they can be managed; however, experience does not solve all problems, and it's better to learn from other peoples' mistakes than from your own.
5. We're myopic about past disasters, preferring to relegate them to the sock drawer of forgetfulness, but we shouldn't. Never forget that a disaster is just around the corner and that it's brightest just before the sun goes out.
6. Our decision making is driven, for very good reason, by emotion. Being coldly emotionless about our investments is the best possible state, but is never entirely achievable. However, adopting a carefully mindful state about our decisions is helpful and if we're too tired to be mindful we should go and do something else.
7. Even if we do everything right sometimes stuff just happens. Accept this and move on—emotional resilience is critical for all good investors.

I hope it's becoming clear that many of the biases that unconsciously influence our investing decisions are actually quite healthy in a normal human being. So making mistakes is perfectly natural—it's just that we really don't want to go on making them!

Now we're going to look at what happens when the outside world starts to take an interest in us as advisers. Thus far, we've focused on disposition; now we're going to take a more detailed look at situation.

NOTES

1. Emily Pronin and Matthew B. Kugler, "Valuing Thoughts, Ignoring Behavior: The Introspection Illusion as a Source of the Bias Blind Spot," *Journal of Experimental Psychology* (2006): 565–578.
2. Ola Svenson, "Are We All Less Risky and More Skillful than Our Fellow Drivers?" *Acta Psychologica* 47, no. 2 (1981): 143–148. CiteULike:1371150.
3. Stanley Milgram, "Behavioral Study of Obedience," *Journal of Abnormal and Social Psychology* 67, no. 4 (1963): 371–378. doi:10.1037/h0040525, PMID: 14049516.
4. Günter Bierbrauer, "Why Did He Do It? Attribution of Obedience and the Phenomenon of Dispositional Bias," *European Journal of Social Psychology* 9 (1979): 67–84.
5. Brad M. Barber and Terrance Odean, "Online Investors: Do the Slow Die First?" *Review of Financial Studies* 15, no. 2 (2002): 455–488. doi:10.1093/rfs/15.2.455.
6. Markus Glaser and Martin Weber, "Overconfidence and trading volume," *The Geneva Risk and Insurance Review* 32, no. 1 (2007): 1–36.
7. Don Guyon, *One-Way Pockets: The Book of Books on Wall Street Speculation* (Wells, VT: Fraser Publishing Company, 1965). Reproduction of the 1917 edition.
8. Alfred Cowles, "Can Stockmarket Forecasters Forecast?" *Econometrica* 1, no. 3 (1933): 309–324.
9. *Quantitative Analysis of Investor Behavior 2008*, www.qaib.com/public/default.aspx.
10. Steffen Meyer, Maximilian Koestner, and Andreas Hackethal, "Do Individual Investors Learn from Their Mistakes?" (August 2, 2012). Available at SSRN: http://ssrn.com/abstract=2122652 or http://dx.doi.org/10.2139/ssrn.2122652.
11. Daniel Kahneman and Amos Tversky, "Prospect Theory: An Analysis of Decision under Risk," *Econometrica* 47 (1979): 263–291.
12. Lee D. Ross, Teresa M. Amabile, and Julia L. Steinmetz, "Social Roles, Social Control, and Biases in Social-Perception Processes," *Journal of Personality and Social Psychology* 35, no. 7 (1977): 485–494.
13. Hersh Shefrin and Meir Statman, "The Disposition to Sell Winners Too Early and Ride Losers Too Long: Theory and Evidence," *Journal of Finance* 40 (1985): 777–790. doi:10.1111/j.1540-6261.1985.tb05002.x.
14. Devin G. Pope and Maurice E. Schweitzer, "Is Tiger Woods Loss Averse? Persistent Bias in the Face of Experience, Competition, and High Stakes" (2009).

Available at SSRN: http://ssrn.com/abstract=1419027 or http://dx.doi.org/10.2139/ssrn.1419027.

15. Peter Locke and Steven C. Mann, "Do Professional Traders Exhibit Loss Realization Aversion?" Working paper (2000).
16. Dan Ariely, *Predictably Irrational: The Hidden Forces That Shape Our Decisions* (New York: Harper Perennial, 2008).
17. Kent Daniel, David Hirshleifer, and Avanidhar Subrahmanyam, "Investor Psychology and Security Market Under- and Overreactions," *Journal of Finance* 53, no. 6 (1998): 1839–1885.
18. B. Fischhoff, "Hindsight ≠ Foresight: The Effect of Outcome Knowledge on Judgment under Uncertainty," *Quality and Safety in Health Care* 12, no. 4 (2003): 304–312. doi:10.1136/qhc.12.4.304.
19. William N. Goetzmann and Nadav Peles, "Cognitive Dissonance and Mutual Fund Investors," *Journal of Financial Research* 20, no. 2 (1997): 145–158.
20. P. E. Tetlock, "Correspondence and Coherence: Indicators of Good Judgment in World Politics," in *Thinking: Psychological Perspectives on Reasoning, Judgment and Decision Making*, ed. D. Hardman and L. Macchi (Chichester, UK: John Wiley & Sons, 2005): 233. doi:10.1002/047001332X.ch12.
21. Joseph R. Radzevick and Don A. Moore, "Competing to Be Certain (but Wrong): Market Dynamics and Excessive Confidence in Judgment," *Management Science: Journal of the Institute for Operations Research and the Management Sciences* 57, no. 1 (2011): 93–106.
22. Don A. Moore, Paul J. Healy, "The Trouble with Overconfidence," *Psychological Review* 115, no. 2 (2008): 502–517. doi:10.1037/0033-295x.115.2.502.
23. Antonio R. Damasio, *Descartes' Error: Emotion, Reason, and the Human Brain* (New York: Penguin Books, 1994).
24. A. Bechara, A. R. Damasio, H. Damasio, and S. W. Anderson, "Insensitivity to Future Consequences Following Damage to Human Prefrontal Cortex," *Cognition* 50, nos. 1–3 (1994): 7–15.
25. Nassim N. Taleb, *The Black Swan: The Impact of the Highly Improbable* (New York: Random House, 2007).
26. Yao-Chu C. Chiu, Ching-Hung H. Lin, Jong-Tsun T. Huang, Shuyeu Lin, Po-Lei Lee, and Jen-Chuen Hsieh, "Immediate Gain Is Long-Term Loss: Are There Foresighted Decision Makers in the Iowa Gambling Task?" *Behavioral and Brain Functions* 4 (2008): 13. doi:10.1186/1744-9081-4-13.
27. Jonathan Levav and Peter A. McGraw, "Emotional Accounting: How Feelings About Money Influence Consumer Choice," *Journal of Marketing Research* 46 (2009): 66–80. Available at SSRN: http://ssrn.com/abstract=1553907.
28. Terrance Odean, Michal Ann Strahilevitz, and Brad M. Barber, "Once Burned, Twice Shy: How Naïve Learning, Counterfactuals, and Regret Affect the Repurchase of Stocks Previously Sold," (July 31, 2010). Available at SSRN: http://ssrn.com/abstract=611267 or http://dx.doi.org/10.2139/ssrn.611267.
29. Yoav Ganzach, "Judging Risk and Return of Financial Assets," *Organizational Behavior and Human Decision Processes* 83, no. 2 (2000): 353–370.
30. Paul Slovic, David Zionts, Andrew K. Woods, Ryan Goodman, and Derek Jinks, "Psychic Numbing and Mass Atrocity," in *The Behavioral Foundations of Public*

Policy, ed. E. Shafir (Princeton, NJ: Princeton University Press, 2013), 126–142; NYU School of Law, Public Law Research Paper No. 11–56. Available at SSRN: http://ssrn.com/abstract=1809951.

31. Meir Statman, "Martha Stewart's Lessons in Behavioral Finance," *Journal of Investment Consulting* 7, no. 2 (2005): 52–60.

32. Kathleen D. Vohs, Roy F. Baumeister, Brandon J. Schmeichel, Jean M. Twenge, Noelle M. Nelson, and Dianne M., Tice, "Making Choices Impairs Subsequent Self-Control: A Limited-Resource Account of Decision Making, Self-Regulation, and Active Initiative," *Journal of Personality and Social Psychology* 94, no. 5 (2008): 883–898. doi: 10.1037/0022-3514.94.5.883.

33. Richard H. Thaler and Shlomo Benartzi, "Save More Tomorrow™: Using Behavioral Economics to Increase Employee Saving," *Journal of Political Economy* 112, no. S1 (2004): S164–S187.

34. Karl E. Weick, Kathleen M. Sutcliffe, and David Obstfeld, "Organizing for High Reliability: Processes of Collective Mindfulness." in *Research in Organizational Behavior*, Volume 1, ed. R. S. Sutton and B. M. Staw (Stanford: Jai Press, 1999), 81–123.

CHAPTER 3

Situational Finance

It will, obviously, take quite a lot of therapy for us to come to terms with our egos' requirements to believe that we're a better than average investor. But with time we'll no doubt manage it, at which point we will be set to start reaping our investment rewards, no?

Well, probably not. It depends on the situation we find ourselves in because it turns out that different situations cause us to behave differently. In normal life this is done so naturally that we don't even notice, and if we do we put it down to our internal decision-making processes rather than the influence of our environment.

However, it turns out that the way we invest is heavily influenced not just by our own beliefs but by the situation we find ourselves in. Time for the tour bus to visit the highly irrational land of situational finance.

DISPOSITION VS. SITUATION

In Western societies we're brought up to think of ourselves as ruggedly individualistic, ploughing our personal furrows through life. In many ways this is typified by the idea of the American Dream, the idea that anyone can achieve anything if they just try hard enough. As it happens, the United States has one of the lowest rates of social mobility in the Western world:[1] if you're born poor or rich, you're likely to die that way, another example of how we prefer attractive stories to hard statistics.

It's also the central thesis behind the advertising industry: we live in a world bathed in advertisements, attempting to influence us from all sorts of angles and in all sorts of ways. Although generally we feel that we rise above the marketers' attempts to part us from our hard-earned or ill-gotten dollars the mere existence of the multi-multibillion-dollar advertising industry ought to be sufficient to convince us otherwise. Come on, do we believe the corporations spending their cash on marketing are *that* stupid?

So, if advertising really influences us but we tend to ignore the fact that it does, what does that imply about other, less obvious, forms of influence on our behavior? And, in the context we're interested in, what does it imply about the effects of these influences on our investing returns?

The issue comes down to a point we've already discussed, the idea that there's a difference between our innate disposition and the situation that we find ourselves in, and that we frequently get muddled between the two. As we saw earlier, people often believe that game show hosts are smarter than they are because they know the answers to the questions—which, given that they're written down in front of them, shouldn't be very hard.

What's even more remarkable about that research is that the participants continued to persist in this belief even when they themselves set the questions! This confusion between the situation—the game show host has the answers written in front of them—and our interpretation of their disposition—they know the answers so they must be clever—overrides what you might think ought to be a commonsense appreciation that the intelligence of the person with the answers isn't deductible from the situation.

As it turns out, this is just the tip of a very peculiar iceberg of irrationality: situation often dominates disposition to an extent we find hard to accept, bathed as we are in the belief that we're in control of our lives. To a surprising degree, we're not, and figuring out how to avoid being unduly influenced by external pressures is an important addition to our armory of investing weaponry.

BEAUTY IS IN THE EYE OF THE INVESTOR

When you meet an attractive person what do you think?

Well, obviously, you may feel attracted to them, but you're also likely to assume that they're clever. Or, at least, more clever than they actually are. And they'll almost certainly earn more than someone else less favored by good looks but doing the same job. This odd fact is known as the beauty premium and was demonstrated by Daniel Hamermesh and Jeff Biddle,[2] who showed that physically attractive people earn 10 percent more than the more average lookers among us.

A more detailed study[3] showed that 20 percent of this premium was due to confidence, 40 percent due to the visual perception of supervisors, and the rest due to the beautiful elite having better conversational skills—something usually regarded as an outcome of greater confidence. Unsurprisingly the study also showed that the premium was unjustified in terms of output, because simply being better looking doesn't make you any better at what you do.

Judging people by their external appearance is another naturally occurring facet of our behavior—most likely due to the way we go about judging each other's fitness to reproduce with. It's yet a further example of anchoring, as we latch onto a single feature and then use that as a basis for a more wide-ranging assessment of a person. But it's the way this assessment creeps into other areas that raises cause for concern, the so-called halo effect, because there's no real reason why we should trust someone more because they're attractive. It's another example of how we tend to confuse situation with disposition.

The rough lesson here is that if your adviser seems to know what they're talking about, but has the charisma of a skunk and the looks of a warthog then your assessment is probably good. On the other hand, if you think they're the most attractive person you've met in the past month you probably want to ask them for a date, but not for advice.

LESSON 1

We prefer attractive people to ugly ones, and tend to read across their attractiveness into other areas. Any sensible adviser is going to make themselves look presentable; this is one area where content trumps appearance every time.

ANGELS OR DEMONS?

Now, a little bit of lateral thinking might take you in the following direction. If the halo effect can cause us to impute qualities to another person based on a single, probably irrelevant, factor, what can it do when we start looking at corporations? We've already touched on one industry that uses it extensively—the advertisers, who happily use celebrities to promote goods and services that they've probably never even heard of, safe in the knowledge that a celebrity endorsement will see the halo effect kick in. Do you really believe that some of the richest and most beautiful women in the world use mass market makeup?

As far back as 1920, Edward Thorndike[4] identified the halo effect in operation when he noticed that army officers tended to see their subordinates as either all good or all bad, with few shades of gray in between. However, it was a study by social psychologists Richard Nisbett and Timothy Wilson[5] in 1977 that confirmed the effect in operation and, in particular, that it operates entirely unconsciously—even when presented with overwhelming evidence people simply refuse to believe that they can be influenced in this way, which is fortunate for advertisers and scammers everywhere.

Some corporations clearly have their own halos, often unrelated to their investment potential. Historically we've seen all sorts of booms where the valuation of a corporation has been dramatically inflated for no good reason. Perhaps the most obvious example in recent times was connected to the huge boom in dot-com stocks around the turn of the century. Although this originated in some genuine insight into the way the world was going to be changed by the wide availability of the Internet, it also caused some of the worst examples of overinvestment and bizarre investor behavior in living memory.

In the gold rush mentality that accompanied dot-com fever many corporations decided to hitch a lift on the elevator to endless riches. Of course, the canny executives of these companies didn't do anything so complicated as actually changing their business models. No, many of them opted for the simpler option of renaming their companies with something that sounded dot-comish—often simply adding ".com" to the company name. Naturally, investors responded to this overt gaming in the only way we should expect— they flocked to buy the renamed stocks.

In a neat bit of research entitled "A Rose.com by Any Other Name," Michael Cooper, Orlin Dimitrov, and Raghavendra Rau[6] showed that the effect of a company changing its name to something Internet-related saw the share price increase by an average 53 percent at the time of the announcement, with the stocks going on to average a rise of 80 percent over the six months following. And, yes, this happened regardless of whether any actual changes occurred to the company involving the Internet.

Of course, when the dot-com bubble burst, the tag of ".com" suddenly became a stigma, and many companies promptly reversed the name change. You would hope that investors would have learned the lesson, but remember that myopia rules, and removing the association with the Internet promptly saw share prices soar once again, this time by an average of 64 percent.[7] And the more remote from the internet the new name was the greater the share price inflation. In fact, this technique is regularly used by the mutual fund industry, which often changes fund names to take advantage of the latest fad in investing.[8] Once again it works, as such funds see a 30 percent increase in investment monies in the year following the name change—with no associated change in their underlying investment performance.

Halos may be good for short-term share price performance, but they all too often slip and turn into a very unpleasant necktie. The shared willingness of the marketing and investment industries to exploit halo effects is no accident, either. They're both in the business of attracting money from gullible members of the public. Which is fine, because those people aren't going to be us from now on. Are they?

LESSON 2

Halos are no basis for making an investment decision, but the investment industry will ruthlessly exploit popular trends to bring in funds.
Don't be fooled, we need numbers not halos.

MERELY FAMILIAR

So, how many animals of each kind did Moses take on the Ark?

We can be reasonably certain that the tendency to chase stocks with popular names in particular and the halo effect in general is down to familiarity.
Familiarity in the psychological sense is very similar to the normal one; it's
about the things we easily recognize and is an aspect of availability. The
general idea is that familiarity breeds fluency, or ease of neural processing:
we can easily access the relevant information.

One of the odder aspects of familiarity is known as the mere exposure
effect and was first identified by Robert Zajonc back in 1968.[9] What he
showed was an outcome of the influence of familiarity—that if you repeatedly expose someone to something they will increase their preference for
the something. Cue a thousand feeble, but oddly effective, advertising cam-
paigns. The link between mere exposure and the halo effect was demonstrated in 2010 by Melanie Dempsey and Andrew Mitchell,[10] who managed
to get a majority of people to prefer an inferior product (a pen, to be precise)
by repeatedly showing it to people while accompanied by images of things
we generally feel positive about but which are generally irrelevant to the
main point of purchasing a writing implement.

There's an awful lot of research that shows how fluency impacts the ease
of information processing in our brains. For instance, rhyming aphorisms
seem more true than nonrhyming ones.[11] A stitch in time definitely saves
nine, but it's likely that too many cooks don't spoil the broth. And, of course,
sell in May and go away is obviously true while sell your losers and run your
winners is a much less convincing proposition.

This is the idea behind the Moses Illusion, hinted at above. Research
into processing fluency by Hyunjin Song and Norbert Schwarz[12] used this
little trick to analyze how we process familiar and unfamiliar information. The thing about the Moses Illusion itself is that the question is familiar but a trick, so that's why we get it wrong, because we rely on fluency
to come up with an answer rather than actually trying to analyze it. If
we're asked a difficult question in a nonfluent form we're more likely to

get it right, because it forces us to really think about what the question means. Of course, we innately prefer the easy option, and this is probably why most investors seek easy answers to the difficult question of what to invest in—follow someone else, look for easy-to-read signals like halos (which everyone else can read, too), or employ a convincing looking and sounding expert.

In fact, it seems that this effect leads neatly back to the dot-com naming studies we saw in the previous section. When Adam Alter and Daniel Oppenheimer looked at short-term price movements in stocks they discovered that companies with easy-to-pronounce names outperformed those with less fluent ones.[13] Presumably this is a combination of fluency and availability, because nonfluent names aren't easily available, but it's still an extraordinary finding.

Alter and Oppenheimer went on to do what I think is some even more remarkable research looking at the way in which the presentation of information affects people's ability to process it.[14] They presented people with a mathematical test in which the actual answers weren't quite so obvious as they first appeared, but they did it in two forms—an easy-to-read font and one that was difficult to read. The results were astonishing. Only 10 percent of the people in the easy-to-read sample got the test completely correct, compared to 65 percent in the hard-to-read sample. So there's a simple lesson—make sure you don't use easily understood fonts when you analyze firms, it lulls you into a false sense of familiarity, and a more complicated one—actually analyze the data, and don't rely on short-cuts and simple rules; real-life is not so simple.

LESSON 3

Moses never had an Ark, don't trust questions posed by innocent looking psychologists, and familiarity is no basis for making investment decisions. Anything that forces us to process information properly is to be encouraged, so print all your notes out in really hard-to-read fonts (or if you have my handwriting, write them out by hand . . .).

LEMMING TIME

Now, one of the other observations we might make about the halo effect on dot-com stocks is that it suggests a certain sort of herd mentality. After all, it takes more than one or two people deciding that a renamed company is worth buying to make its price more or less double more or less overnight. This can only happen as the result of concerted action by a whole bunch of people. You might even note that the whole of the dot-com debacle was caused by such activities. We've met this peculiar behavior before, in Chapter 1: it's known as herding, and we saw it there as an internally driven behavior caused by us searching for certainty in an uncertain world, and following what everyone else does in the hope that this will protect us.

However, herding has another aspect, because the idea that we all suddenly synchronize and behave the same way is clearly not something that can just be explained by each of us as individuals reaching for certainty—after all, we might all do so by copying something different. It's the fact that we all suddenly seem to do the *same* thing that's peculiar, and suggests that there's something else going on, something that's about us confusing situation with disposition.

There's not much doubt that we do synchronize our behavior—Dion Harmon's research into volatility around financial panics shows this—in essence, rapid price declines cause increases in volatility in stock prices but the reverse isn't true, increased volatility doesn't cause prices to fall. Basically, when prices in their favorite stocks fall people rush to sell them—which is exactly the opposite of what you might expect. After all, if your favorite beer suddenly goes on sale you don't immediately start selling the contents of your fridge at a knockdown price; more likely, you go out and stock up on the stuff. Money does weird things to our thinking. Really weird; we're wired for wrongness.

This mimicry is quite common in the periods leading up to market crises, as share prices become detached from real news. In the parlance of psychologists these crises are described as *self-organized*, because they don't rely on external information, but are caused by people copying each other's behavior, while simultaneously ascribing it to their own individual beliefs, a clear case of situation trumping disposition. Essentially it's all in our heads, folks.

Herding has a long and terribly undistinguished history—as far back as 1688 Joseph de la Vega was describing it at work in the Dutch stock market (which at the time consisted of just two companies).[15] As de la Vega pointed out, when emotions run high, reason runs out the window, and this is fundamental to human nature, not something about the modern information age we currently live in, because it's less about information overload and more about our implicit tendency to panic when the uncertainty in the world is revealed in all its gory glory.

There's a nasty technical term for the way that people all suddenly start copying each other—it's assumed that they exhibit *complementarities*, which is a fancy way of saying that people coordinate their behavior and cause the very uncertainty that they're so scared of. This is one of the more bizarre manifestations of human nature—our innate disposition to want to exhibit control over the world around us leads us into unconsciously coordinating our behavior with lots of other people in response to external events. It's known as a self-fulfilling prophecy, and the world is full of them when you start looking.

Just such coordinated effects have been seen in U.S. mutual funds, where relatively illiquid funds can see investors synchronizing withdrawing their cash in response to poor performance.[16] The more likely investors are to think there's a problem the more likely they are to cause one. And, once again, this often has very little to do with fundamentals and has everything to do with how the illusion of control can be triggered in large groups of people by the uncertainty of the world around us.

LESSON 4

Investors can demonstrate lemming-like herding behavior because they're all reacting to the same situation in the same way. Our innate disposition is to seek control, and this can lead us into coordinated behavior, which can cause the very problems we seek to avoid.

STORY TIME

An obvious corollary to the idea that we all react in a similar way to uncertainty in the world is that we're all dependent on the way that uncertainty is presented to us, and often it's presented in the form of stories in the mass media. As we saw in Chapter 1, popular media stories are often highly salient and therefore highly available to our brains, which become sensitized to the narratives being presented, seeing a pedophile in every playground and terrorists in every trattoria. But the mass media is also part of the wider environment in which we're all immersed, and it's therefore an important part of the story about how disposition and situation can get mingled and confused.

A public policy paper from the Boston Fed by Anat Bracha and Elke Weber has pinpointed stories—narratives—as critical to the way we seek to understand and control the world around us, and a key aspect of mass financial panics.[17] They argue that this is an aspect of our illusion of control problems, as we look for control over the world and create narratives that allow us to feel that control is within our reach. When we experience events that undermine these models our basic mode of operation is panic, and this kind of emotional trauma can lead to real pain. Neuroscientists Naomi Eisenberger, Matthew Lieberman, and Kipling Williams have shown the basis of social pain is similar to that of physical pain—when we're rejected by a lover that feeling of pain is real, not some mental confusion.[18] Similarly, the fear and sense of loss that accompanies financial panics is likely to be based on the same type of process: it hurts, and we want to escape the pain.

The mass media, in its many forms, is designed to create these narratives of control—the talking heads on the business channels are all there to explain why every minute change has a reason and an explanation—although when rare, sensational events occur they're inevitably as shocked as the rest of us. The evidence that traditional news channels have been able to influence investor behavior is quite strong—historical records of regional U.S. newspapers have been used to show that business reporting influences stock buying and selling patterns, and that negative news has more effect than positive news.[19]

In fact, the researchers went further than this. In many cases they were able to show that there was a time delay between the actual news being announced and it being published in the papers, and this allows them to assert that the media effects they identified are several times more influential over investor trading decisions than the actual information itself. People aren't reacting to a change in a company's fortunes but to the way in which it's reported.

All of which suggests, once again, that investors are ignoring the fundamentals and focusing on the salience of the stories being presented. And, once again, they're doing it en masse, presumably operating on the basis that they're behaving in accordance with their own beliefs when, in fact, they're being manipulated by the situation created for them.

However, this isn't the whole truth by any means. Although the salience of media stories has a part to play in herding behavior it turns out that the fundamental idiocy of many investors has a part to play as well. And, oddly enough, this part is often deemed to be why markets work properly, rather than why they fail horribly.

LESSON 5

Our drive to seek narratives to explain and control the world around us exposes us to the dangers of manipulation by mass media stories. Our tendency to react to these in a similar way, regardless of the underlying fundamentals, is a sign we're reacting to our environment and not analyzing the data. Keeping abreast of the real news and doing our own thinking is the only way we can allow our analysis to trump a manufactured situation.

WISE CROWDS?

Back in 1907, Francis Galton, cousin of Charles Darwin and founder of the eugenics movement, published an article on a peculiar statistical event he'd spotted at a local country fair.[20] In one of those quaint customs the English have, the locals were having a "guess the weight of the ox" contest. Galton, who was an inveterate collector of odd bits of information, noticed that although none of the individual guesses was right the distribution of answers tended to cluster around the correct result. The idea that a group of people can arrive at the right answer even though no individual is exactly correct has since been popularized by James Surowiecki and is known as the wisdom of crowds.[21]

It's sometimes suggested that stock markets are examples of environments in which the wisdom of crowds is prevalent, because a stock price is the result of thousands of people attempting to weigh the evidence and guess the correct value of a company. However, wisdom of crowds models depend on the people doing the weighing being independent—that is, they need to come to their judgments independently of each other. In a perfect world this would be the way we invest, each of us carefully analyzing the data and coming to our own opinions but, as the evidence of herding suggests, this isn't true.

In fact, the evidence actually seems to suggest that people are quite happy to trade on the basis of what everyone else is doing, without paying a great deal of attention to the actual underlying fundamentals of a corporation. These people have been termed "noise traders" by the economist Fischer Black, who's argued that these investors were obscuring what was really going on in markets by trading on irrelevant information.[22] However, although these noise traders may be idiots they can be surprisingly coordinated—herding together to cause mass movements in the markets.

When Brad Barber, Terrance Odean, and Ning Zhu studied the effect of these traders on markets they uncovered a range of herding behaviors that cause them to move in synchronicity.[23] They tend to both buy and sell stocks with strong past returns, they tend to focus on stocks with unusually high trading volumes, and they're net buyers of stocks with recent extreme returns—either negative or positive. All of this suggests that these types of investors are likely to herd, an effect that's underpinned by a bunch of other behavioral biases, of which our old friend the disposition effect is prominent.

However, other effects also seem to play a part. Researchers think that the representative heuristic—remember the feminist librarian Linda?—is implicated. Typically, noise traders are relying on representative examples based on extrapolating recent past experience and performance and, as they have all had the same recent exposure to markets, this is responsible for causing similar beliefs to be generated across this investor cohort.

Salience and availability are also suspects, because the focus on stocks with recent extreme performance suggests that attention-grabbing stocks are highly salient to this type of investor. They're not trying to analyze the wider market but are instead relying on gut feel, and therefore depending on availability as a way of narrowing down their stock selection. Of course, if enough people are doing this then there's money to be made out of predicting this, but the ability of individuals to outperform institutions over the short-term is highly suspect.

In truth, noise traders aren't demonstrating the wisdom of crowds, but rather their foolishness, not because they're directly communicating with each other but because they're relying on the same signals from stock price movements and being betrayed by a common heritage of psychological weakness. It's richly ironic that we create our own environments and are then betrayed by them, but disposition often creates situations which affect disposition. It's an effect known as reflexivity, and it's this we'll turn to next.

LESSON 6

Noise trading by uninformed individuals can result in herding behavior as common behavioral biases dominate proper investing decisions. Ensuring that we're not duped by the disposition effect and suckered by saliency is the best defense against the unwashed masses.

ADAPTIVE MARKETS

As we can see, people tend to get a bit confused between the situation they find themselves in and their innate behavior, often leading to some very bizarre investing decisions. However, the puzzle that is the disposition effect is even more complicated than it might seem, because very often it's our dispositions, en masse, that create our situations. And our situation then drives us to change our minds. Confusing, yeah?

One of the recurring themes you'll find in stock market commentary is the idea that markets are somehow predictable. After all, if they're not, the vast amount of time and money spent on analysts, expert commentary, tip sheets, business channels, and so forth is simply wasted. Which would be ridiculous, were it not largely true. The point is, of course, that we crave certainty and we're prepared to pay people who pander to that craving.

The truth is rather more difficult to accept, that short-term market trends and movements are impossible to predict and that the long term doesn't offer much certainty either. However, it does offer some, which is fortunate because otherwise you and I would both be wasting our time.

Andrew Lo has developed an idea that he calls the Adaptive Markets Hypothesis.[24] This is an in-joke, because the standard economic theory of markets is called the Efficient Markets Hypothesis and essentially says that everything is predictable as long as people are rational. The trouble is people aren't entirely rational, so nothing is predictable, and Lo builds his theory on this concept.

The idea is that markets and people interact in a complex and unpredictable way, such that people move markets and the movement of markets then causes the behavior of people to change, which then changes the way the market behaves. This is typical of a class of systems usually called "adaptive," where it's impossible to precisely predict the outcome with certainty. The global weather is a naturally occurring example, which is why longer range weather forecasts are so often wrong. These sorts of systems are unstable and are prone to something called the butterfly effect, the idea being that if a butterfly somewhere in the Amazon decides to flap its wings in an especially aggressive fashion we may end up having tornados in Omaha.

In truth, there's not much doubt that markets are adaptive; we know that they tend to exhibit extreme behavior, and we know that this causes people to do stupid things, like sell their stocks when the market is at a low and then buy when it's at a high. This change in mass psychology is caused by something called reflexivity, and it's an important feature of the human cognitive system, because it means we can adapt to changes in our environment. It's how we learned to adapt to the last Ice Age.

We're learning machines, and our ability to change our behavior in response to changes in the world around us is a key facet of our survival, but without proper training we can end up learning the wrong lessons. Sometimes it's just a cold snap, not long-term climate change.

LESSON 7

We're reflexive, capable of adapting our behavior in response to changes in our environment. However, markets are also adaptive, changing as we change our behavior. So we need to be careful not to continually modify our behavior in response to short-term market changes. Usually it's just a bad winter, not a new Ice Age.

GEORGE SOROS'S REFLEXIVITY

George Soros is famous for being fabulously wealthy, often described as the man who broke the Bank of England when he bet huge on the United Kingdom being forced out of the predecessor to the common European currency. Soros is one of the great exponents of the Babe Ruth effect; he loses far more often than he wins, but when he wins he wins huge. This means that he's managed to overcome the dubious designs of the disposition effect and will happily sell his many losers quickly but will run his few winners to fabulous effect.

As you'll recall, at the heart of the disposition effect is confusion between disposition and situation—we think we're buying and selling because of our innate good sense, but often we're doing it because we're unduly influenced by the situation. Somehow Soros overcomes this and at the heart of his bias-beating approach to investing is a philosophy he describes as economic reflexivity, which in essence accepts the idea that markets are adaptive and people react to those markets in ways that cause the markets to change, and so on, and so on.

He believes that when we think about markets we tend to get confused and treat them like inanimate objects. For instance, if a scientist predicts that an earthquake is about to happen we don't need to worry that the prediction will stop the upheaval because the planet gets in a huff and decides it's not going to be told what to do by some geek with a seismograph. Yet if some supposedly competent expert predicts that markets may collapse it's entirely possible that they may cause the very behavior they're predicting.

This is the basis of Soros's general theory of reflexivity: market behavior is essentially a self-fulfilling prophecy—because we don't just observe markets, or simply participate in them: we *are* the markets.[25] The problem with this is that, as he points out, our understanding of the world is always flawed, limited, and partial. He calls this the principle of fallibility, but it means that markets never just reflect the fundamentals of a situation but also embed our psychological weaknesses, and these flaws themselves drive the movements of the markets. If enough people believe markets will fall, they will fall. And if enough believe that they'll rise, then they'll rise. And the markets create an environment—a situation—within which the disposition has full reign to cause havoc.

So we need to be aware that the very act of buying or selling changes our mental expectations of the stocks involved. As we've seen, sometimes a lot of traders will do this simultaneously based on the same signals and we can find ourselves unexpectedly part of a losing herd of bewildered steers teetering precipitously along a canyon's edge. Soros builds this into his mental toolkit for surviving the madness of markets; we need to too.

LESSON 8

George Soros has a mental model of markets that argues that fundamentals are often displaced by people implementing self-fulfilling prophecies about the way that markets work. Yet he doesn't confuse situation with disposition, and has no problem selling his losers and keeping his winners. Remember that markets are simply the outcome of mass psychology, and don't let yourself become a reflexive part of the herd.

GROW OLD QUICKLY

Interestingly, there's one factor that does seem to help improve our likelihood of falling prey to the disposition effect. Unlike other problems such as hindsight bias, experience does seem to improve our ability to resist the depredations of disposition, although even this isn't unquestioned. If someone is especially lucky they're likely to be a spectacularly bad role model for others.

You can see this in the way we treat spectacularly successful entrepreneurs or businessmen. Clearly, people who are very successful are very attractive role models, but in a world in which everyone is trying everything, it stands to reason that some people will succeed. It doesn't mean that they have any special insight into the way in which they became successful, it just means that they're the last ones standing. The rate of failure of entrepreneurs is spectacular, so anyone deciding that they want to be one because they've seen that a handful of people can make billions is about as sensible as someone who decides the route to fame and fortune is appearing on a celebrity TV show (which doesn't stop more than one in six British teenagers from thinking just that[26]).

In a similar fashion there's an argument, expounded by Juhani Linnainmaa that people are as much biased by their own experiences as by biases like the disposition effect.[27] The idea is that people learn from their own experiences but because those experiences, especially for many inexperienced investors, are essentially random, the beliefs we develop about our investing abilities are also essentially random. On the other hand, the more investing we do the more experience we get, and eventually luck ought to even out a bit.

And this is exactly what Amit Seru, Tyler Shumway, and Noah Stoffman uncovered—one of the benefits of experience is that we're less prone to the disposition effect.[28] They also identified a range of associated changes in behavior—as we get older we tend to diversify more and focus more on larger capitalized, less risky stocks (although this may be because we have more to lose), and they specifically identified the groups of people most likely to have learned from experience.

What they found suggests that three particular groups are most likely to improve their ability to invest with age. Firstly, unsophisticated investors improve markedly—perhaps because they have few preconceptions to start with and don't overtheorize. Secondly, people who start out with consistently poor returns tend to make better investors in the long term—because many of this group will simply give up so the ones that persist are likely to have an above average determination to learn from their mistakes. And the third group is one that we'll return to later: women, who seem to be less erratic and situationally compromised than male investors.

Of course, the best answer would be to grow old, in investing terms, quickly rather than going through the pain of getting there slowly. But mostly we don't do that, we chase the returns of other, supposedly better, investors without having a clue how they achieved them. And, as it turns out, they weren't always so smart themselves . . .

LESSON 9

Perhaps the best defense against situational biases is to gain experience. Whether it's because only half-decent investors stick at investing or because the experience of repeated failure forces us to improve our methods one benefit of age is a reduction in the power of the disposition effect. Once again, however, we'd be better off learning the lessons of growing old from those who've already done it.

SPEAKING ILL

The startling idea that investors may actually communicate with each other directly is partly behind the understanding that wisdom of crowd type effects don't really apply to stock markets. If we share the same ideas about stocks or markets we're not going to be operating independently of each other, and our decisions will be linked. This leads to an interesting line of thought, which suggests that these conversations themselves may be biased and that the world view we obtain through conversations with other people may be equally flawed.

So, for instance, we all have a tendency to present ourselves in the best possible light. Arguably this is part of the introspection illusion but in truth we all like to gild the lily a little bit when talking about ourselves. It's much more satisfactory to tell everyone about our investing triumphs than it is to highlight our failures. This type of conversational bias means that investors operating in an environment comprised of other investors—bulletin boards, investing clubs, and so on—are far more likely to be exposed to positive information than negative, and this will in turn reduce our willingness to share our errors. Few of us want to look foolish in front of our peers, especially when none of our peers ever seems to make a mistake.

What's worse is that we don't seem to adjust our thinking to take account of this problem. Given that we ought to know that we're exaggerating our own successes and downplaying our failures you might think we would recognize that other people are doing the same. But we don't. When Jeffrey DeMarzo, Dimitri Vayanos, and Peter Zweibel looked at this issue, they identified something they labeled as persuasion bias, which suggests that being repeatedly exposed to the same views from the same source gradually increases our belief that the view is correct.[29] So if we constantly read the opinion of one journalist, for instance, we will treat each article they write as independent. This, of course, is the mere exposure effect and familiarity in operation.

In our Internet connected world we're linked into a network of opinions and we often simply fail to recognize that we're being repeatedly exposed to information from the same source—because in networks of this type there are often a few critical opinion formers whose views are repeated by others, such that we're frequently presented with the same opinion from apparently different sources. Timur Kuran and Cass Sunstein[30] have shown that you can explain the buildup of irrational market beliefs simply by modeling the effect of information availability in social networks: we speak ill and it does none of us any good.

LESSON 10

We need to discount information obtained through social networks where people will tend to present themselves in the best light possible. If we can't critically analyze the information we're being presented with we'd be better off cutting ourselves off from it, because once we allow ourselves to be influenced by the lies of others we're exposed to a whole range of very dangerous biases.

THE POWER OF PERSUASION

If our financial decision making can be influenced irrationally by the situation we happen to find ourselves in, because we fail to recognize that we're not independent of our environment, then it stands to reason that we're at risk of being manipulated by people who seek to exploit these weaknesses. After all, if we constantly and unconsciously adapt to the world around us because we have to, in order to survive, it's a small step to suggest that maybe we could be equally influenced by people attempting to deliberately manipulate our environment. And, of course, this is true because the world is full of people attempting to separate us from our cash—scammers, fraudsters, bankers, advertisers . . . and all too often they do it and leave us craving more.

Perhaps the heart of the problem is that we now live in a world that's too complicated for us to understand and our brains have to take shortcuts simply in order to survive. In the gap between reality and our limited processing power lies the void that conmen repeatedly seek to exploit. It's less that we're being conned and more that we're conning ourselves, and this is the skill of the truly great persuader who exploits the range of behavioral biases that we offer up.

The scammers seem to target a specific set of biases, in particular our well documented inclination to defer to authority figures and our emotional instincts: greed, pain avoidance, and the desire to be liked seem to be high on the list according to an extensive study carried out in the United Kingdom, where people are estimated to lose over $5 billion a year to various scams.[31] There's no reason to believe the United States is any better in this regard, nor is there any evidence that financial literacy helps; having investment experience is no guarantee that you won't be a victim.

The classic book on the subject of persuasion is *Influence*, by Robert Cialdini, which is essential reading for anyone with half a brain.[32] Cialdini's main point is that we need to recognize the hidden persuaders and prepare our defenses against them in advance. It's the same advice I give here: only by understanding that the world is full of people using our own weaknesses to separate us from our valuable time and money can we even begin to start the process of becoming a better investor.

One of the best examples is typified by an exploitation of something called the contrast principle. This is the reason people will buy stocks that have fallen significantly after they've sold them without doing any analysis; they're contrasting the previous price with the new one, without really analyzing why the change has occurred. Scammers will exploit this by initially making a higher priced offer before retreating and then making a lower offer, in the knowledge that the contrast between the two prices will convince some people that they're getting a bargain.

We simply can't analyze all of the data we're presented with and we need to identify some safe and simple shortcuts in order to navigate our way through the investment jungle. Yet we need to be constantly aware that there are people and organizations out there that will seek to exploit those shortcuts for their own benefit. So our investment management needs to include ways of identifying and filtering out the scammers, regardless of the form they come in: the worst offenders often come in the most beguiling forms.

LESSON 11

Our investment environment can be manipulated by those who understand the confusion we suffer between situation and disposition. The willingness of people and organizations to exploit us should never be underestimated. Remember, most of this manipulation is perfectly legal and we fall into it naturally; this is the art of the great persuaders. Our job is to recognize when we're being exploited, and reject the advances.

SAD INVESTORS

A lot of people are afflicted by a condition known as Seasonally Affective Disorder or SAD. In essence, they become depressed due to lack of sunlight, a condition ameliorated by the onset of longer days. SAD was originally identified by Norman Rosenthal and colleagues, who suggested that the effect is an evolutionary hangover from earlier times, when the rhythms of the seasons were markers for determining reproductive and hibernation periods.[33] Whatever the reason, some people are seriously affected by the seasons, which led some researchers to wonder if this has an effect on investors.

Now, at one level this is plainly ridiculous. No matter how biased we are, and how much we confuse our innate control over our behavior with external influences, it stands to reason that share prices aren't going to be particularly impacted by the hours of daylight. Ultimately this is a world dominated by the doings of corporations, their earnings and prospects, not by irrelevant factors such as the weather. Well, you'd think so, wouldn't you?

Of course, the truth is rather different. Just as we find it impossible to differentiate between our own self-generated patterns of behavior and those imposed on us by the behavior of others, we also find it impossible to overcome the legacy of our evolutionary history and the physical environment we exist in. So when Lisa Kramer started to investigate the impact of seasons on investing it shouldn't have been a great surprise to find that there are astonishing variations in seasonal returns: U.S. Treasuries, for instance, have an 80 basis point change in monthly returns between April and October.[34] Kramer and colleagues can find no explanation for this other than a correlation with SAD.

SAD investors tend to be risk averse during the winter months, and the effect is clearly seen in both Northern and Southern hemispheres (which has its summer during the Northern winter), so this isn't an accident of the data or some other unseen causal effect. The condition affects around 20% of the population, which, on the face of it, wouldn't be sufficient to affect markets as a whole. However, as we've seen, if a subset of investors all suddenly start behaving the same way this can cause herding effects and it's quite likely that this explains the fact that investors tend to shift money into government bonds in the fall and back to equities in the spring.

The idea that our physical environment has an impact on the way we invest shouldn't be a great surprise, but the majority of investors have no idea that they may be affected like this. If you're a sufferer from SAD then you need to be particularly careful about your decision making in the winter months, and during the turn of the seasons. The rest of us just need to be careful about following trends.

LESSON 12

Our physical environment can change the way we invest. Being aware of the external causes of our investing inclinations and having a plan that we keep to regardless of the length of the daylight hours is a critical part of managing our investing psychology.

SELL IN MAY . . .

SAD doesn't seem to be the only environmental factor implicated in irrational investing decision making. For instance, there's the January effect, which sees small cap stocks outperforming during January on a regular basis. We don't know why this is, but there are quite strong suggestions that there are other underlying seasonal patterns of human behavior that we don't really understand.

Here's an odd example: people born in the summer are luckier than those born in the winter.[35] Yes, you read that correctly. Richard Wiseman, a UK psychologist who specializes in the quirky side of human nature, has run some experiments on the unlikely topic of luck. In one experiment he got people to rate how lucky they were and then got them to scan a newspaper. Halfway through was a large advertisement offering a substantial reward for bringing it to the attention of one of the researchers. The people who noticed this were overwhelmingly from the lucky group, which was itself overwhelmingly made up of people born in the summer, and this was true even if they're born in the Southern hemisphere, where the summer is the winter in the north.

We don't know why this is, it may be some kind of underlying causal effect we can't imagine, but one idea is that summer babies tend to be less wrapped up than winter ones, and have more freedom of movement and more opportunity to explore. Unlikely as it sounds it's not impossible; small changes in the environment in the early months can have a disproportionate affect on character.

Whether or not there are real seasonal variations in underlying behavior there's no doubt that there are some quite strong seasonal effects in the stock market. The January effect[36] is one of the most marked, where small cap stocks experience marked outperformance at the turn of the year. A theory is that this is due to the end of the tax year in the United States, when investors buy back stocks they've sold to take capital gains during December, but the effect seems to apply to all stock markets, even in countries with different tax year end dates.

In fact, the old adage "Sell in May and go away" actually seems to be backed up by some evidence. When Ben Jacobson and Wessel Marquering analyzed the data they couldn't find any conclusive evidence that there was any external influence on investors, but they still reckoned that a policy of selling in May and waiting until the fall would yield outsize returns.[37] Alternatively, the so-called Halloween effect, start buying at the end of November, works well, too.

We can be fairly sure that there's some underlying influence on investor behavior triggered by seasonal changes, but it's one area where we really don't have much of a clue why. The best advice is to ignore the simple aphorisms and concentrate on actual valuations. After all, if buying in November yields such great returns you ought to be able to find cheap stocks galore, and wondering why is pointless. Why look a gift horse in the mouth?

LESSON 13

Although being born in the summer leads to a luckier life it doesn't offer any easy investment returns. Seasonal effects are real but not understood, and should be countered by focusing on valuation, not wise old sayings.

THE MYSTERY OF THE VANISHING ANOMALIES

One of the fallacies of the average private investor—and most of us are very average—is that there's some way to directly exploit the anomalies we've been discussing in order to get an edge, to allow them to beat the markets in the short term. This is the dream of day traders everywhere, but unfortunately it's likely to be impossible because we're all faced with the behemoths of the investment industry who can throw billions of dollars at technology, which automates trading on any kind of signal that we can think of. The idea that technical analysis, the modern equivalent of reading tea leaves, was ever any use has been utterly overwhelmed by the rise of the automated trading machines.

Here's one instructive example. Back in 1996, a researcher named Richard Sloan managed to get a paper published on something called the accrual anomaly.[38] Accruals are the part of a company's profits that they actually haven't received yet, they're promises rather than actual cash and, like all promises, they often don't get delivered on. But very often the market treats profits from accruals as though they're cash in the bank when really they're just glorified IOUs.

What Sloan showed was that earnings persistence—the ability of a company to consistently raise its profits—is highly correlated with the cash component of earnings, and that companies that have higher accruals components of earnings are far more likely to produce profit warnings. After all, not all IOUs ever get repaid so it's not surprising that earnings based on such promises are more likely to turn out to be illusory than earnings based on actual cash in the bank. This not entirely surprising finding generated a lot of heat from economists who insisted that such an obvious mispricing issue couldn't possibly exist. But they were wrong, and follow-up studies confirmed the anomaly.

At this point, Sloan, and other colleagues in the area, got poached by hedge funds seeking to exploit the accrual effect and the net result is, after a decade or more, that the anomaly has more or less disappeared.[39] This is Andrew Lo's adaptive market in action, as soon as something becomes well known it becomes a target for arbitrage. More pertinently it emphasizes the point I made earlier: the investment corporations can bring far more money and automation to bear on the challenge of investing than any group of private investors. This is an arms race with only one loser, and in such a situation it's best not to even bother competing because the environment is toxic.

LESSON 14

There's no point in taking investment short cuts because private investors can't possibly win in an investment environment where financial institutions can buy up the best brains and back them with the best technology. There is no anomaly we can exploit better than the corporations, so don't even try.

TWEET AND INVEST

There's perhaps no modern situation more modern than the Internet. We've already seen that giving people access to an Internet trading account makes them trade twice as much and correspondingly lose more money, but the main focus of the World Wide Web is communication, and there's nothing investors like more than information, even if they haven't got a clue what to do with it.

Increasingly, it's not just the Internet but the use of social media such as Facebook and Twitter that provides us with virtually instantaneous links to those people with whom we share interests. Unsurprisingly these innovations have been seized on by traders, desperate for any tiny dribble of data that might give them an edge in the dogfight to make a dollar. This is noise trader heaven, although a little more analysis might suggest that it's more the work of the devil.

Yet the emerging research on the use of Twitter to predict stock market movements suggests that the apparently witless warblings of thousands of tweeters is startlingly accurate. In a paper aptly titled "Twitter Mood Predicts the Stock Market," Johan Bollen, Huina Mao, and Xiao-Jun Zeng have shown that a model based on tweets has an 87.6 percent success rate in predicting the daily up and down changes in the Dow Jones Industrial

Average.[40] In fact, the method appears to be astonishingly successful, and will therefore not survive the publicity it's been given: reflexivity will see to that.

This is what happened to the accrual anomaly, and it seems to be a common theme: the more well-known such a technique is the more people will start to use it and, remembering that people are reflexive, the market adapts and destroys the anomaly by arbitraging it away: essentially, the more people that use the method the less successful it is. In fact, though, it's at least as questionable as to whether the twitter information anomaly is there to start with. To understand why this is we need to investigate the strange case of the Bangladeshi butter.

In a famous piece of research the statistician David Leinweber set out to show that most of the predictive models used for stock markets are figments of the various analysts' imaginations.[41] He went looking for something—anything—that predicted the movement of the S&P 500 and found that the best correlate for the index was the level of butter production in Bangladesh, which could predict 75 percent of the variation of the index over a year. By adding in U.S. butter and cheese production and the sheep population in the two countries, he was able to improve the accuracy to 99 percent. The point being, of course, is that no one in their right mind would believe that this set of variables had any predictive power for U.S. stock markets, no matter what the statisticians claimed. As Leinweber remarked:

> *If someone showed up in your office with a model relating stock prices to interest rates, GDP, trade, housing starts, and the like, it might have statistics that looked as good as this nonsense, and it might make as much sense, even though it sounded much more plausible.*

This is the same sort of error we saw with the Super Bowl effect, but on a much larger scale, caused by mining vast sets of data within which there will always be random patterns of information that look like they're somehow related. The idea that social media can really predict the movement of markets is doubtful in the first place, and even if it exists it will be arbitraged away by all-too-eager investors seeking an edge. And the whole idea is scary anyway, as it's bad enough letting noise traders loose in the markets in the first place, without pandering to their day-trading fantasies on Twitter.

But they'll do it anyway; we should ignore them and just use social media for its intended usage, tracking the Kardashians and making rude remarks about the British Royal Family.

LESSON 15

Social media is not an environment for a sensible investor: even if it does predict markets, which is doubtful, the advantage will soon be lost. More likely it's just another stupid data mining fallacy.

FIRE!

As this chapter has attempted to show, investors are not irrational in a vacuum, but are heavily influenced by the environment around them—whether this be the changing of the seasons in the real world, the tweeting of fellow investors on the Internet, the way that we're unconsciously influenced by external factors via the halo effect, or by the deliberate exploitation of our flawed psychology by people setting out to scam or defraud us. One of the great ironies of all of this self-defeating behavior is that we're usually attempting to act in our own best interests; it's just that the effect of our behavior changes that of other people, and produces an end result somewhat different from what we imagined.

The classic example of this is what happens in a crowded theater when someone shouts "Fire!" The best chance of most people escaping to safety is for everyone to remain calm and orderly and to file out in a sensible fashion. Unfortunately, this isn't in the best interests of the people at the back of the queue who are getting toasted, and for whom jumping on the heads of the people in front of them is far and away the best move. Therefore, by panicking they run the risk of scaring everyone else, and causing a rush for the exit, wherein most people get hurt and far fewer escape. And if you think this sounds like what happens in markets when they collapse you wouldn't be far off.

This type of behavior, where each individual acts in their own best interests yet ends up losing out because when this behavior is scaled up to the level of a crowd it causes a wide-scale failure has a name—it's called the fallacy of composition.[42] There are many funny examples of how this can lead to erroneous conclusions but my favorite is: atoms are colorless, dogs are made up of atoms, therefore dogs are colorless. Or maybe even better: sodium and chloride are both dangerous to people, so sodium chloride will be dangerous to people. Yeah, whatever, just pass the salt, but has anyone seen the dog recently?

So when stock markets fall there's a tendency for individual investors to dump their stocks, often because they've borrowed money to buy them in the first place. Unfortunately, what is good for these individual investors is often bad for the market as asset prices fall, people start saving more and spending less, and the economy goes into a tailspin. Being caught in a market fall having borrowed lots of money is a particularly bad situation to find yourself in and it's one reason I always urge investors to avoid borrowing to invest: the last time you want to be forced into selling is when everyone else is, even if everyone has a perfectly valid reason to be doing it. Fire!

LESSON 16

Don't borrow money to invest in stocks; you'll be caught out by the fallacy of composition the next time the market has one of its periodic breakdowns.

THE RISE OF THE MACHINES

I want to end this chapter by touching on one other situational factor that most private investors seem to ignore when figuring out how to invest: the power and intelligence of the investment institutions. We collectively pour billions of dollars into these organizations every year and although most of this goes out to the executives and employees in bonuses and expense accounts they still retain enough moulah to invest in the brightest minds and the best technology that the planet has to offer.

It's easy to scoff at institutions—and I often do—but we should never forget that if we think of some clever technique to find surefire winners then chances are that they have already done it, invented an algorithm to exploit it, and have loaded it into a supercomputer that is engaged in some form of high-frequency trading at speeds that no human can truly comprehend, let alone compete with. In fact, the institutions have resorted to the theory of relativity in order to figure out where to situate their computers in order to get the tiniest, fractional edge over their competitors.[43]

The death of the accrual anomaly is only one example of apparently guaranteed trading methods that failed once the institutions got their hands on them and started implementing computer-based strategies to capture the excess or so-called abnormal returns. The idea that any private investor can compete on level terms with the automated trading machines is an absolute joke; the only edge that we have is that we can exploit the uncertainty and adaptiveness of the markets because these cannot be modeled by any computer system. In the short or medium term, markets are completely unpredictable, and can create huge paper-based losses, and the investment industry, obsessed by short-term returns, has no choice but to respond in kind. But we, the private investors,

don't have to—we can take the longer view, and take the regular market de-
pressions as an opportunity to invest in good companies for the long term.

Unfortunately, most private investors do exactly the opposite, and fixate
on short-term market movements that they have little if any chance of making
a decent return from. This is due to a range of underlying biases, but is mostly
because of our unwillingness to learn the lessons of history. These offer a clear
lesson: don't attempt to beat the markets in the short term, because we can only
do so through luck. True skill comes from a long-term, consistent approach.

LESSON 17

Investment institutions aim to exploit the same short-term trends as
private investors but have many more dollars and much more com-
puting power with which to do it. No sensible investor attempts
to compete with this, and we should instead focus on longer-term
approaches, where our ability to ride out and exploit uncertainty gives
us an edge.

THE SEVEN KEY TAKEAWAYS

This chapter has introduced how situational factors, and our tendency to
convince ourselves that it's our disposition and our personal decision making that are in control, rather than the way that our environment biases us
towards certain behaviors, can lead us astray.

To finish, let's draw together a few key ideas from this chapter before we
move on. The main takeaways are:

1. We are all impacted by the disposition effect, which in its common form
   causes us to sell our winners and keep our losers, but more broadly
   causes us to confuse our situations with our dispositions.
2. We need to beware of halo effects, where particularly prominent features
   of an investment, or a person, can bias us into believing that it or they
   are great at other things as well. This is an availability bias, where ease
   of access of certain features bleeds across into other areas.
3. Uninformed, so-called noise investors, can cause significant market movements by herding and trading together using external signals from highly
   available events and corporations. These price changes hold no signifi-
   cance at all, and should be disregarded by logical investors everywhere.

4. External environmental conditions like the hours of sunlight and the weather have noticeable effects on the way markets behave, probably because significant cohorts of investors herd together based on these conditions during these periods. Try to avoid changing your investment techniques in response to external conditions.

5. Markets do not behave the same way throughout history because they change in response to the way that people trade, and traders change their behavior in response to the way that the market behaves. Because of this there are no long-term, surefire techniques for making money, and as soon as someone finds one and makes it public it's likely to disappear as everyone moves to take advantage of it—this is the fallacy of composition.

6. The investment industry has far more firepower to throw at short-term trading than private investors, and this is an arms race we can only ever lose. Avoid competing with the industry on its own terms and focus on longer-term approaches where its weaknesses lie.

7. Be very wary of people who come up with some new method of investing, often dependent on some technical innovation and incontrovertible data, because these results are often a result of judicious data mining. Bangladeshi butter production does not predict the U.S. stock market, and it's unlikely that Twitter will, either.

So now we've seen how our senses can deceive us, how our emotions can betray us, and how our situational awareness can cause our investing to go awry. Next up for analysis are our social traits, because humans are, if nothing else, intensely social creatures. And, of course, this too can lead us astray in markets.

NOTES

1. Lawrence Mishel, Josh Bivens, Elise Gould, and Heidi Shierholz, *The State of Working America* (New York: Cornell University Press, 2012).
2. Daniel S. Hamermesh and Jeff E. Biddle, "Beauty and the Labor Market," National Bureau of Economic Research, NBER Working Paper No. 4518 (1993).
3. Markus M. Mobius and Tanya S. Rosenblat, "Why Beauty Matters," *The American Economic Review* (2006): 222–235.
4. Edward L. Thorndike, "A Constant Error in Psychological Ratings," *Journal of Applied Psychology* 4, no. 1 (1920): 25–29.
5. Richard E. Nisbett and Timothy D. Wilson, "The Halo Effect: Evidence for Unconscious Alteration of Judgments," *Journal of Personality and Social Psychology* 35, no. 4 (1977): 250.
6. Michael J. Cooper, Orlin Dimitrov, and P. Raghavendra Rau, "A Rose.com by Any Other Name," *The Journal of Finance* 56, no. 6 (2001): 2371–2388.

7. Michael J. Cooper, Ajay Khorana, Igor Osobov, Ajay Patel, and P. Raghavendra Rau, "Managerial Actions in Response to a Market Downturn: Valuation Effects of Name Changes in the dot.com Decline," *Journal of Corporate Finance* 11, no. 1 (2005): 319–335.

8. Michael J. Cooper, Huseyin Gulen, and Raghavendra Rau, "Changing Names with Style: Mutual Fund Name Changes and Their Effects on Fund Flows," EFA 2003 Annual Conference Paper No. 293 (2004). Available at SSRN: http://ssrn.com/abstract=423989 or http://dx.doi.org/10.2139/ssrn.423989.

9. Robert B. Zajonc, "Attitudinal Effects of Mere Exposure," *Journal of Personality and Social Psychology* 9, no. 2, part 2 (1968): 1–27.

10. Melanie A. Dempsey and Andrew A. Mitchell, "The Influence of Implicit Attitudes on Choice When Consumers Are Confronted with Conflicting Attribute Information," *Journal of Consumer Research* 37, no. 4 (2010): 614–625.

11. Matthew S. McGlone and Jessica Tofighbakhsh, "Birds of a Feather Flock Conjointly (?): Rhyme as Reason in Aphorisms," *Psychological Science* 11, no. 5 (2000): 424–428.

12. Hyunjin Song and Norbert Schwarz, "Fluency and the Detection of Misleading Questions: Low Processing Fluency Attenuates the Moses Illusion," *Social Cognition* 26, no. 6 (2008): 791–799.

13. Adam L. Alter and Daniel M. Oppenheimer, "Predicting Short-Term Stock Fluctuations by Using Processing Fluency," *Proceedings of the National Academy of Sciences* 103, no. 24 (2006): 9369–9372.

14. Adam L. Alter, Daniel M. Oppenheimer, Nicholas Epley, and Rebecca N. Eyre, "Overcoming Intuition: Metacognitive Difficulty Activates Analytic Reasoning," *Journal of Experimental Psychology: General* 136, no. 4 (2007): 569.

15. Joseph de la Vega, *Confusión de Confusiones* (Boston: Harvard Graduate School of Business Administration, 1957).

16. Qi Chen, Itay Goldstein, and Wei Jiang, "Payoff Complementarities and Financial Fragility: Evidence from Mutual Fund Outflows," *Journal of Financial Economics* 97, no. 2 (2010): 239–262.

17. Anat Bracha and Elke Weber, "A Psychological Perspective of Financial Panic," FRB of Boston Public Policy Discussion Paper 12-7 (2012).

18. Naomi I. Eisenberger, Matthew D. Lieberman, and Kipling D. Williams, "Does Rejection Hurt? An fMRI Study of Social Exclusion," *Science* 302, no. 5643 (2003): 290–292.

19. Joseph E. Engelberg and Christopher A. Parsons, "The Causal Impact of Media in Financial Markets," *The Journal of Finance* 66, no. 1 (2011): 67–97.

20. Francis Galton, "Vox Populi," *Nature* 75 (1907): 450–451.

21. James Surowiecki, *The Wisdom of Crowds* (New York: Random House Digital, 2005).

22. Fischer Black, "Noise," *The Journal of Finance* 41, no. 3 (1986): 529–543.

23. Brad M. Barber, Terrance Odean, and Ning Zhu, "Systematic Noise," *Journal of Financial Markets* 12, no. 4 (2009): 547–569.

24. Andrew W. Lo, "The Adaptive Markets Hypothesis," *The Journal of Portfolio Management* 30, no. 5 (2004): 15–29.

25. George Soros, *Open Society: Reforming Global Capitalism Reconsidered* (New York: PublicAffairs, 2007).
26. "Kids Seeking Reality TV Fame Instead of Exam Passes," Learning and Skills Council press release, January 13, 2006.
27. Juhani T. Linnainmaa, "Why Do (Some) Households Trade So Much?" *Review of Financial Studies* 24, no. 5 (2011): 1630–1666.
28. Amit Seru, Tyler Shumway, and Noah Stoffman, "Learning by Trading," *Review of Financial Studies* 23, no. 2 (2010): 705–739.
29. Jeffrey H. Zwiebel, Dimitri Vayanos, and Peter M. DeMarzo, "Persuasion Bias, Social Influence, and Uni-Dimensional Opinions," Research Paper, Stanford University, Graduate School of Business, No. 1719 (2001).
30. Timur Kuran and Cass R. Sunstein, "Availability Cascades and Risk Regulation," *Stanford Law Review* (1999): 683–768.
31. S. Lea, P. Fischer, and K. Evans, "The Psychology of Scams: Provoking and Committing Errors of Judgement," Report for the Office of Fair Trading (2009). Available at www.oft.gov.uk/shared_oft/reports/consumer_protection/oft1070.pdf.
32. Robert B. Cialdini, *Influence* (New York: HarperCollins, 2009).
33. Norman E. Rosenthal et al., "Seasonal Affective Disorder: A Description of the Syndrome and Preliminary Findings with Light Therapy," *Archives of General Psychiatry* 41, no. 1 (1984): 72.
34. Mark J. Kamstra, Lisa A. Kramer, and Maurice D. Levi, "Seasonal Variation in Treasury Returns," Rotman School of Management Working Paper 1076644 (2012).
35. Jayanti Chotai and Richard Wiseman, "Born Lucky? The Relationship between Feeling Lucky and Month of Birth," *Personality and Individual Differences* 39, no. 8 (2005): 1451–1460.
36. Mark Haug and Mark Hirschey, "The January Effect," *Financial Analysts Journal* (2006): 78–88.
37. Ben Jacobsen and Wessel Marquering, "Is It the Weather?" *Journal of Banking & Finance* 32, no. 4 (2008): 526–540.
38. Richard G. Sloan, "Do Stock Prices Fully Reflect Information in Accruals and Cash Flows About Future Earnings?" *Accounting Review* (1996): 289–315.
39. Jeremiah Green, John R. M. Hand, and Mark T. Soliman, "Going, Going, Gone? The Demise of the Accruals Anomaly," *Management Science* 57, no. 5 (2009): 797–816. Available at SSRN: http://ssrn.com/abstract=1501020 or http://dx.doi.org/10.2139/ssrn.1501020.
40. Johan Bollen, Huina Mao, and Xiao-Jun Zeng, "Twitter Mood Predicts the Stock Market," *Journal of Computational Science* 2, no. 1 (2011): 1–8.
41. David J. Leinweber, "Stupid Data Miner Tricks: Overfitting the S&P 500," *Journal of Investing* 16, no. 1 (2007): 15–22.
42. Jörg Mayer, "The Fallacy of Composition: A Review of the Literature," *The World Economy* 25, no. 6 (2002): 875–894.
43. A. D . Wissner-Gross and C. E. Freer, "Relativistic Statistical Arbitrage," *Physical Review E* 82, no. 5 (2010): 056104.

CHAPTER 4

Social Finance

Once we've disentangled the complex interaction between situation and disposition we will be ready to face the next set of challenges. Situation is one aspect of our environment, but there is another one, one that we're so immersed in we hardly recognize it at all.

Humans are social creatures, we rely on our social relationships and social networks to function properly, and we're so embedded in these that we react to the behavior of other people in entirely unconscious ways. And, of course, these ways are generally not going to make us wealthier than we already are.

Our tour, folks, is entering the land of social finance, where what your neighbor, your friend—even your unmet Facebook friend—and your family does is far more important to your investing decision making than anything you analyze in your own head.

CONFORM—OR DIE

The British Prime Minister Margaret Thatcher once opined that there was "no such thing as society," but we can be fairly sure that she was wrong. We are totally and utterly immersed in our societies, to an extent that's astonishing once you start trying to unpick it. Our behaviors are conditioned by the expectations of the people around us, and we respond to those expectations by, largely, seeking to conform.

As we saw in Chapter 3, the idea of the wisdom of crowds doesn't tend to apply to investing situations because people's decision-making processes are often linked, sometimes in surprisingly obscure ways. But you'll also find people all making the same decision for another reason—in order to conform to their peer group's expectations. This was famously shown by Solomon Asch, whose conformity test is still a staple of college psychology courses.[1]

Asch had a group of stooges and a single valid participant compare the lengths of lines in a test in which the correct result was always obvious.

He had the real participant answer last and his stooges deliberately got 75 percent of the answers wrong, but such that they were all in agreement with each other. Remembering that the correct answer was *obviously* the correct answer, regardless of the decisions of the stooges, the results showed the power of conformity—three quarters of the participants conformed at least once rather than trusting the evidence of their own eyes.

Why people do this isn't hard to understand. Faced with concerted agreement by a group of peers, there aren't many of us who are prepared to go our own way, and if we are we're likely to end up on the outside looking in. In our modern age that may not be the worst thing that can happen, but a few thousand years ago it was likely a death sentence. Our inclination to conform to social pressure exerted on us by our peers is a very powerful drive indeed. Unfortunately, groupthink is not a good basis for investing decision making.

LESSON 1

There may be safety in conforming in everyday life, but in investing the people who follow everyone else are simply setting themselves up for failure.

GROUPTHINK

The idea that we tend to conform to the beliefs of the majority is usually known as groupthink, a striving for what its original discoverer, Irving Janis,[2] described as "concurrence seeking." And the more in tune with the rest of the group we are the less likely we are to engage in thought processes of our own, which all too often leads to poor outcomes.

One spectacular, and tragic, example of this occurred on January 28, 1986, when the Space Shuttle *Challenger* broke up after takeoff. In a famous piece of independent analysis, aided and abetted by insider information, the Nobel Prize–winning physicist Richard Feynman uncovered the technical problem, caused by the failure of a single component known as an O-ring, responsible for sealing joints between separate parts of the spacecraft.

Feynman[3] estimated, given the complexity of the Shuttle, that one in every hundred flights would fail, compared to the management estimate of one in a hundred thousand. It was not that any specific component failed—although given the O-ring design weaknesses were known and apparently ignored this was a problem in itself—it was that the entire process of risk management was flawed. When, 17 years later, the Space Shuttle *Columbia* failed it became evident that lessons hadn't been learned and that many of the management issues identified by Feynman were still at work and, as Claire Ferraris and Rodney Carveth have pointed out, groupthink figured high among them.[4] The NASA management team was operating in a way that made it almost impossible for information that didn't meet their desired outcome to even be discussed, let alone acted upon.

In everyday life, groupthink is powerful because of our addiction to group conformity. You shouldn't be at all surprised to be told that it's an equally powerful force in investment. Unlike the kind of herding processes we discussed in the previous chapter this has nothing to do with people reacting to similar external signals, but is entirely about them reacting to each other. Roland Bénabou[5] suggests that the effect of group conformity and groupthink is that it frames how people use new information. What he calls a "Mutually Assured Delusion principle" leads to investors ignoring bad news, either because the overconfidence of their peer group is providing them with (temporarily) positive returns or because their losses drive them into denial, which is itself contagious.

Perhaps even worse than groupthink-led collective denial is that the same effect leads to willful ignorance. This is the same behavior we see in people avoiding health checkups that might save their lives because they'd rather not know the truth, because the outcome might not be pleasant. In all of these processes, our decision making is distorted by a nastily contagious form of motivated reasoning.

LESSON 2

Investing groupthink leads to losses: groups will delude themselves into ignoring bad news. If you want to check if groupthink is in operation try pointing out some negative information about the group's favorite investing idea and wait for the deluge of denial. Groups can give you good ideas, but they don't offer any safe haven.

MOTIVATED REASONING

The idea behind motivated reasoning is quite simple: we feel before we think. This is the affect heuristic again, that faint whisper of emotion that guides our decision-making processes and colors our choices. The problem is, largely, that we have to believe something before we can understand it and that gives us a bit of an issue, because it means that if we want to analyze two contradictory positions we somehow have to believe both of them simultaneously, and that's taking keeping an open mind a step or two too far.

The basic idea goes back to a seventeenth-century philosopher named Benedictus de Spinoza,[6] who argued that if an idea is abhorrent to you then at best you'll ignore it and at worst you'll attempt to twist it to conform with your own beliefs. This is often seen in the backfire effect, where people will take evidence that proves the opposite of what they believe and use it to propose exactly the opposite. The point being is that we can't simply think that evidence that disproves the dominant theories of the group will actually have the expected effect—it may simply serve to drive the collective delusion to a new peak.

Harvard's Daniel Gilbert[7] has analyzed the issue in depth and has come to the conclusion that Spinoza's ideas are roughly correct. We first have to believe an idea before we can analyze it and then we have to unbelieve it in order to get to the correct position, assuming it's wrong. And if you think the idea of unbelieving something sounds hard you're dead right—Gilbert has also shown that it's relatively easy to interrupt the unbelieving process, by putting people under time pressure or forcing them to multitask. This is yet another aspect of information overload.

The broad conclusion we can draw from these findings is that we need to avoid becoming part of a larger investment group, we need to minimize the number of decisions we need to make and, we need to make the process as mechanical as it's possible to achieve. Above all, we need to do all of this without subjecting ourselves or being subjected to unnecessary time pressure or while making other difficult decisions. We can't take away the whisper of emotion, but we can at least relegate it to a backseat somewhere. Of course, if it were that simple to avoid social biases then it wouldn't be hard at all to avoid some terrible investing mistakes. But, as it turns out, groupthink is only the beginning of a very twisted tale.

LESSON 3

Analysis of an investing idea leaves you open to the problem of liking what you're investigating so much you forget to finish your analysis. Try to make analysis as mechanical a process as you can, and never invest under time or emotional pressure. You may end up forgetting to unbelieve your own analysis.

POLARIZED

If you take a random group of people, put them in a room together and ask them to come to a decision over some matter on which everyone has an opinion, what do you think will happen? Well, for a long time the belief was that the group view would tend to the average and that the more extreme views would be filtered out and watered down. Eventually, James Arthur Finch Stoner of MIT thought it might be worth testing this idea out and discovered, rather to his surprise, that this is not the case, not at all.[8] In fact, the group will usually move toward a more extreme position than that of the average group member. The effect is known as group polarization and, when added to groupthink, it forms a potent and dangerous cocktail for investors.

The move towards an extreme position is known as a risky shift, and while that may sound like a daring item of ladies underwear it's actually a thoroughly scary type of behavior, because groups of people tend to advocate more risky behavior than they would have as individuals. It's almost as though the presence of other people emboldens the group to embrace danger. None of us will walk the tightrope over the canyon on our own, but as a group we might just manage to egg each other on to do exactly that.

Harvard Law Professor Cass Sunstein's analysis of risky shifts shows that they're more likely to happen in some situations than others.[9] Where the group members are relatively diverse and randomly selected—a jury for instance—then the effect is less powerful, but where there are shared interests, prior beliefs, and some form of shared social identity—political groups, terrorist cells, or investment clubs, for instance—then a shift to risk is more likely and likely to be more pronounced.

Associated with this is an effect we've seen before, our tendency to outsource our thinking when someone expresses a strong view with great force and precision: a particularly strong-minded individual can often sway the whole group. On the other hand, even if the group is minded to take a particularly strong position then a single person with a strongly held opposing view can ameliorate this effect.

Steven Utkus, who runs the Vanguard Center for Retirement Research, has proposed a four-stage model of stock market bubble formation that draws on group polarization and other effects.[10] Firstly, he suggests that the representative heuristic, where we form opinions on whatever we can easily bring to mind (Linda the feminist again), lures us into chasing short-term success stories. Secondly, he thinks that overconfidence then kicks in and causes unrealistic extrapolation of short-term trends into the distant future. Thirdly, large groups of like-minded investors then undergo a risky shift caused by groupthink and group polarization effects and then, finally, when the bubble bursts then everyone shifts to a risk averse position and sells all their stocks.

This is a fascinating model because it builds on sensory issues—the representative effect—followed by issues of self-awareness into social effects. And there's good reason to suggest that situation in the form of modern technology may be increasing the problem. Eli Pariser has argued that Internet search technology is creating a bubble of experience for like-minded individuals based on their web profiles, where only information that fits that profile is served to us.[11] If we all start with a similar viewpoint and all receive similar feedback we're more likely to be polarized into a more extreme position to start with.

In short, we need to be very, very wary of investing opinions formed by groups. Any type of shared investment forum brings with it a combination of issues. Of course, they may give us access to information and investing opportunities we might otherwise not have found but they also bring us group opinions that we may not be able to ignore. More information is good, up to a point, but outsourcing our critical thinking is not. And don't just trust a single Internet search engine when you're doing your research, because it's quite likely to show you what it thinks you want to see—and it may well be right, even if it isn't in your best interests.

LESSON 4

Any group is likely to form a more extreme opinion than that of the average investor. If you choose to conform with the group you may end up making riskier decisions than you otherwise would have. And don't trust your Internet search engine either, it's as biased as you are.

A PERSONAL MISSION STATEMENT: SOCIAL IDENTITY AND BEYOND

As you can see, the possible effects of social groups can be very powerful. However, there's a strong argument that states we are only really influenced by people with whom we identify with. If you're a dyed-in-the-wool Democrat you're highly unlikely to be influenced by someone with strong Republican views. Indeed, the evidence of group polarization suggests quite strongly that our group or social identity is heavily implicated in how we make decisions.

Roughly, social identity is a concept about how we anchor our identities by linking them to social groups: political parties, football teams, racial groups, and so on. It's also bound up with how we interact with our employers and colleagues. George Akerlof and Rachel Kranton have shown that how an employee relates to his or her fellow workers and managers is far more important than simple incentives when it comes to motivated performance.[12] Of course, this runs completely counter to the modern approach to employee management where people are treated as resources, are hired and fired at will, and it's assumed they can be incentivized to do things regardless of whether they believe in them or not.

The truth, as usual, is more complex, more nuanced, and far, far more interesting. While it's possible to incentivize people to do very specific things there are consequences in doing so, because if you direct people's focus on to one specific area of interest then they'll spend a lot of time attempting to ensure that they achieve that specific goal, and will quite often miss or even deliberately bypass the bigger picture. So, for instance, when the headmaster of a private school was given a bonus for every new fee-paying child he recruited the numbers of new starters suddenly soared. It was only later that the school governors discovered that he'd been heavily discounting the fees in order to boost numbers. Consider the contract offered to Ken O'Brien, a football quarterback, which stipulated a penalty every time he threw the ball to the opposition.[13] In consequence, he rarely got intercepted, but that was largely because he rarely threw the ball at all, not a great quality in a quarterback. Be careful what you wish for.

The same is true of investing, although the incentives are often far more difficult to discern. Although we may start out investing because we want to become rich, we often get diverted by other issues along the way. As we've seen we may do it for reasons of self-esteem, or because we're fooled by our situation or, as it turns out, because we want to be at one with our social group: these are all real incentives for humans and it's important that we recognize this and take account of it. Kranton and Akerlof's employment-based research points the way—they argue that you have to make people identify with their employers rather than simply incentivize them, because by doing this you align the goals of the individuals with the goals of the organizations.

So, we need to start out with a manifesto that states what our organization's goals are. It's a personal investing mission statement that will provide us with the structure to socially identify with our own lives, and to provide us with a benchmark against which to measure our own behavior. You have to create your own, based on your own interests and approach to investing; there is no single way of doing this. Here's mine:

> *My mission is to invest in high quality corporations when they are undervalued relative to the market, and to hold them until such time they become extremely overvalued relative to the market.*

This statement contains a whole bunch of difficult to untangle concepts that we'll need to analyze further: What, for instance do "high quality" or "market" or "overvalued" mean? But the general point is easily understood and provides a basis for evaluating any particular investment both before and after a purchase. Moreover, it provides a quick and dirty checkpoint for whenever I get carried away with some awesome new investing idea offered by someone whose ideas I value from within my investing cohort. I seek to actively construct my social identity as an investor, I don't just leave it to random chance to form it.

One other thing, though. This definition is not absolute. Those "relative" terms are important, because they provide an element of flexibility. Remember that markets are reflexive, an investing style that works today will probably not work in 10 years' time, and getting drawn into a single method of analysis that's set in stone will guarantee that you fall off a cliff at some point. So don't do it.

LESSON 5

We need to be very clear about what we're investing for and why we're doing it. Unless we identify with our own mission statements we will be easily persuaded and fooled into doing otherwise. Our brains, our egos, our environments, and our peers will make sure we lose.

GAMING THE SYSTEM

The process by which people manipulate incentives to their own financial advantage is known as gaming the system—basically, we manipulate the rules, staying within them technically but betraying the spirit of the game. Closed groups with a cohesive social identity can often lose sight of the bigger picture, and fail to remember that their little world is actually part of a bigger one in which there are other rules, ones enforceable by law.

The United Kingdom had such an example in 2010, when it became clear that its politicians were gaming their expenses system by claiming for things that they weren't actually purchasing and then pocketing the difference. Some of the claims were simply bizarre, one parliamentarian claimed for a duck house, another for horse manure (no, seriously, I am not joking), and another to have the moat of their castle cleaned (only in England!). Some claims were simply illegal and, eventually, a few representatives ended up going to prison, but throughout the whole episode, the entire body of politicians seemed to be unable to accept that their game was illegal within the context of laws that they themselves had enacted. They could see nothing wrong in acting in a way that saw other citizens imprisoned for fraud.

There have been many similar examples in an investing context, where managements simply ended up out of touch with the real world, operating to their own code of conduct, seemingly unaware of the wider context of their actions. The infamous failures at Enron and Worldcom seem, in part, to be due to this kind of group issue.

This type of willful blindness is not confined to politicians and corporate executives. In fact, Dan Ariely argues that it's the type of behavior we all might be guilty of given half a chance.[14] His research suggests that the more removed from actual money our fraud is the more likely we will be to try and get away with it, and we will try to find ways of rationalizing our behavior to ourselves to avoid admitting our guilt. This process was dubbed *moral disengagement* by Albert Bandura, and is a particular issue in corporate fraud as Anand, Ashforth, and Joshi have shown—white collar criminals will tend to acknowledge their behavior but simply deny that it's criminal.

You're probably thinking "so what?" Well, if you think about private investors as a group with a shared social identity—and let's face it, most of us share the same basic beliefs about capitalism and democracy—then it's not hard to see how we can easily end up being polarized in our thinking and subject to groupthink. Moral disengagement is part of the very fabric of shareholder democracy, because we expect our corporations to aim to maximize their returns on investments while staying on the right side of the law.

The problem with this is that the incentives to maximize return on investment can often cause unintended consequences: corporations who have too much of a focus on the short term and who have overly incentivized their managements to meet these aims tend to underperform in the longer term. CEOs tend to operate to maximize their own returns and, given that the lifespan of a CEO is often comparable to that of a mayfly in a frog farm, that may not be in our best interests as shareholders.

So we shouldn't be surprised that when Daniel Bergstresser and Thomas Philippon examined CEO compensation they discovered that the more heavily biased incentives were toward earnings-related elements like stock options the greater the probability there was of earnings manipulation.[15] Of course, it's an unworthy thought that CEO remuneration packages may induce them to direct our great corporations to maximize their own personal compensation but CEOs are nothing if not good at playing the game.

Remember, again, that in the short term we are likely to be outcompeted by investment institutions. Focusing on corporations with longer-term aspirations will provide us with better returns, even if they take longer to realize. Our moral disengagement may lead to executives gaming the system, something that's not in our interests. We need to frame our investment approach to suit our personal goals, not those of the wider group or faceless corporations.

LESSON 6

Don't simply accept the general idea that we should be focusing on making money regardless of the consequences. This leads to extreme short-term thinking, tempts executives to game the system, and puts us in competition with organizations we can't hope to outperform. We're here to make money, but on our terms, not other people's.

YOU'VE BEEN FRAMED

And so we come to the odd, but infinitely powerful topic of framing. If you still have any faint residue of hope that you're an independent individual capable of insightfully overcoming your biases then ready yourself to abandon them now. Framing is how politicians bend us to their wills, how lovers overcome our objections, and how children get their way. We don't lose our jobs anymore; we experience career upgrading or are right sized. At other times we're redeployed, reorganized, displaced, or, startlingly, experience career upgrading. We're being framed, to fit with a general approach toward moral disengagement.

The idea of framing comes out of the work of the twentieth-century sociologist Erving Goffman, who used the metaphor of a stage and drama for our various roles: as a parent, a partner, a child, an employee, an employer . . . the roles we play are infinite, while we are not.[16] The way we present ourselves depends upon the situation and the situation frames us through our interaction with others. And this isn't something we can avoid doing because we have to frame situations in order to give ourselves the social context within which we operate; all of that unconscious processing that goes on below the surface that we're rarely aware of but without which life becomes nearly impossible.

The way we look at things colors our perceptions.

The idea of framing has been popularized by the cognitive linguist George Lakoff, mainly in relation to politics.[17] He's studied the way in which politicians frame situations to create an environment that's conducive to their own ambitions and ideologies. They manipulate frames in order to change our perspective—remember that the U.S. Army wasn't engaged in a long-term occupation of Iraq but was involved in a short-term "surge."

In particular, Lakoff proposes that Wall Street frames itself in a particular way: self-interest is always right, we are individually responsible for our actions but not for their social consequences, and success defines moral authority—by definition if you're successful you must be doing something right—and these principles are ones we should live with in daily life, not just in our financial dealings.[18] Of course, this is not the only way of framing yourself, but it is one that is commonly propounded. And, of course, from this comes the mantra of short-term earnings maximization and the moral disengagement of shareholders, with all the problems that this brings.

In terms of actual investing there's striking evidence that framing has deep consequences for individuals.[19] Think about this:

A: You've found the calculator you want in a local store. It costs $15. However, a bit of judicious Internet surfing shows that you can purchase the same calculator for $10 in a store that's a 15-minute drive away. Would you get in your car or buy locally?

B: You've found the tablet PC you want in a local store. It costs $125. However, a bit of judicious Internet surfing shows that you can purchase the same table PC for $120 in a store that's a 15-minute drive away. Would you get in your car or buy locally?

When Amos Tversky and Daniel Kaheneman investigated this problem they found that in A the majority of people would drive to get the cheaper calculator, but in B most people would buy locally. Yet the saving ($5) and the effort (15-minute drive) was identical in both cases. What's different is the frame, which is constructed on the value of the item under consideration.

In fact, Tversky and Kaheneman were able to show reversals of preferences in a wide variety of situations simply by manipulating the frame. Traditionally, economists didn't expect this, because they assumed our behavior was consistent across time. But it isn't, so it wasn't surprising that when Alok Kumar and Sonya Lim looked at the effect of framing on stock investment choices they discovered that framing has a massive impact on the way people make investing decisions.[20] The more narrow the frame, the more likely they were to invest badly.

In this sense a "narrow" frame means one that's constructed in a very focused fashion—maybe on one particular stock or a single investing decision. Wider frames based on portfolios or overall wealth tend to be better diversified. If we think about how the disposition effect works—our behavior changes whether we are dealing with a gain or a loss—then this isn't especially surprising. If you narrowly frame based on every single investment then you'll be letting the disposition effect run rampant on every single stock. If you widely frame based on your entire portfolio then the effect will only really work at the overall portfolio level and you're less likely to be triggered into short-term fight or flight reactions.

LESSON 7

Narrow portfolio framing—especially focusing on individual stocks— is likely to be disastrous for us as private investors. Avoiding such frames reduces our exposure to the worst types of behavioral bias. And sometimes avoidance is the best we can hope for.

BEHAVIORAL PORTFOLIOS

One of the lessons of framing should be to ensure we manage our money as a whole, not as separate and different sets of accounts. As we saw with the concept of mental accounting we tend to assign money to different buckets and then manage those buckets separately, even though it's all the same pot of money in the end. We often do this quite consciously to ensure we save money for specific purposes such as holidays or Thanksgiving, but we often also do it unconsciously on a much broader scale.

It has long been noted that people will buy both lottery tickets and insurance. We're simultaneously both risk seekers and risk averse. Most of us probably can't see any issues with that but it's puzzled economists who recognize that this is inconsistent. You may be getting the idea that economists have a lot of trouble with the real behavior of people, and you would be right.

As individuals we have no trouble differentiating between the pleasure of a small gamble and the safety of a small outlay for large downside protection. Meir Statman[21] has pointed out, however, that our love of gambling can cause problems for investors—because investors confuse the negative sum game of stock trading for the positive sum game of stock holding. In particular, stock trading exposes us to a raft of costs that stock holding doesn't but with every decision comes trailing behavioral consequences that are hard to manage.

Even so, this doesn't explain all of this lottery-insurance behavior. The people who can least afford to gamble on the lottery are the people who are most likely to buy tickets. The people who can most afford the losses they're insuring against are the people who are most likely to purchase insurance. Harry Markowitz,[22] the economist who almost single-handedly invented the Efficient Market Hypothesis, suggested a simple reason for this—we're very, very concerned about our social status relative to our peers. We aspire to move up the social ladder and we struggle to avoid moving down it. The keeping up with the Joneses effect is very powerful indeed.

The idea is that our dominant frame, one caused by our society's focus on financial rewards, is that financial status is equivalent to social status and this is all that's needed to trigger this sort of risky behavior. After all, if you're at the bottom of the heap with no way out then a lottery ticket may be a rational, if very low-probability, option for seeking a way up and out.

Hersh Shefrin and Meir Statman[23] have proposed that this strange risk seeking/risk avoidance behavior lies behind the way that people build their investment portfolios. Traditional economic theory says that we worry about diversification within our portfolio, and there's a bit of a myth based on this idea that 15 stocks are all you need to get sufficient diversity to avoid most foreseeable risks. Behavioral economics says that this may (or may not) be true but it's not what real people actually do. Instead they create a downside protection (insurance) portfolio and an upside opportunity (lottery) portfolio and then they manage them separately, as the theory of mental accounting suggests they should.

Into the insurance portfolio people will pour cash, bonds, mutual funds, maybe even some blue chip stocks or whatever meets their particular definition, while in the lottery portfolio you may find higher-risk stocks and a range of weird and wonderful derivatives. And people react differently to different events in these portfolios—unexpected losses are okay in a lottery but anathema in insurance, while unexpected gains are bizarre in insurance but quite likely to be gambled away in a lottery. These different reactions are guided by framing, of course.

The older we are the more likely we are to favor insurance over the lottery, unless we suddenly realize we don't have enough to retire on, whereupon we may start gambling. As you can tell, the whole framing thing is fraught with difficulty, but anchoring against what your peers do seems to be a major part of the problem. Nothing makes us more unhappy than seeing the brother-in-law or the neighbors become richer than us, and the temptation to try and keep up can sometimes be overwhelming. Social effects often trump every other type of bias.

However, investment shouldn't be treated as a relative thing. We need to measure against sensible benchmarks, not ones we can't test against. And we especially need to test against ones the hoard of behaviorally compromised investors in the market can't directly impact. Something like a dividend, maybe?

> **LESSON 8**
>
> Deciding how we invest based on how the neighbors or the in-laws are doing is a one-way ticket to lottery hell. This is madness; we need to set ourselves sensible, measurable goals, not ones determined by the luck or skills of others.

DIVIDEND DILEMMAS

One of the odder bits of framing, suggest Hersh Shefrin and Meir Statman,[24] has to do with how we treat dividends from stocks. People tend to get very, very angry at dividend cuts, even though these are often in their best interests, because sometimes retaining funds that would otherwise be paid out to shareholders is the best way for a corporation to raise money to invest in new ideas. The researchers propose that although stocks are treated by most people as belonging to the lottery portfolio, the same people tend to treat dividends as belonging to the insurance portfolio—which is peculiar, but no more so than a range of other behaviors we've seen.

In fact, dividends may offer an interesting route out of some of our more damaging psychological traits. Shinichi Hirota and Shyam Sunder[25] have shown that the difference between vaguely rational investors and very irrational ones can be explained by the way in which they use dividends to anchor their expectations. Investors who use dividends as a starting point for valuation analysis are basing it upon something they can't affect, and this provides a basis for rational analysis of future earnings. The alternative seems to be to base valuation analysis on share price and this leads to the nasty issue of market reflexivity we discussed earlier: share prices can be a self-fulfilling prophecy under certain circumstances.

Further evidence supporting this idea shows that where there is unusual uncertainty about the future trajectory of dividends it's quite likely that the share price of the stock will get out of whack with its fundamental valuation. Basically, the anchor of the dividend is no longer reliable, and no longer a basis for rational analysis. Of course, stocks that don't pay a dividend will also be harder to value: as many of these are high growth or speculative corporations to start with it's easy to see that the valuations of these can often disappear on a tangent of their own, regardless of reality, whatever that may be.

Given this type of extrapolation from dividends to future earnings it's not hard to see why people get a bit upset at dividend cuts, as they cut across rational analysis. Nonetheless, valuation methods that include dividends are far less susceptible to social pressures than those merely based on share price. A dividend is generally not determined by how much investors want it to be, but a share price may be.

LESSON 9

All things being equal—and they're often not, of course—a dividend-paying stock is easier to value than one that doesn't make payments. Remember that for every popular, wildly successful growth stock you've heard of, there are hundreds that don't succeed. Dividends are a good anchor for sensible investors.

THE LANGUAGE OF LUCRE

Of course, the main way in which social interaction is conducted by humans is through language. We frame things through language and we communicate through language. So it's not surprising that a lot of the social biases we're concerned about have their roots in the way we speak to each other and in the stories we tell. In fact we seem to be designed to tell each other stories—narratives—and then to act on those stories. The psychologist Dan McAdams[26] actually suggests that we construct our social identities out of narratives, and then follow these narratives to their logical conclusions.

Language has many effects on investors but one of the most common is the way in which it allows memes to be transmitted from brain to brain. A meme is an idea coined by the biologist Richard Dawkins[27] by analogy with a gene, it's an idea that propagates from brain to brain through social interaction, and like a gene it has a life of its own.

Investors seem peculiarly prone to accepting these socially propagated ideas without subjecting them to anything like proper scrutiny. In fact, the market is generally full of memes that no one ever really analyzes. To take one, there was the fantastic idea back in the go-go nineties, during the dot-com boom, that you should always "buy on the dips." The idea was that the market would carry on going up forever, so if it took a dip it would be temporary and that was the time to fill your boots (another meme, by the way). In truth, this meme was, at best, only valid during the temporary insanity of the age and when the market decided to take a decade long dip it took some people quite a long time to come to terms with this. Years, in fact, and some people probably still haven't quite accepted that it doesn't work.

Building on this, the economist Robert Shiller, who famously predicted the great stock market crash of 2000 when most experts were sagely expecting the continuation of the greatest bubble since, well, the last one, has proposed that markets sometimes change behavior for reasons that have nothing to do with economics and everything to do with people's shared perceptions of the world.[28] He suggests that the way in which prices of all sorts of assets shot up in the 1990s was due to the lowering of nominal interest rates, the idea being that people feel that they can afford to borrow more to invest. However, as Shiller points out, this is actually a meme that's based on a fallacy caused by people framing their ideas based on nominal rather than real interest rates; it's the base rate fallacy in another form. However, the power of the idea is that it's shared, sitting in the heads of all those like-minded investors out there.

These shared ideas form the core of our ideas about how we invest and are incredibly powerful because they're virtually unconscious, they're simply part of the fabric of how we go about doing our investing business. Yet when they're wrong they can drive whole cohorts of investors into major error, often for a generation or more. To counter this we need to construct our own memes, and to develop approaches that aren't easily influenced by fashion and fads. We need to be logical investors, not trendy ones.

LESSON 10

Memes drive us to invest in a similar fashion to one another and they're so ingrained we often don't even notice them. Shared perceptions are great for everyday social behavior, where what we believe is close to reality, but stocks don't care about our beliefs, so we need to protect ourselves. Invest on the basis of fundamental principles, not "obvious" ideas.

EMBEDDED INVESTING

The idea that we invest in a world based on shared ideas mediated by social relationships, and the biases they bring with them, has a specific name—it's called embeddedness. Embeddedness argues that the way we deal with economic transactions isn't simply about making money but is very powerfully governed by our relationships with other people. At a simple level this is easy to understand—we will trust people who have previously demonstrated that they're honest and we will avoid dealing with people who've cheated us in the past.

In fact this idea is so obvious that it's largely been ignored by most of economics but is well known in the not-obviously related discipline of sociology, where Mark Granovetter has outlined the basic principles of the concept.[29] The idea is that the economic relationships between people and companies are embedded in social networks, but that these networks simply aren't part of any normal kind of economic analysis, and certainly aren't considered by investors.

Because we're all embedded in complex sets of social relationships we can't avoid being influenced by them. And this influence will sometimes lead us into error, when we trust someone who trusts someone else who trusts another person who happens to be wrong. We often cross-check our own behavior by looking at what other people in our social network are doing—we're being consciously reflexive but in so doing we usually don't recognize that our peers are doing exactly the same to us.

An extreme example of this, and one that demonstrates that even the most advanced computer modeling technology can't stop people being people, was identified by Daniel Beunza and David Stark, who analyzed what happened when groups of professional traders who try to make money by exploiting takeover situations got things badly wrong.[30] In 2001, the European Commission blocked a merger between GE and Honeywell, a decision that collectively cost the traders about $3 billion.

What's really odd about this particular massive cock-up is that these traders are specifically aware of their own weaknesses and go out of their way to continually question their own beliefs: they're an active, ongoing demonstration of the benefits of reflexivity. However, what the researchers suspected was that reflexivity on its own isn't enough, because the only way that anyone can check their beliefs is by reference to someone else, and if everyone is embedded in the same network of social interactions then the net result will sometimes be disaster.

This is exactly what happened in this case. These reflexive traders were carefully checking each other's views but because they were all working on the same set of assumptions everyone lost, big time. Organizational management experts Daniel Beunza and David Stark question whether simple reflexivity is enough to prevent the kinds of major errors that we frequently see: it's not that people are blindly making errors, it's that we're so embedded in social interactions that we are cognitively interdependent.[31]

In normal life, this is a good thing, because the alternative is pretty scary, but in investing life this can lead to wildly unfortunate outcomes.

LESSON 11

Cross-checking what we're doing against what other people are doing—even when those others are genuinely insightful and careful investors—is no guarantee of success. We probably can't help but calibrate ourselves against such comparisons, but we must limit the impact of getting that calibration wrong.

FINANCIAL THEORY OF MIND

We know at least one alternative to being socially interconnected, and it's a common symptom of autism. Autistic people suffer from a variety of problems, which manifest themselves as an inability to interact with others. There are lots of ideas about why this might be, but the overarching problem seems to be that autistics suffer from a lack of theory of mind.

The psychologist Simon Baron-Cohen has proposed that we are all, in a limited sense, mind-readers.[32] It's our ability to know what someone else is thinking, and to know that they know that we know this, that allows us to effectively interact. As it turns out, a lot of human social behavior isn't directly mediated by language, which sometimes causes unusual problems such as the wild nineteenth-century belief in animal telepathy, caused by the apparent mind-reading abilities of a horse called Clever Hans.[33]

Clever Hans could seemingly provide the answers to simple mathematical sums by tapping his hoof the correct number of times. His owner made a living demonstrating this and Clever Hans became the subject of a bewildering array of scientific theories. When it was shown that the horse could answer questions when someone other than his owner was asking the questions, thus proving it wasn't some kind of signaling trick, the speculation exploded into a fever, with many otherwise serious scientists suggesting that this was evidence of animal telepathy.

Eventually, however, someone had the idea of getting someone who didn't know the answer to the questions to ask them, at which point Clever Hans stopped being clever. It turned out that the horse was just unusually good at reading the body language of the questioner, which told him when to stop tapping.

We all perform this kind of trick unconsciously and naturally and, along with a whole array of other natural skills such as joint attention, they allow us to form common beliefs and to act upon them. We are very, very good at figuring out what other people are thinking and it's this ability that allows us to operate in the complex social networks that form human society. And this is also the way we like to try and invest, as John Maynard Keynes[34] demonstrated back in the 1930s.

Keynes is primarily famous for being the economist who argued that in recessionary times governments should man the pumps of financial priming and push loads of cheap money into the markets. This is partly behind the idea of quantitative easing that central banks have been pursuing for the past few years. As such, Keynes's name is enough to send half the world's financial experts into apoplexy.

But when he wasn't coming up with entirely original ways of thinking about economics he was also a highly successful investor,[35] and one who spent a lot of time thinking about how people actually went about investing. To this end he came up with the metaphor of a newspaper beauty contest, in which the winner is the person whose choices correspond to the preferences of the competitors as a whole. So to win you need to pick the contestants you think other people will pick, not those you personally find most attractive.

By analogy, Keynes suggested that this was how most people go about investing: they pick the shares that they think other people will pick, rather than the ones they themselves would choose. In essence they're relying on theory of mind to figure out what stocks people will buy rather than simply relying on fundamental analysis. As theory of mind is the basis of most human social interaction we can easily imagine that it is very, very difficult to turn off, even in a world such as investing where you're more likely to be rewarded for independent thought, rather than Clever Hans–like attempts to read the minds of others.

In fact, Keynes, who started out as a beauty contest style investor, gradually adopted his style to become much more focused on fundamentals. Unsurprisingly his returns improved dramatically, as will yours, once you stop worrying about what other people are going to do.

LESSON 12

Beauty contest style investing is a one-way street to penury. Clever Hans wasn't clever, but we can't help trying to mind read. The best investors almost certainly learn to avoid second-guessing other people's intentions; we need to do the same.

TRUST ME, RECIPROCALLY . . .

A theory of mind is great for figuring out what other people are thinking but it's also very useful for another purpose—deceit. The psychologist Paul Ekman, who's the prototype for the protagonist in the TV series *Lie to Me*, has made a career out of analyzing liars and their filthy lying ways, which, unfortunately, tends to mean most of us. In fact, one of the theories about why we have such large brains relative to our size is that we're engaged in an escalating war of deception in which the person with the biggest brain wins. Certainly Richard Byrne and Nadia Corp[36] have done some convincing experiments with primates, which suggests the larger the brain and the more complex the social group the more scope there is for deception.

Unfortunately, detecting liars isn't as simple as checking out their hat size. Most of us can't figure out when someone is lying. In fact, as Paul Ekman and Maureen O'Sullivan[37] have shown, most experts can't detect someone who's lying, which shouldn't really come as a surprise after everything else we've seen. Because of this, it's likely that our evolutionary response to detecting deception was to exclude the liars from the social group—a punishment that would often have been a death sentence.

However, the evolutionary benefits of deception are significant, because anything that allowed our ancestors to freeload on their peer groups was a way of ensuring survival and more breeding opportunities. If you make a daily diary and truthfully record every partial truth and piece of downright dissembling that you do you'll be astonished by how often you don't really speak the truth.

The issue of trust looms large in human social relations, and never more so than in the area of finance, where we all too often have to trust others to invest our money for us. In a world in which liars abound trust is difficult to achieve and we have evolved techniques for managing this asymmetry of information. Here's a little test.

Imagine you're playing a game with a stranger. You're given $100 and are told that you have to offer the stranger some of this money. If he accepts, he gets to keep the money you offered and you get to keep the rest. If he rejects your offer, neither of you get a penny.

How much do you offer?

Well, the standard answer in economics is that you should offer 1 cent. The reasoning is that as far as the stranger is concerned they're getting a cent for nothing, and are better off, and as far as you're concerned then you should be seeking to maximize the amount you make. And as the stranger realizes this, he should accept.

In real life, of course, as Armin Falk, Ernst Fehr, and Urs Fischbacher[38] discovered, when they carried out the above experiment, anyone offering one cent will probably be told to take a hike and may well get a punch on the nose in the bargain. A low-ball offer will offend the stranger's sense of fairness and they'll reject it—we expect people to demonstrate reciprocity, we are highly attuned to concepts of social justice, and will tend to rage against perceived injustice. It's likely that this sense of fairness comes out of our need to create and maintain social networks and our rejection of unfair offers is probably based on our innate reaction to being given something: we'll feel obliged to reciprocate and we calculate that what's being offered doesn't make that worthwhile.

Of course, this is a framing effect: we're deciding to reject the offer on the grounds of unfairness rather than that of an overall increase in wealth. So, startlingly, it seems that there's more to money and investment than simply becoming wealthy: we expect people to be fair in their dealings with us as well. Yet the unvarnished truth is that investing is only about making money, and when we get ourselves confused by moral and social issues the only damage we do is to our own finances.

Don't misunderstand me, I absolutely believe that we should live moral lives according to an ethical code of conduct. I believe equally as strongly that the managements of the corporations I invest in should also—I absolutely hate executives who preach one thing, do another, and then disclaim all responsibility when some underling is caught breaking the rules. Responsibility for ethical behavior starts at the top.

However, when it comes to our money we cannot afford to get confused by social biases that are irrelevant to the entirely unsocial world of stock market investment. Reciprocate all you want in the rest of your life, but when it comes to investing, stick to the point, take the low-ball offer, and move on. We're here to make money, not friends.

LESSON 13

While we need to make sure that we don't get fooled into taking a short-term approach to our investments we also shouldn't ever forget that investing is about making money. Don't expect faceless corporations to reciprocate our trust—don't expect to be loved for investing. We are here to make money, friends we can find elsewhere.

AKERLOF'S LEMONS

Unfortunately there are financial situations where fairness is important and you do need to be able to detect liars and charlatans. Financial advisers, lawyers, bankers, insurance salespeople—there are lots of situations in which the ability to figure out whether we can trust someone is critical. In these situations we're faced with an issue of trust due to the asymmetry of information in the marketplace: the problems of lying and reciprocity give us immediate problems when we're dealing with experts who may know more than us or may be simply very good liars and are pretending that they know more than us. This type of situation is very common, even outside of finance when we're faced with an expert who knows lots and we're like tourists abroad. Take used cars, for instance, an area renowned for being populated with charlatans and worse.

George Akerlof famously won the Nobel Prize for Economics for his work on this particular problem.[39] Normally we'd expect that the price of something like a used car would be set by supply and demand: the more cars on offer the lower the price, and so forth. In the case of used cars, however, this turns out not to be the case because they're all cheap regardless of availability. Supply-demand pricing works whenever we get situations where there is clear and transparent information. Unfortunately, when it comes to used cars most of us are less able to judge the actual state of a particular car than the smooth talking salesman pitching to us, and simply don't know when we're being sold a lemon. So we discount the price of all used cars and end up with what's known as a market failure—market forces simply fail to deliver clear and transparent pricing.

The overall effect on the used car market is chilling, because owners of good used cars can't get a fair price for them, and therefore the only cars on the market are lemons. This type of asymmetry in risk isn't as rare as you might think—for instance, the only older people who want health insurance tend to be the ones who know they have something wrong with them, because the price of health insurance increases rapidly with age. Of course, one of the reasons it increases rapidly with age is because only sick people want the insurance, while all the healthy people decide it's too expensive. . . .

This particular issue is known as adverse selection, and means that those elderly people who aren't ill and simply want to protect themselves are unfairly penalized. It's actually a problem in all sorts of situations: many corporations find themselves with a similar problem of how to distinguish themselves from inferior competitors, and their solution is one based in the psychology of humans. Robert Cialdini, in his book *Influence*,[40] provides an anecdote that illustrates the principle—a gift shop owner accidentally doubled the price of some hard-to-sell items instead of putting them on a half-price sale and was amazed to find that they were all snapped up in short order. The purchasers were relying on a very simple heuristic—expensive means quality.

This type of external flag is known as a signal, which are often used by corporations to establish the unobservable quality of their goods. Amna Kirmani and Akshay Rao[41] have come up with a range of such signals, but make the point that signaling only works when the gains for the high-quality firm are higher than for other strategies, while low-quality firms get a better payoff by not signaling—otherwise, the lower quality company can compete on signaling. So think of branding as a signaling mechanism—spending large amounts of money on advertising may not be about the messages supplied but the overt signal that the corporation can afford to splash out in this way.

Our use of these types of signals can reach over into investment activities. People will often buy stocks because the share price has gone up or sell them because it's gone down, a practice often labeled "momentum investing." Whatever you call it, however, if it's being practiced simply based on the signals emanating from the share price itself, it's simply stupid investing and should be avoided.

More pertinently, the issue of information asymmetries is one faced by investors every day. Managements, advisers, mutual fund managers; they all know more than we do. Although technically trading on inside information is illegal there's no doubt that it does happen, and it disadvantages the private investor. Again this is why we often see speculation about what movements in share prices mean—because although they're often random sometimes they are signaling that something is going down.

Unfortunately, share price movements unaccompanied by public disclosure of information are not safe signals upon which to base trades. We operate in a social world of murky behavior and uncertain outcomes, where our lie detecting capability often leads us astray, but we need to be clear about what information we can trust and what we can't. If you trade regularly on the signals given off by share prices you will lose money. Occasionally it will work, but don't fall for the occasional reinforcement of a bad idea. Just focus on learning how to spot the lemons in the first place—because even in a market full of them there'll still be the odd peach, if you're smart enough to find it.

LESSON 14

Signals are an easy way of determining whether we want something or not. However, the signals given off by stocks are not a good basis for investing, because they're as likely to come from a lemon as a peach.

THE PEACOCK'S TAIL

The idea that our mechanisms for social trust fail in certain market situations and lead us into other ways of attempting to establish the quality, or
otherwise, of goods or stocks arises from an unexpected source: evolutionary biology. In particular, it comes out of some very counterintuitive analysis
about the point of some of the most stupidly extravagant displays in nature.
Take, for instance, the peacock's tail.

However you look at it, carrying around an enormous set of tail
feathers so that you can impress the lady peacocks must carry some kind
of handicap: it's a burden in every way and it's not going to help you run
away or fight when a fox comes calling. So the idea is that the handicap must be worth the burden—otherwise peacocks with extravagant tails
would get eaten and the rather less showy male birds would get their pick
of the females. And, in the thinking of Amotz Zahavi,[42] the handicap is
itself a signal.

The idea is that the ridiculous plumage of the handsome male peacocks
is actually making a statement that they're so darned fit that they can survive
regardless of the handicap that nature has conferred on them. The females
aren't being wooed by the display but are using it as a proxy—a signal—
for overall fitness of the individual. Not only that, potential predators and
competitors are making the same calculation—a bird with that amount of
baggage has got to be a pretty tricky customer, so better go find a less fit one.
It's a maddeningly perverse idea, but it seems to be correct.

The same idea appears to apply to corporations who use advertising for
signaling purposes. Back in 1961, George Stigler[43] pointed out that it can be
actually quite difficult for people to figure out the correct market price for
things, and that advertising may be a practical way for producers to reduce
consumer search costs. Phillip Nelson[44] then showed that people don't just
use advertising to find the best price but also to establish what he called "experience qualities." It's not that advertising carries any useful information,
it's that it *is* the useful information. It's a handicap and we respond to it.

The use of handicaps and advertising as a short-cut to doing any actual
research is a common problem for private investors. It's far easier to latch
onto some popular meme about an investing trend or some powerful signal
from a well-known corporation than it is to do the hard work of analyzing
stocks. The odd thing is that this trait is actually caused by our underlying
mechanisms for trying to establish the truth or otherwise of information
we're being presented with in situations where we really don't want to be
fooled by others. And yet again we find our evolutionary mechanisms betraying us as they're exploited to trick us into deploying our money in the
wrong way.

The layering of different biases on top of each other—salience, availability, social trust failures—compound the issues that we're faced with. It's not sufficient to defend ourselves against specific individual issues, but we need to arm ourselves more broadly against the world.

LESSON 15

We are built to look for the equivalent of the peacock's tail: we look for signals that indicate fitness. Unfortunately the easy ones are marketing and advertising, which don't take any effort to find. The proper signals of corporate strength are in the strength of the balance sheet and the competitive advantage. We're not peahens, so let's not act like we have their brains.

FACEBOOKED

If you wanted an example of a corporation that marketed itself using a gigantic plume of feathers you need look no further than Facebook, the social networking company. So spectacular was its marketing that investors were prepared to pay almost any price for the stock when it launched on the market and almost inevitably suffered short-term disappointment. It was a classic example of Keynesian beauty contest investing, and went badly wrong for a whole variety of reasons.

But Facebook itself is a prime example of another social trend, because the sheer interconnectedness of social media offers widely separated groups of people ways of interacting in near real-time, which have not been possible until now. And given our propensity for overlaying our evolutionary heritage on top of modern inventions you won't be surprised to know that this seems to be quite a dangerous thing for us to do.

As we've seen, the idea is that financial memes can spread through social networks in what one commentator has called "a sort of social epidemic." We come with inbuilt social intelligence, ready-made for social interaction, and we'll use this every chance we get. David Hirshleifer's idea that we disproportionately prefer to discuss our triumphs over our disasters—a feature known as self-enhancing transmission bias—leads to the suggestion that the more actively interconnected we are the more we will hear about the investing successes of our peers and the more inclined we will be to become active investors.[45]

When David Simon and Rawley Heimer[46] investigated a Facebook-like social network this is precisely what they found. Successful short-term traders were more likely to start broadcasting their results, and the more successful they were the more likely people were to start copying them. However, because this type of investor normally tends to take significant risks and outlier positions, a few of them, purely by chance, will become disproportionately successful. And this group will demonstrate disproportionate influence in a social network.

What's really interesting about this is that it suggests that more efficient forms of communication can actually lead to less efficient investing. The challenge is to separate out the lucky from the skillful and the self-aware from the high-risk gambler. The next time you're inclined to follow the teachings of some networked-up guru, ask them what their last complete disaster was, and what they learned from it. Investing in stocks involves a great deal of luck as well as skill. We need to distinguish the purely lucky from the genuinely skillful, because skill works for a long time and luck will always run out.

LESSON 16

Social networks are designed to allow people to spread the information that they want to spread. This is not the same as the unvarnished truth and when you have a whole network of people who are only telling you about their successes you're likely to end up unduly influenced by people whose main skill is self-promotion. This is not a good basis for investment success.

BE KIND TO AN OLD PERSON

Let's end this journey through social biases with a really odd one, our social interactions with our future selves. One of the many interesting facets of our social interconnectedness is that most of us are imbued with a sense of social responsibility. We are inclined, all things being equal, to help people in need when we can.

This doesn't always play out the way you'd want. Famously, Kitty Genovese was repeatedly attacked in New York within earshot of lots of people who could have helped her but didn't.[47] The theory was that everyone left it to someone else to do something about it, the so-called bystander effect. In fact, there's quite a lot of doubt as to what really happened, sufficient to cast doubt on the whole theory, but there's absolutely no doubt at all about what you should do if you ever find yourself in trouble in a crowd and need help: you need to focus on one person and appeal directly to them. If one person comes to your aid others will follow, but otherwise everyone may leave it to someone else.

More generally it seems that we're naturally imbued with an instinct to connect with others. There are lots of studies about the connection between happiness and money, the general idea being that buying lots of consumer goods doesn't promote any lasting improvement in general well-being but that investing in experiences does. Supplementary to this Elizabeth Dunn, Lara Aknin, and Michael Norton[48] suggest that spending money on other people makes us more happy than spending it on ourselves—and follow-up research indicates that spending that money on people with whom we have strong social ties makes us happier still.[49]

Coming from a world in which social links are everything, it's not hard to imagine that this type of behavior is generally beneficial in strengthening the social bonds. So the closer we feel connected to someone the more likely we are to act on their financial behalf (and in lots of other ways too, but we'll stick to the knitting on this one). This leads to a puzzling observation—that we often fail to act in our own financial interests because we don't seem to relate very well to our future selves.

The observation comes out of the evidence that we don't save enough for our retirement—in fact, we're generally very unwilling to make short-term sacrifices for ourselves in order to reap long-term benefits.[50] In addition, we tend to procrastinate over difficult decisions and avoid making any choice at all, and as Ted O'Donoghue and Matthew Rabin have shown, the more choices and the more important the decision the less likely we are to make any choice at all.[51]

However, a slightly different theory posits a different reason for our procrastination over retirement savings; that we simply don't feel any psychological connectedness to that strange, old person who we will become one day. Christopher Bryan and Hal Hershfield[52] have suggested that this lack of connectedness means we don't feel any social responsibility to our future selves, which means that when we save for retirement it feels like we're giving money away—to a stranger.

Odd though this is—and it is undeniably strange—it really looks like there's something to this idea. If you appeal to someone's sense of social responsibility about their future self—if you pick yourself out in the crowd and appeal directly to yourself for help—many people respond. It's a framing issue: frame the future you as a stranger and you won't bother helping them, frame them as a friend and you just might. And, to be honest, we'd all be better off helping an old person, especially when that old person is ourselves.

LESSON 17

Look on your future self as the best friend you'll ever have, and plan for that eventuality. One day you'll thank yourself.

THE SEVEN KEY TAKEAWAYS

This chapter has introduced how social interaction is a critical and unconscious influencer of our investment decisions. We are hopelessly embedded in an intricate network of social relationships; we are social creatures by definition, and we can't avoid the impact of this, however undesirable it might be. Mostly it's not desirable at all, but when we are investing sometimes it pays to be a little self-absorbed.

To finish, let's draw together a few key ideas from this chapter before we move on. The main takeaways are:

1. We take our cues from other people. We like to conform. Never stop asking awkward questions—and if the other people don't like it, then tough.
2. Beware of investment groups, they'll tend to experience a risky shift due to group polarization. Use them by all means, but don't be afraid of being the one opposing the group's preferred view. You'll be doing everyone else a favor as well as yourself.
3. Framing is something we all do, unconsciously. We need to make a specific effort to frame our portfolios widely and to avoid unnecessary mental accounts. It's one big pool of capital, treat it all with equal respect.
4. Basing our investing decisions on second-guessing what other people would like—Keynes's beauty contest style of investing—is very common and not very successful. Keynes himself lost lots of money this way and learned this lesson the hard way: make it easier on yourself.
5. Our normal ways of detecting honesty and cheats and distinguishing between them won't always work in the world of finance. We can't rely on signals for fitness because they are deliberately contrived, not an evolutionary statement. Getting confused between the two can be very expensive.
6. Social interactions can lead us into behavior that seems sensible but leads to negative results. Comparing our decisions to those of others, and relying on the positive spin from other people about their successes, can lead us into profoundly dangerous investments.

7. Try to relate to yourself as an older person, to perceive your future self as a friend you need to try to support. The better you can relate to the future you the more you're likely to take care of your investing needs.

Social biases brings us to the end of our brief trawl through the Outer Limits of psychological bias in investment. Mostly you'll have picked up the idea that we're all somewhat open to unexpected influences, but you may not have recognized that this is a general problem. The normal solution to this kind of difficulty is to call in the experts, but as we are about to see, that isn't as much of a solution as you might hope.

NOTES

1. Solomon E. Asch, "Effects of Group Pressure upon the Modification and Distortion of Judgments," in *Groups, Leadership, and Men,* ed. H. Guetzkow (1951): 222–236.
2. Irving L. Janis, *Victims of Groupthink: A Psychological Study of Foreign-Policy Decisions and Fiascoes* (Boston: Houghton-Mifflin,1972).
3. Richard P. Feynman, "Personal Observations on the Reliability of the Shuttle," *Report of the Presidential Commission on the Space Shuttle Challenger Accident* 2 (1986): 1–5.
4. Claire Ferraris and Rodney Carveth, "NASA and the Columbia Disaster: Decision-Making by Groupthink?" Proceedings of the 2003 Association for Business Communication Annual Convention (2003).
5. Roland Bénabou, "Groupthink: Collective Delusions in Organizations and Markets," *The Review of Economic Studies* 80, no. 2 (2013): 429–462.
6. Benedictus de Spinoza, *The Ethics and Selected Letters*, ed. Seymour Feldman, tr. Samuel Shirley (Indianapolis: Hackett, 1982).
7. Daniel T. Gilbert, Romin W. Tafarodi, and Patrick S. Malone, "You Can't Not Believe Everything You Read," *Journal of Personality and Social Psychology* 65, no. 2 (1993): 221.
8. James Arthur Finch Stoner, "A Comparison of Individual and Group Decisions Involving Risk," dissertation, Massachusetts Institute of Technology, 1961.
9. Cass R. Sunstein, "Deliberative Trouble? Why Groups Go to Extremes," *Yale Law Journal* 110, no. 1 (2000): 71–119.
10. Stephen P. Utkus, "Market Bubbles and Investor Psychology," Vanguard Research, Vanguard (2011).
11. Eli Pariser, *The Filter Bubble: What the Internet Is Hiding from You* (London: Penguin, 2011).
12. George A. Akerlof and Rachel E. Kranton, "Identity and the Economics of Organizations," *Journal of Economic Perspectives* 19, no. 1 (2005): 9–32.
13. Canice Prendergast, "The Provision of Incentives in Firms," *Journal of Economic Literature* 37, no. 1 (1999): 7–63.

14. Dan Ariely, *Predictably Irrational: The Hidden Forces That Shape Our Decisions*, revised and expanded edition (New York: HarperCollins, 2009).
15. Daniel Bergstresser and Thomas Philippon, "CEO Incentives and Earnings Management," *Journal of Financial Economics* 80, no. 3 (2006): 511–529.
16. Erving Goffman, *The Presentation of Self in Everyday Life* (New York: Anchor, 1959).
17. George Lakoff and Mark Johnson, *Metaphors We Live By* (Chicago: University of Chicago Press, 2008).
18. http://georgelakoff.com/2011/12/11/how-to-frame-yourself-a-framing-memo-for-occupy-wall-street/.
19. Amos Tversky and Daniel Kahneman, "The Framing of Decisions and the Psychology of Choice," *Science* 211, no. 4481 (1981): 453–458.
20. Alok Kumar and Sonya Seongyeon Lim, "How Do Decision Frames Influence the Stock Investment Choices of Individual Investors?" *Management Science* 54, no. 6 (2008): 1052–1064.
21. Meir Statman, "Lottery Players/Stock Traders," *Financial Analysts Journal* 58 (2002): 14–21.
22. Harry Markowitz, "The Utility of Wealth," *Journal of Political Economy* 60, no. 2 (1952): 151–158.
23. Hersh Shefrin and Meir Statman. "Behavioral Portfolio Theory," *Journal of Financial and Quantitative Analysis* 35, no. 2 (2000): 127–151.
24. Ibid.
25. Shinichi Hirota and Shyam Sunder, "Price Bubbles sans Dividend Anchors: Evidence from Laboratory Stock Markets," *Journal of Economic Dynamics and Control* 31, no. 6 (2007): 1875–1909.
26. Dan P. McAdams, "What Do We Know when We Know a Person?" *Journal of Personality* 63, no. 3 (1995): 365–396.
27. Richard Dawkins, *The Selfish Gene* (New York: Oxford University Press, 2006).
28. Robert J. Shiller, "Low Interest Rates and High Asset Prices: An Interpretation in Terms of Changing Popular Economic Models," NBER Working Paper No. 13558. National Bureau of Economic Research, 2007.
29. Mark Granovetter, "Economic Action and Social Structure: The Problem of Embeddedness," *American Journal of Sociology* (1985): 481–510.
30. Daniel Beunza and David Stark, "Models, Reflexivity and Systemic Risk: A Critique of Behavioral Finance." Available at SSRN 1285054 (2010).
31. Ibid.
32. Simon Baron-Cohen, *Mindblindness: An Essay on Autism and Theory of Mind* (Cambridge, MA: MIT Press, 1997).
33. Oskar Pfungst, *Clever Hans (the Horse of Mr. Von Osten): A Contribution to Experimental Animal and Human Psychology* (New York: Holt, 1911).
34. John Maynard Keynes, *The General Theory of Employment, Interest, and Money* (New Delhi: Atlantic Books, 2006).
35. David Chambers and Elroy Dimson, "Keynes the Stock Market Investor." Available at SSRN 2023011 (2012).
36. Richard W. Byrne and Nadia Corp, "Neocortex Size Predicts Deception Rate in Primates," *Proceedings: Biological Sciences* (2004): 1693–1699.

37. Paul Ekman and Maureen O'Sullivan, "Who Can Catch a Liar?" *American Psychologist* 46, no. 9 (1991): 913.
38. Armin Falk, Ernst Fehr, and Urs Fischbacher. "On the Nature of Fair Behavior,"*Economic Inquiry* 41, no. 1 (2003): 20–26.
39. George A. Akerlof, "The Market for 'Lemons': Quality Uncertainty and the Market Mechanism," *Quarterly Journal of Economics* 84 (1970): 488–500.
40. Robert B. Cialdini, *Influence: The New Psychology of Modern Persuasion* (New York: Morrow, 1984).
41. Amna Kirmani and Akshay R. Rao, "No Pain, No Gain: A Critical Review of the Literature on Signaling Unobservable Product Quality," *Journal of Marketing* (2000): 66–79.
42. Amotz Zahavi, "Mate Selection—A Selection for a Handicap," *Journal of Theoretical Biology* 53, no. 1 (1975): 205–214.
43. George J. Stigler, "The Economics of Information," *Journal of Political Economy* 69, no. 3 (1961): 213–225.
44. Phillip Nelson, "Advertising as Information," *Journal of Political Economy* 82, no. 4 (1974): 729–754.
45. David Hirshleifer, "Self-Enhancing Transmission Bias and Active Investing," unpublished working paper, 2010.
46. David Simon and Rawley Heimer, "Facebook Finance: How Social Interaction Propagates Active Investing," AFA 2013 San Diego Meetings Paper (2012).
47. Rachel Manning, Mark Levine, and Alan Collins, "The Kitty Genovese Murder and the Social Psychology of Helping: The Parable of the 38 Witnesses,"*American Psychologist* 62, no. 6 (2007): 555–562.
48. Elizabeth W. Dunn, Lara B. Aknin, and Michael I. Norton, "Spending Money on Others Promotes Happiness," *Science* 319, no. 5870 (2008): 1687–1688.
49. Lara B. Aknin, Gillian M. Sandstrom, Elizabeth W. Dunn, and Michael I. Norton, "It's the Recipient That Counts: Spending Money on Strong SocialTies Leads to Greater Happiness than Spending on Weak Social Ties," *PloS ONE* 6, no. 2 (2011): e17018.
50. Shane Frederick, George Loewenstein, and Ted O'Donoghue. "Time Discounting and Time Preference: A Critical Review," *Journal of Economic Literature* 40, no. 2 (2002): 351–401.
51. Ted O'Donoghue and Matthew Rabin, "Choice and Procrastination," *Quarterly Journal of Economics* 116, no. 1 (2001): 121–160.
52. Christopher J. Bryan and Hal E. Hershfield, "You Owe It to Yourself: Boosting Retirement Saving with a Responsibility-Based Appeal," *Journal of Experimental Psychology: General* 141, no. 3 (2012): 429.

CHAPTER 5

Professional Bias

Normally, when we're faced with a situation where our knowledge and expertise are plainly not sufficient for our needs we'll call in the experts. We go and see a dentist about our toothaches, our doctor about that nagging pain in our stomachs, and a psychologist about our inability to sleep at night due to worries about monsters in the wardrobe. And very often we'll turn to professional investment experts when it comes to handling our finances.

All of these different types of experts suffer from errors of judgment of one kind or another, but financial experts are almost unique in not being professionally overseen: your plumber may be better qualified than your investment adviser. It's not surprising, then, that the professionals often fall prey to the same biases the rest of us suffer from. What is really worrying, though, is that they're often more affected than we are, because their incentives and ours are not the same: the thing that marks out the professionals from the amateurs is that they're paid for their services, rather than simply rewarded, or punished, through their successes or failures at investing.

And this, dear reader, exposes them to a whole new set of biases. So, if you're reliant on expert help for your investment decisions it's time to steel yourselves for a bracing dose of reality. Welcome to the world of professional bias.

MUTUAL FUND MADNESS

It's an astonishing and remarkable fact that not once in the whole history of American mutual funds has an investor's money ever been improperly invested, at least according to the courts. This is in spite of a raft of investigations, mainly initiated by the ever-vigilant, if nocturnally overenthusiastic, ex-Attorney General of New York, Eliot Spitzer, who alleged that many of the advisers running these funds had deliberately siphoned profits from long-term private shareholders to institutional clients.

In fact many advisers run two sets of funds—one for us private investors and one for institutional investors, with the latter paying significantly
lower fees. Unfortunately, according to legal precedent, it's impossible
to pay the wrong price for a security because the market price is always
the correct one—this is the Efficient Markets Hypothesis, once more. The
problem with this is that the market for mutual funds isn't self-evidently
free functioning.

Take, for instance, the peculiar problem of survivorship bias. Classically
this is an issue that occurs when examining historical investing data where
securities drop out of the record because of some failure or another. For
example, if you were to study the record of stock markets over the past
50 years or so but fail to take into account the many, many companies that
go broke then you would end up with an overinflated expectation of how
successful markets have been.

For stocks and stock markets this tends to be a data mining issue,
because the historical records aren't complete, although the best analysts
correct for this issue. However, the mutual fund industry has exploited this
particular statistical issue to deliberately inflate its apparent success stories.
Often this simply takes the form of merging underperforming funds with
successful ones so that the laggards disappear. Burton Malkiel, in *A Random
Walk Down Wall Street*[1] (a book all logical investors should read), showed
that 15 percent of mutual funds simply disappeared between 1988 and
1991. A UK study by Lukas Schneider[2] identified that of 1,008 funds available to investors in 1992 only 491 were still around 11 years later.

Research by Savant Capital/Zero Alpha[3] indicates that there are no sectors of the mutual fund industry for which this silent slaying of the laggards
is not a problem. The performance of the survivors is exaggerated by up to
2 percent a year, which may not sound like much, but when compounded
over many years can make a huge difference—over 100 percent in a single
decade in one case quoted. But exploiting survivorship bias is far from the
only curveball funds throw at us.

A second trick is known as instant history bias. This sees a fund company launch a raft of new funds without marketing them to investors. You
then ditch the ones with poor records and promote the odd one that has
been successful—which is as likely to be due to luck as it is to skill. Or
there's easy data bias, where specific low points in the market or a fund's
history are used as baselines for performance records—this is harder to pull
off these days, but you'll still find funds marketed more heavily when the
records start to fall in their favor.

There's also backfill bias, wherein a new manager is added to the lists of
mutual fund reporting, which funnily enough only happens when the manager has a good record. All of this is bad enough really, but unfortunately we

private investors are apt to be fooled by historical data and the fund advisers are simply exploiting our weaknesses. Of course, we then make the problem worse by buying and selling our funds at exactly the wrong moments.

LESSON 1

Mutual funds are very clever at manipulating historical data to make their performance look better than it really is. Historical data is no real guide to future performance, and we should treat it as a minor data point in deciding what mutual funds to buy, if we buy them at all.

IS PASSIVE PERSUASIVE?

These days we have an alternative to the rafts of mutual funds and their tricky managers: we can take advantage of the burgeoning passive investment industry. William Sharpe demonstrated back in 1991, using only the most basic mathematics, that actively managed funds underperformed their passive brethren by the amount they charged in fees.[4] You would imagine, therefore, that I would suggest that passive funds are the way for the know-nothing investor to go.

And, in general, I would agree. All things being equal, passive funds are more appropriate for private investors than active ones, and a well balanced portfolio of such funds, covering a wide range of sectors, types of security, and geographies, developed over a long period of time is almost certainly the best option for anyone who doesn't want to spend their life pouring over balance sheets and cash flow statements.

That said, there is increasingly persuasive evidence that the sheer amount of money flowing into passive funds is beginning to shape the markets, and if this continues it's likely to cause a problem. Randall Morck and Fan Yang, for instance, point out that the value of S&P 500 stocks is unfathomably high, unless you include the effects of indexing.[5] The issue is about the original purpose of these funds, which were set up to track the market or subsectors within it. This removes many of the biases that cause active investors so much trouble and leads to less of the kneejerk reactions to short-term events that damage investment performance over the long term.

However, the point of these funds is that they are parasites on active investors whose buying and selling creates a market which is based, imperfectly to be sure, on some analysis of the true valuation of the securities involved. Index trackers, and the people who invest in them, are all to some extent relying on the hard work of other people to ensure that they're paying a fair price: a classic free-rider problem. From time to time this goes spectacularly wrong, but most of the time it's more or less right, and most passive funds will buy stocks in proportion to their market capitalization.

However, if passive funds become hugely successful a strange inversion happens, where the sheer volume of funds flowing into them, which is then invested in the market in proportion to the existing valuation of stocks, leads to the biggest stocks becoming bigger, regardless of the actual underlying economics of the business in question. And, as Morck and Yang suggest, there is evidence that this is actually happening to the biggest stocks in the biggest indexes.

It's impossible to see how this particular problem will play out in the longer term, but one thing is certain. If a security, sector, or index becomes massively overvalued due to some technical issue like this it will eventually end badly. Private investors need to take care to diversify their passive portfolios of index trackers, because one day this bubble will burst.

LESSON 2

Index tracking funds are a good, cheap method for private investors to get exposure to the markets. However, they aren't a panacea for all investing ills. Diversify across different types of assets, markets, and geographies and don't go overboard on generalist trackers focused on the largest markets.

LOSING TO THE DARK SIDE

One of the themes of this book is the idea that markets are heavily biased against private investors over the short term. I think that both logic and the evidence is compelling, and certainly it's been shown that very short-term investors—so-called day traders—overwhelmingly lose money. To expand on this I'd like to discuss a couple of modern institutional innovations that simply highlight the problem. Let's take a moment to look at the dark side of institutional investment.

Firstly, we have the peculiar world of high-frequency trading where automated computer programs execute transactions with bewildering speed, buying and selling stocks based on minute changes in valuation, and arbitraging between different markets to squeeze out every last penny. In fact, this process has now got to the point that the institutions are using relativistic physics to figure out where to site their computers[6] in order to minimize the distance to the trading exchanges, because the nanoseconds saved in communication time can make a difference of millions of dollars!

The proponents of high-frequency trading argue that it improves the liquidity in markets, which means there's always someone to buy or sell our stocks. Unfortunately the real evidence suggests that these programs are mainly in the interests of trading houses who are moving vast amounts of stocks about for no good economic reason. In fact, by manipulating trades the automated systems can discover the price that the ordinary trader—that's you and me—is willing to pay for a stock. That's known as asymmetric, differential price discovery in the jargon, and as a rigged game to everyone else.

Even worse, because these trades are automatically executed by supercomputers there's the ever present risk that something will go wrong, as happened to Knight Capital Group in 2012 when an error in updating their high-frequency trading program caused the almost instant execution of several hundred million dollars' worth of unintended and loss-making trades, which severely disrupted markets and left the company in financial difficulties. There's also compelling evidence that high-frequency trading programs are behind some of the so-called flash-crashes in markets, where the systems go into meltdown for no apparent reason.

Allied to these whizzy computer programs are so-called dark pools, which are markets in which institutions trade anonymously with each other, outside of the normal market mechanisms.[7] These black markets allow trading to happen in securities at much lower prices than any private investor can ever achieve and are completely transparent to the markets, so that huge quantities of stock can change hands without anyone being any the wiser.

The problem with this is twofold—firstly, it means that markets are denied information about the true value of stocks and secondly, dark pools parasitize the real markets by using the prices set by the likes of us buying and selling. And sometimes information leaks—traders will fish for dark pool buyers by using dark pool trades and may then trade in the open markets to move the price against the buyers—after all, if someone knows that there's significant black market activity it's very tempting to try to move the real market to affect the prices being achieved.

The real problem with all of this institutional innovation is that it denies us, the private investors upon whose money all markets are built, access to what's really going on. However, far from regarding this as a bad thing I rather regard it as the opposite—because anything that convinces the average private investor that they're disadvantaged in the markets in the short term is to be welcomed.

Our edge is time—we don't need to make a short-term turn. Careful analysis and simple patience are the only skills we need to win at investing.

LESSON 3

Investment markets are run by people to make money for themselves, rather than for us. In the short term there is almost no market trend that we can exploit that will give us an edge, as witnessed by the vast amounts of dollars poured into innovations like high-frequency trading and dark pools, which private investors have no access to. Leave short-term trading to the professionals.

FORECASTING—THE BUTTERFLY EFFECT

If the issues with mutual funds, index funds, dark pools, and high-frequency trading weren't enough to make you wary of the professional world of institutional investing then a brief trawl through the strange world of investment analysis and forecasting ought to serve as a warning. Professional analysts are paid to analyze corporations and make forecasts about their likely future earnings, and these forecasts often drive the market performance of stocks and are eagerly followed by hordes of investors, both professional and private. Unfortunately, they're often wrong. Very wrong.

In fact, I tend to regard earnings forecasting as a triumph of accounting over reality. Anyone who's ever worked in a corporation of any complexity knows full well that no one is really in charge, and the end earnings results are an outcome of a myriad of interconnected and unforeseeable events. As we've seen the markets are really a complex, adaptive system and it's the nature of such systems to be fundamentally unstable.

Similar reasons make the weather forecast unreliable at any distance in the future. Back in the 1960s a mathematician called Edward Lorenz accidentally discovered that if you change the starting conditions of a weather forecasting program by a tiny, tiny amount, the end result is startlingly different.[8] This completely overturned the scientific expectations of the day, which assumed that a small difference at the start would make a small difference at the end. Lorenz showed that for certain types of systems this was simply not true—and this is the behavior we saw in Chapter 3 that eventually became known as the butterfly effect, where the tiniest flap of a butterfly's wings in the Amazon can change the weather in Des Moines.

Similar issues apply to earnings forecasting but as analysts are paid to analyze and produce forecasts they do it anyway. This causes a whole heap of trouble for corporations—as Lawrence Brown and Ling Zhou[9] have shown, the analysts regularly introduce errors and the companies then need to issue guidance to correct them. It's like having to constantly correct for a whole flock of madly flapping, half-witted butterflies. In any case, it's also been shown that[10] professionals are no better than amateur investors at detecting artificially inflated earnings statements.

Ivo Welch and Amit Goyal[11] have conducted some wide-ranging analysis of various investment forecasting techniques, which included (deep breath): dividends, earnings, stock variance, cross-sectional premia, book value, net issuing activity, T-bills, long-term yield, corporate bond returns, corporate bond yields, inflation, investment-to-capital ratio, a combination of all of the aforementioned variables, and consumption, wealth, and income ratio. And they've come to the conclusion that none of these methods are particularly good.

In fact, about the only predictable things about forecasters is that they're nearly always wrong and nearly always unwilling to admit the fact. Paul Söderlind's[12] research showed that a panel of economists demonstrated no ability to predict the movements of the stock markets but nevertheless remained convinced that they had some skill in what is essentially an exercise in coin-tossing, which goes to show that economists are just as fallible and subject to behavioral bias as the rest of us.

Oddly, despite the logical impossibility of analyst forecasts being correct they very often are. Unfortunately this isn't because analysts are any good at analyzing but is because corporations are very good at manipulating their accounts to make their results fit the analysts' expectations. As Dawn Matsumoto[13] has described, some firms use accruals to massage earnings to avoid surprising the markets. Accounting is a very inexact science, and open to all sorts of perfectly legal manipulation.

In fact, as Edward Lorenz concluded, you can't predict the results of these types of systems with any accuracy—so if corporations keep on hitting the analysts' numbers it's a warning sign: sometimes surprises are good, even if they're a bit negative. Better to have results that are roughly genuine than ones that are definitely manipulated, regardless of the short-term consequences.

LESSON 4

Markets and stocks are subject to unpredictable events, so any attempt to accurately predict the short-term trajectory of either is fraught with risk. Most forecasts should be treated with caution, if not outright disdain.

FORECASTER BIAS

Leaving aside the fact that it's probably impossible to accurately forecast earnings because of the nature of markets, it's also probably impossible to accurately forecast earnings because of the nature of forecasters. They're human, and therefore they're biased. Ergo, they tend to make the same mistakes as everyone else.

We saw an example of this previously when the analysts herded together frantically in the wake of BP's calamitous collapsing oilrig, *Deepwater Horizon*. As behavioral finance experts Hersh Shefrin and Enrico Cervellati were able to show,[14] the analysts were all uniformly positive about BP prior to the disaster—despite the company having by far the worst safety record of any oil major—and then subsequently their forecasts converged rapidly as they sought safety in a crowd. Of course, their forecasts remained too positive and wrong even as the scale of the crisis and the political fallout became obvious.

James Montier, who is an analyst himself (and you should search out anything he's written, as he's marvelously astute on behavioral bias from the professional perspective), is dryly dismissive of the relationship between analysts and corporations.[15] He notes that they're both very bad at seeking disconfirming information and that they're quite poor at detecting when someone is lying—and the result is that most analysts tend to follow the stories peddled by corporate management. In general, there are no such things as independent analysts.

The evidence that analysts are biased has a long history, going back to Werner De Bondt and Richard Thaler's classic paper, "Do Security Analysts Overreact?"[16] Their finding was that these professionals tend to exhibit unrealistic optimism about firms' prospects and they argued that this was an agency issue—the problem being that the incentives of the analysts and the incentives of their private investor clients aren't aligned. Analysts and their employers tend to get rewarded for publishing overoptimistic forecasts, so they're hardly likely to stop doing it.

In any case, we're naturally prone to unrealistic optimism. Neuro-research by Tali Sharot, Christoph Korn, and Raymond Dolan has shown that this is connected to asymmetries in belief updating.[17] Or, to put it in plain English—we tend to ignore information that ought to reduce optimism and to take notice of information that reinforces it. In fact, we learn more effectively from the former than the latter, which rather sounds like an issue known as confirmation bias.

Given the general impossibility of forecasting anything very much due to the unpredictability of markets and the inherent bias of being human you might well wonder how come anyone takes any notice of any financial prediction. A clue to the answer comes from the famous magician and de-bunker of charlatans, James Randi.

Every morning before he left home, Randi would take a piece of paper and write on it "I, James Randi, will die today." He'd sign and date it and put it in his pocket. If he had died he would have been proclaimed a psychic, although being Randi one assumes he'd have had a last laugh planned from beyond the grave. This is an example of what J. Scott Armstrong calls the seer-sucker illusion—there's an endless supply of suckers prepared to stump up good money for the illusionary visions of seers.[18] On this simple insight, a whole industry has been created.

Even within the investment analyst community there are variations: it's been shown, for instance, that younger analysts are more prone to herd-ing than older colleagues.[19] They're more heavily punished for getting their forecasts wrong, so they prefer to huddle together for safety. Unfortunately, this doesn't mean that experienced analysts necessarily get better results—as Armstrong's results indicate, forecasting accuracy seems to drop once a certain level of experience is attained. Novices can generally be persuaded to cross-check their analyses, but experts don't think they can be wrong, so what would be the point?

Ben Graham, the famous value investor summed up the correct attitude of an analyst toward the market in a sexist parable (although this was in the 1930s so perhaps he can be excused . . .):

> *The correct attitude of the security analyst toward the stock market might well be that of a man toward his wife. He shouldn't pay too much attention to what the lady says, but he can't afford to ignore it entirely. That is pretty much the position that most of us find our-selves vis-à-vis the stock market.*

Which leads us neatly into another investment brick wall: women as investors.

LESSON 5

Analysts are as prone to behavioral bias as everyone else: they get rewarded for optimism so why would they not be optimistic? Often, their forecasts will be uncannily accurate but they'll never see the car crash coming: overreliance on analyst forecasts is dangerous; we can't outsource our thinking.

FEMININE FINANCE

A lot of studies have shown that women make better investors than men. They're less inclined to overtrade, suggesting that they take a more realistic and less overconfident approach to trading than their male counterparts. The standard explanation is to assume that women are simply less rash then men, but I reckon that a lot of it has to do with upbringing rather than genetics. But regardless of the reason, women do seem less prone to rash decisions, so you might think that they would make good professional advisers and fund managers.

Indeed, it does seem to be the case that women are much less likely to chase returns irrationally but this also means that they run into a different nasty little problem because the people who make huge returns tend to be the ones that take huge risks. Most of the managers who take huge risks lose money but the ones that succeed are massively successful, and tend to attract investors' money. By and large, the more level-headed approach espoused by women means that they don't fall into this bracket of apparently brilliant managers.

In any case, a study by Robert Durand, Rick Newby, and Jay Sanghani suggests that it's not whether you're male or female that determines your appetite for risk, but your masculinity.[20] Women with a more masculine attitude to risk take similar chances but, of course, tend to be fewer in number. Brad Barber and Terrance Odean (them again) report that men trade 45 percent more than women and correspondingly make less money.[21] So it's likely that it's this propensity for risk taking that's driving the gender difference in returns.

Unsurprisingly this different attitude to risk flows over into the world of professional investment. Alexandra Niessen and Stefan Ruenzi have shown that female investment managers are more risk adverse, tend to be less likely to modify their investment styles than their male counterparts, and achieve more persistent performance.[22] Overall they don't find any significant variation in returns between male and female managers, but women generally achieve their results with a lot less fuss and volatility.

So, if women are calmer and more reliable you'd expect that they'd be among the most popular fund managers and advisers. Of course, they're not—overall, women only manage about half the funds that men do and tend to work for the larger, more established management companies, which are likely to be more cautious about antidiscrimination lawsuits. The researchers suggest that women tend to manage less attractive funds, and hypothesize that the problem is due to gender stereotyping.

This may be the case, but I reckon that it's about risk taking as well. But if you want a safe pair of hands you'd probably do a lot worse than applying a bit of stereotyping yourself, and seek out female fund managers. If you want to take risks go skydiving, but leave your money at home.

LESSON 6

Female investment managers are less likely to achieve sky-high returns but they'll tend to help you sleep at night. If you want lower-risk management use female managed funds—if you can find them.

TRADING ON A HIGH

Our propensity for risk taking is one that occupies a lot of researchers. As we saw in Chapter 2 with the Iowa Gambling Task, it's linked with emotions, and is probably deeply integrated into our wetware. Hormones are one area that have received a fair amount of attention, as they're known to be linked with risk-taking behavior.

Serotonin, for example, is implicated in triggering areas of the brain that generate positive or negative emotional reactions such as anxiety or excitement when risk taking is anticipated. Research has shown that different versions of the gene for serotonin transportation lead to different financial risk-taking profiles.[23] In fact those people with one version of the gene tend to focus on the potential negative outcomes of any investment and avoid complex investments altogether.

However, increasingly the wavering finger of suspicion has come to rest on some of the areas of the brain that manage the hormone dopamine, which is associated with control of the reward center of our nervous systems. It's implicated with the anticipation of the reward—whether these are big profits or a nicotine fix or something stronger—rather than the reward itself.

Interestingly, some analysis of brain scans suggest that when we're represented by someone else—a congressman, a CEO, a platoon leader—then their dopamine reward system is triggered when they're successful on our behalf.[24] This is one explanation for altruistic behavior and explains why a financial adviser may get a kick out of making money for their clients.

Generally, though, some people seem to be peculiarly sensitive to the anticipation of rewards and studies of people with compulsive gambling problems have found a link with the dopamine system. These people are driven by the need to take risks and take increasingly mad gambles in order to fuel their addiction—it's the uncertainty that gives them their reward, not success itself.

Steven Sapra and Paul Zak think that in a world where 90 percent of market trades are carried out by professional investors and we frequently see the markets lurching this way or that without apparent reason we may be seeing the impact of a self-selecting bunch of risk takers driven by dopamine.[25] On the positive side they also suggest that the longer the traders had worked the more likely they were to balance risk and reward in a sensible fashion, which accords with other evidence we've discussed that indicates that more experienced traders are less emotional.

This is far from conclusive—traders who are successful early in their careers may simply drop out of the records as they retire to gamble away their huge earnings, but it certainly adds weight to the proposition that more experienced advisers are safer than younger ones. In addition, if you're particularly inclined to like a bet and find the thrill of expectation a lot of fun you probably don't want to be doing your own investing. The most successful investors are calm, rational, and calculating, not risk junkies on a one-way trip to financial penury.

LESSON 7

It's quite likely that a lot of irrational market movements are caused by hormone-fueled traders, taking risks in order to obtain the thrill of anticipation. For us, investing should not be about thrills or gambling. If you must use a professional, look for someone who's been around a while, and if you like gambling you should probably avoid playing the markets.

MARRIAGE AND MONEY

We've already covered a lot of unexpected findings, but here's a doozy: in general, you should want any financial professional you have dealings with to be married and in a stable relationship, because they'll take less risks with your money. It all has to do with sex, you see. But on some level, doesn't everything?

One of our main biological imperatives is to pass on our genes, and the evidence suggests that when we're confronted with this need we tend to become quite aggressive risk takers in pursuit of a partner, preferably one of higher status. Michael Baker and Jon Maner's research backs this up.[26] Men who were shown pictures of attractive women promptly started taking more risks.

Of course, as we've already seen, anything that promotes risk taking in our financial advisers is something we should be very wary of, so if this behavior extends into the world of investing it's something we should concern ourselves with. And, no surprises here, it seems that it does. Nikolai Roussanov and Pavel Savor have found a direct link between the marital status of CEOs and the risk profiles of their corporations—companies run by singletons pursue more aggressive investment policies, although the effect reduces with age.[27]

They also found a similar correlation for mutual fund managers who take on more so-called idiosyncratic risk, which, essentially, tends to come down to irrational risk taking in an attempt to stand out from the crowd. It's the opposite of herding, and done in an attempt to generate greater returns. Which is a nice idea, as long as it's done intelligently. Unfortunately, it rarely is.

So, mutual funds run by single people—men mainly—are usually less well diversified than those run by married people. Interestingly the same effect is seen with investors—so if you're single and looking for a partner you'll probably be taking more risks with your portfolio than if you're happily married. Of course, correlation is not causality—single people will also tend to be younger and less experienced and both of those factors tend to lead to more risk-taking behavior.

The evidence also suggests that this is another area in which women are less inclined to be irrational risk takers than men. This may simply be the nature of the dating game, but it all adds up to the general advice. For financial advice look to married men or to women and leave the risk-taking single males to sort themselves out.

LESSON 8

People in general, and men in particular, exhibit risk-taking behavior when on a quest for a mate. The best money managers are older, in a stable relationship, and unlikely to be attempting to impress anyone with the size of their portfolios. You have been warned.

MUDDLED MODELERS

One of the ways in which the professional investing industry addresses the complexity of risk taking and decision making in what is a fundamentally uncertain environment is through the use of so-called quantitative models. These are usually computer simulations of the way that the markets work and are used to make both human and, increasingly, automated investing decisions. The problem with these is that they're based on an assumption that doesn't really stand up to close inspection—that we can actually come up with something that accurately models the markets.

When I write online about investing issues it's amazing how often this particular problem appears, often in disguised form. It's terribly, terribly easy for even very good professional investors to end up reliant on models which are, at best, a very imperfect way of predicting the future. This was one of the problems behind the big sub prime bank bust in 2007, when markets went into a tail spin and, for a while, it appeared that the world's economy was going to crash and burn.

As Emanuel Derman, who has experienced this first hand as a quantitative analyst, describes in his article "Model Risk," there are all sorts of ways in which models can be wrong.[28] They can be incorrect because they don't actually model what you're trying to describe, they're used wrongly, they use bad data, or a whole host of other issues that are dizzyingly complex but which boil down to a single factor: if you rely on a model that you don't understand then you are taking on trust that the people who built the model know what they're doing. All too often it turns out that trust is misplaced, and frankly if you're prepared to put your trust in some method that someone is peddling to you but can't explain then you deserve everything you get.

It's actually worse than this, in fact, because the very existence of a model can change the way that markets work. It's that darn reflexivity in action again. This can happen in some very peculiar ways—take, for instance, the famous (and sometimes infamous) Black-Scholes method of pricing share options. Share options allow people to take a bet on the future price of some asset like a share without actually going to the trouble of buying it: they're a form of derivative, and can be very useful if you want to insure yourself against the markets moving against you. So if you have a portfolio of stocks but may need to access the money in the short term you can buy options that protect you against the market falling.

Of course, derivatives have a bad name, being associated with many of the bad things that have happened in markets, but there's nothing essentially bad about them—it's just that investors use them badly. Anyway, the Black-Scholes model tells investors what the "proper" price for an option should be and is used widely in the market. What's really odd is that prices only started to conform to the model after it was invented: it appears that it was traders using the model that made it work—because it made their jobs easier![29]

Anyway, many critics including Nassim Taleb and Warren Buffett believe that Black-Scholes is usually an accident waiting to happen, because markets do all sorts of strange things that the model doesn't take account of. The inventors of the method were involved in what was at the time one of the world's largest bankruptcies when their firm Long-Term Capital Management went bust in 1997. In what is now a classic case, but is also only one of many such incidents, their model failed when it encountered unusual market conditions. And this is the problem—markets are governed by uncertainty which is, by definition, unpredictable: And how can you build a model that predicts the unpredictable?

Generally speaking, a logical investor shouldn't go anywhere near these kinds of models. In the right hands, at the right time, they have their place but that place is largely in the world of professional investing. At least the institutions can usually afford the massive losses that occur when things go wrong. Although, as Lehman Brothers discovered in 2007, sometimes even that's not true.

LESSON 9

Lots of professional investing decision making is based on computer models. These are only as good as their programmers and users. Generally they're not for private investors, but if someone is trying to convince you to use one make sure they can explain how it works.

CEO PAY—BECAUSE THEY'RE WORTH IT?

Not only do investment institutions act against our best interests but, all too often, so do the corporations that we invest in. Again this is often about incentives, where executives feel that they're above the rules that apply to us normal folk. Research by Joris Lammers, Diederik Stapel, and Adam Galinsky has shown that powerful people think that it's okay if they break the rules, but unacceptable when minions behave in exactly the same way.[30] Many of us who've worked on the corporate treadmill will have no difficulty finding examples of similar hypocrisy among managers.

Given this underlying tendency it ought to be no surprise that many managers regard shareholders as pretty much irrelevant when it comes to making a decision. In fact, quite often, the only people they seem to be interested in are themselves.

At the root of many problems with executives are stock options, which give managers the right, but not the obligation, to purchase stock if certain price levels are hit. The idea is that this aligns the interests of the managers of the company with those of ours, the shareholders. This is a good thought, but in practice tends to mean that executives run the company to push up the share price. And what, you might think, is wrong with that?

Well, when Daniel Bergstresser and Thomas Philippon looked at corporations where CEO compensation is heavily biased toward stock options they discovered—surprise, surprise—a high incidence of earnings manipulation.[31] Unsurprisingly, heavily incentivized CEOs were extremely anxious to hit the targets, which ensured a hefty payday, and were quite happy to achieve this by vaguely foul, if legal, means.

This isn't a minor issue for us shareholders—corporations engaging in earnings manipulation are firstly not representing themselves correctly, making analysis difficult—and secondly are exposing themselves to dramatic collapses. Xerox, Waste Management, Enron, and Tyco were all guilty of this kind of problem, and all turned into disasters for everyone involved. Perhaps even worse, the incredibly well-aligned bank executives who led their corporations into financial oblivion in 2007 and 2008 apparently had no idea that the firms in their charge were about to crash and burn.[32] All the executive alignment in the world won't help shareholders if executives don't understand the businesses they run.

You might think that the answer to this is to rein in CEOs, and you're probably right. But while it's true that powerful CEOs can lead to dreadful performances it's also true that they can lead to outstanding results.[33] For every Jeffrey Skilling there's a Warren Buffett, but look for the leader who admits mistakes—because every one makes them, it's just that some don't realize it.

LESSON 10

CEOs are inclined to self-promotion, and are certainly very interested in making lots of money for themselves. Be very wary of corporations whose CEOs have lots of stock options, because the temptation to run the company to hit the option targets is all too great for some of them.

CORPORATE MADNESS

CEOs don't just get their kicks from large remuneration packages, they also get them from the exercise of power. After all, you don't tend to claw yourself to the top of a corporation without having an excess of animal spirits. So given that this trend to self-selection will tend to select overly optimistic, rather aggressive men (and they are, largely, men), we should probably expect some overly optimistic, rather aggressive behavior from them.

Perhaps the most obvious way in which CEOs can make their tendencies clear is in the field of mergers and acquisitions—M&A, as it's known in the jargon. There's nothing like buying out the competition to make a CEO feel good, the only problem being that it's often a short-term fix to the problems of boosting earnings. Typically, as economist Robert Bruner has shown, the main winners from any corporate acquisition are the shareholders of the company being taken over, who tend to walk away with a 20 to 30 percent premium over expected value.[34]

Certain types of acquisitions work better than others. Those that aim to diversify the purchasing company usually fail: firms are good at what they do and are quite poor at integrating with firms that do other things. Those that aim to extend the existing business often do very well, but purchases that aim to capture large amounts of market share are less successful, usually because regulators step in and make things difficult.

Most notably, in the area of investor and management irrationality, purchases that are pitched in excess of the stock's 52-week high price are more likely to succeed.[35] This looks like a simple case of anchoring, where the shareholders of the target corporation aren't willing to sell below their most recent high-water mark. This also tends to explain, partly, why there are more purchases of companies near stock market peaks—it's the point at which the 52-week high price can most easily be justified to the acquiring company's shareholders.

By and large, though, we need to be wary of large corporate acquisitions. There's often a lot of ego and not enough analysis involved. There aren't many strong sell signals in the corporate world, but a large acquisition, especially one that aims to diversify the core business, is one helluva good one.

LESSON 11

Successful M&A usually involves bolt-on businesses in the same niche as the purchasing company. In particular be wary if the price being paid is in excess of the 52-week high—most large corporate acquisitions are mistakes, fuelled by CEO egos and benefit only the shareholders of the firm being acquired.

BUYBACK BROUHAHA

It's not just M&A where corporations expose to the world the fact that they're about as rational as the rest of us: consider, for instance, the bizarre way that they handle stock buybacks. This is where a corporation buys back its own stock and retires it. This, in theory, is a good thing for shareholders because it means that there are less shares to share the firm's profits, so we should end up with a bigger slice of the pie. Unfortunately, it often turns out that when something can be manipulated it will be manipulated.

One of the good things about dividends, if you're a shareholder, is that they tend to be "sticky": corporations prefer not to cut dividends because this sends a signal to the market that there's a problem and, generally, leads to share prices falling. As executive rewards are usually linked to share prices then executives generally try to avoid doing this.

Share buybacks, on the other hands, are usually at the discretion of the company and are rarely pre planned. So a share buyback is something executives can use to boost corporate earnings and share prices. If you were of a suspicious turn of mind you might wonder if there's some kind of relationship between a CEO's remuneration and the prevalence of share buybacks. This is a suspicious thought, and, of course, one that's very likely to be correct.

Paul Griffin and Ning Zhu examined the relationship between share buybacks and CEO share option plans—which benefit if their firm's share price goes up at the right time—and have found that there is a reliable correlation: the more options that are up for grabs for the CEO the more likely there is to be a share buyback.[36] And this is true, regardless of the value of the buyback to shareholders.

Make no mistake, there are times when buying back stock is a very, very good idea for shareholders. Remember that when a corporation generates profits it can do one of two things. It can give that money back to its shareholders or it can reinvest it. Where a company can reinvest the cash effectively to generate even more profits then this is better, all things being equal, than returning it to shareholders—after all, we would only have to figure out somewhere new to invest it, and as we've seen we're not generally very good at that.

However, occasionally, a stock ends up trading at less than its real value—its intrinsic value. Intrinsic value is something we'll discuss in a bit more detail later on, but the idea is that if you shut the company down and sold off everything it owns then it would be worth more than the current market price. That this can happen is nuts, but it does, and these can be wonderful investment opportunities (but not always).

Anyway, in this kind of situation a company should buy back its own shares because the current shareholders benefit—they end up with even more of the company. Otherwise, share buybacks are a waste of money. Unfortunately, they're all too common and we, as shareholders, should view them skeptically. Incentives don't explain everything in the markets, but they do explain a lot . . . and generally when executives find a way of rewarding themselves that is acceptable to markets, they will tend to use it.

LESSON 12

Corporations pursuing large buyback programs should be viewed with suspicion—look carefully at the executives' share options packages. However, not all buybacks are bad business, and they can be a sign that a firm is trading at a low level. But usually it's more about the executives than the valuation.

OH NO, IPO

One area where the world of institutional investment and corporate management come together is during IPOs—initial public offerings, when corporations are brought to the public market for the first time. As a general rule, private investors should avoid IPOs because of the issue we discussed around Akerlof's lemons: the people selling know a hell of a lot more about the company than we do. And if it's so darn good, why are they selling it?

To be fair, there are a bunch of perfectly good reasons why shares may be offered to the public—the point of stock markets is that they're a way of raising capital for corporations, which can then invest it in order to drive earnings. However, managements will tend to time offerings to coincide with times when their firm is doing particularly well, and it's very difficult for outsiders to judge whether what's being offered is decent value.

Oddly, though, the evidence suggests that most IPOs are underpriced, rather than overpriced. As Jay Ritter, who specializes in research into IPOs, has shown, between 1990 and 2009, IPO'd companies showed a combined gain of over $124 billion in first-day trading, which is value that the owners have left on the table.[37] Unfortunately, all is not as transparent as we might hope because the intermediaries involved in marketing the stocks tend to over allocate stock to potential purchasers, who then end up with less stock than they want and end up chasing it in the market.

IPOs are generally "underwritten" by investment institutions who guarantee to pick up stock that's not wanted. Unsurprisingly the underwriters may want to underprice the stock to make sure they're not left holding an expensive baby, but as Richard Booth has pointed out, they have also tended to allocate stock in order to reward or attract customers.[38] This so-called corruption hypothesis is how Tim Loughran and Jay Ritter explain the IPO boom during the dot-com era of the late 1990s and early 2000s.[39]

However, there's another explanation for this for the period before and after dot-com—it's a psychological issue known as the winner's curse. The idea behind the winner's curse is that the winner in any auction is the person prepared to pay the most—and the person prepared to pay the most is likely the person who least understands what they're buying, so they overpay. It's a classic case of Akerlof's lemons, only one in which instead of avoiding buying used cars because we don't know which one is a dud, we willingly overpay because we think everyone else wants the thing.

All in all, IPOs are tricky to get right, and avoiding them should be part of the basic toolkit of any private investor. It's a simple scenario—where the insiders know more than we do we're unlikely to have any kind of edge. It's hard enough making money from markets anyway, without throwing away the few advantages we have. Ignore IPOs, even if they make money it's unlikely any of it will come our way.

LESSON 13

IPOs pit the sellers—who understand their businesses—against the purchasers—who don't. Even if the firm is a decent business it's very hard to figure this out from the outside. Unless there's some overwhelmingly obvious reason why the float is at a bargain price we should avoid IPOs, the risk is all on the downside.

YOUR 6 PERCENT SELF-INFLICTED TRADING TAX

One of the effects on private investors of all of the confusing professional issues is to cause us to give away a lot of money. Around $170 billion a year, I reckon, when you add everything up.

Yes, you read that right: $160,000,000,000 a year.

To be honest this is an estimate that's replete with possible mistakes, but I'm pretty sure that if you took a zero off the end of it you'd still think it's a stupid amount of money to give away. The evidence comes from a paper on Taiwanese traders published by Brad Barber, Yi-Tsung Lee, Yu-Jane Liu, and Terrance Odean, and then downgraded by assuming American investors are only half as irrational as those in Taiwan.[40] Whether this is true or not, it's one hell of a lot of money and it's being passed from private investors to four different institutional groups: corporations, dealers, foreigners, and mutual funds. But basically, if private investors are stupid there will be someone around to take their money.

The actual losses themselves come from four sources. Firstly, trading losses. These account for over a quarter of the losses as people are generally not very good at investing, and not very patient when it comes to waiting for success. Secondly, nearly a third of losses come from commissions—and the more you trade the more commission you pay. Thirdly, there are transaction taxes and, finally, market-timing losses.

The authors implicate that old favorite, overconfidence, as the main cause of all of this irrational behavior and I think a lot of that is because people simply fail to account for their trading behavior correctly. If we just wrote down what trading costs us any sensible person would rapidly give up investing.

Research by the UK author Pete Comley suggests that we usually start each year with a balance of minus 6 percent: we have to make at least 6 percent on our investments before we break even, once you take inflation into account.[41] This is a bit rough and ready, to be sure, but generally it suggests that most people might be better off leaving their money in a savings account than trying to invest it.

Of course, we're not most people, are we?

LESSON 14

We lose an astonishing amount of money every year in trading stocks. This is how the investment industry funds itself. Track your investments and account for your costs, you may be surprised at what you find.

EXPERT OPINION?

There's no chance that your doctor, dentist, or attorney will be a high school dropout. These are carefully regulated professions, for the good reason that they're dealing in complex subjects that the average person doesn't really understand. Moreover, we don't really have the knowledge to check that these people know what they're talking about, so the regulation is critical to ensuring we receive a decent service.

Unfortunately when it comes to financial advisers there is no such implicit guarantee of even a basic level of service. In fact, most advisers prefer to rely on contracts to define the relationship with their clients—and this is a biased relationship because one party understands the contract and, typically, the other party doesn't. The point is, of course, that if the client could understand the contract then they'd probably not need the adviser in the first place.

Our relationships with other professionals are typically not based on contracts—or at least not wholly. Generally relationships of this sort should be based on the concept of fiduciary duty, rather than a defined contract. The idea of a fiduciary stretches back to the Middle Ages, when knights tended to charge off on various quests, leaving trusted advisers in charge of their property, gold, and the chastity belt keys. A fiduciary's duties are those of loyalty and prudence toward their clients: perfect for the modern day financial adviser, you'd think.

Unfortunately, most financial fiduciaries tend to interpret the requirement for prudence in terms of the Efficient Market Hypothesis, rather than doing their own thinking, which tends to lead to returns, which closely track the market.[42] This isn't so bad compared to losing money on their clients' behalf, but is something the average individual could achieve themselves simply by using index trackers.

There is a small movement toward insisting that all financial advisers accept the role of a fiduciary and that the herd mentality of following the average market position should be dropped.[43] However, until this is enforced by legislation we should continue to be very careful about how we choose our advisers. Unfortunately, we have to assume the worst until we have evidence to the contrary, which means we need to think for ourselves. We don't need to be experts at investment, but we do need to be experts at assessing investment advisers.

LESSON 15

If you want to find a good adviser then you need to work hard. The hints in this chapter suggest the type of person you're looking for—but don't rely on fiduciary duty to ensure you get a good one. You need to know enough to test their knowledge for yourself.

AVOID THE SHARPSHOOTERS

If you're a bit depressed at the way the professional investment industry manages itself, the way that corporate executives prioritize themselves, and the way that expert advice all too often isn't expert, you have my sympathies. Finding ourselves alone with our money is a bit like being stuck on a desert island with a toothache and discovering that we're the only dentist in town.

In fact there's a great deal of useful advice out there, but you need to work hard to sort the wheat from the chaff. By and large, you should treat the vast majority of self-help investment books and websites as great entertainment but not regard them as definitive methods of getting rich by any means, fast or slow. Almost all purveyors of such approaches will be able to point to evidence of success, but the problem is that most of them are trading on the Texan Sharpshooter Effect.

The Sharpshooter Effect works like this: take a gun and blaze away randomly at the side of a barn. Get some paint and slap up a target, centered on wherever your bullets have ended up. Invite friends around to congratulate you on your shooting skills. It's a trick—anyone can appear good if they're allowed to set their goals after they've achieved them. This is how most investing self-help stories work, by using examples to "prove" the success of whatever the sure-fire method is. As we've seen, stories are what we like to hear, but they're not evidence of anything in isolation from the real data.

Instead we should be looking at the evidence from people who don't make a living from this kind of storytelling and, for preference, from those who are more than happy to admit their past mistakes as well as regale us with their successes. Look for anything by Phil Fisher, Ben Graham, Charlie Munger, Warren Buffett, or any of the fund managers out there who are happily making a living already. They don't need our money to feed their families, they're already rich enough.

LESSON 16

All too many investment experts are relying on the Texan Sharpshooter Effect. Anyone can make themselves look good, better to find material from people who've done it for real, in public, over a long period of time. Learn from the best investors, not the best self-publicists.

THE SEVEN KEY TAKEAWAYS

This chapter has discussed a range of themes around professional investing and corporate management and how these intersect with personal incentives. By and large the outcomes aren't good for us as private investors, but with a bit of effort we can help ourselves.

Let's draw together a few key ideas from this chapter before we move on. The main takeaways are:

1. Incentives incentivize—and if we're dealing with people whose incentives are different from ours we need to recognize this and take it into account.
2. The professional investing industry exists to take money from us, and is almost impossible to beat in the short term, so don't try to.
3. Mutual funds and index trackers can both have a part to play in investing strategies but neither offer ready-made solutions. We need to understand the rules of the game if we're going to use them successfully.
4. Investment forecasts are the modern day equivalent of fortune telling. They're right until we need them and then they're wrong. Don't rely on them, markets and earnings cannot be accurately forecasted.
5. There are some simple rules we should take into account about the types of professionals we want to interact with. Being married, experienced, or female are indicators of a lower propensity for risk—but only indicators; you need to do your own due diligence.
6. Incentives and biases in corporate managements, especially CEOs, can lead to bad investment outcomes. Look carefully at stock option packages, stock buyback, and M&A activity before investing.
7. Don't rely on the happy storytelling of self-proclaimed experts; they're probably relying on the Texan Sharpshooter Effect. Look for people who have long track records of actually making money, preferably across a range of different businesses.

So much for the experts. They suffer from all the normal biases and a bunch more as well, triggered by their incentive packages.

NOTES

1. Burton G. Malkiel, *A Random Walk Down Wall Street: The Time-Tested Strategy for Successful Investing* (New York: W. W. Norton & Company, 2003).
2. Lukas Schneider, "Are UK Fund Investors Achieving Fund Rates of Return? An Examination of the Differences between UK Fund Returns and UK Investors' Returns," thesis, July 2007.

3. Amy L. Barrett and Brent R. Brodeski, "Survivor Bias and Improper Measurement: How the Mutual Fund Industry Inflates Actively Managed Fund Performance," Savant Capital Management, March 2006.

4. William F. Sharpe, "The Arithmetic of Active Management," *Financial Analysts Journal* (1991): 7–9.

5. Randall Morck and Fan Yang, "The Mysterious Growing Value of S&P 500 Membership, NBER Working Paper No. 8654, December 2001.

6. A. D. Wissner-Gross and C. E. Freer, "Relativistic Statistical Arbitrage," *Physical Review E* 82, no. 5 (2010): 056104.

7. Hitesh Mittal, "Are You Playing in a Toxic Dark Pool? A Guide to Preventing Information Leakage," *Journal of Trading* 3, no. 3 (2008): 20–33.

8. Edward N. Lorenz, "Deterministic Nonperiodic Flow," *Journal of the Atmospheric Sciences* 20, no. 2 (1963): 130–141.

9. Lawrence Brown and Ling Zhou, "Interactions between Analyst Earnings Forecasts and Management Earnings Forecasts" (2011). Available at SSRN 2002345.

10. D. Eric Hirst and Patrick E. Hopkins, "Comprehensive Income Reporting and Analysts' Valuation Judgments," *Journal of Accounting Research* 36 (1998): 47–75.

11. Ivo Welch and Amit Goyal, "A Comprehensive Look at the Empirical Performance of Equity Premium Prediction," *Review of Financial Studies* 21, no. 4 (2008): 1455–1508.

12. Paul Söderlind, "Predicting stock price movements: regressions versus economists," *Applied Economics Letters* 17 (2010): 869–874.

13. Dawn A. Matsumoto, "Management's Incentives to Avoid Negative Earnings Surprises," *Accounting Review* 77, no. 3 (2002): 483–514.

14. Hersh Shefrin and Enrico Maria Cervellati, "BP's Failure to Debias: Underscoring the Importance of Behavioral Corporate Finance," *Quarterly Journal of Finance* 1, no. 1 (2011): 127–168.

15. James Montier, "Seven Sins of Fund Management," Global Equity Strategy, November 2005.

16. Werner F. M. de Bondt and Richard H. Thaler, "Do Security Analysts Overreact?" *American Economic Review* (1990): 52–57.

17. Tali Sharot, Christoph W. Korn, and Raymond J. Dolan, "How Unrealistic Optimism Is Maintained in the Face of Reality," *Nature Neuroscience* 14, no. 11 (2011): 1475–1479.

18. J. Scott Armstrong, "The Seer-Sucker Theory: The Value of Experts in Forecasting," *Technology Review* 82 (1980): 16–24.

19. Harrison Hong, Jeffrey D. Kubik, and Amit Solomon, "Security Analysts' Career Concerns and Herding of Earnings Forecasts," *Rand Journal of Economics* (2000): 121–144.

20. Robert B. Durand, Rick Newby, and Jay Sanghani, "An Intimate Portrait of the Individual Investor," *Journal of Behavioral Finance* 9, no. 4 (2008): 193–208.

21. Brad M. Barber and Terrance Odean, "Boys Will Be Boys: Gender, Overconfidence, and Common Stock Investment," *Quarterly Journal of Economics* 116, no. 1 (2001): 261–292.

22. Alexandra Niessen and Stefan Ruenzi, "Sex Matters: Gender Differences in a Professional Setting," CFR Working Paper No. 06-01, 2007.
23. Camelia M. Kuhnen, Gregory R. Samanez-Larkin, and Brian Knutson, "Serotonergic Genotypes, Neuroticism, and Financial Choices," *PloS ONE* 8, no. 1 (2013): e54632.
24. John R. Alford et al., "Generosity Is Its Own Reward: The Neural Basis of Representation," Annual meeting of the American Political Science Association, Toronto, Canada, 2009. Retrieved from http://ssrn.com/abstract. Vol. 1451309.
25. Steven Sapra and Paul Zak, "Neurofinance: Bridging Psychology, Neurology, and Investor Behavior," *Neurology and Investor Behavior* (2009).
26. Michael D. Baker Jr. and Jon K. Maner, "Risk-Taking as a Situationally Sensitive Male Mating Strategy," *Evolution and Human Behavior* 29, no. 6 (2008): 391–395.
27. Nikolai Roussanov and Pavel G. Savor, "Status, Marriage, and Managers' Attitudes to Risk," NBER Working Paper No. w17904, 2012.
28. Emanuel Derman, "Model Risk: What Are the Assumptions Made in Using Models to Value Securities and What Are the Consequent Risks?" *Risk* 9 (May 1996): 34–38.
29. Donald MacKenzie and Yuval Millo, "Negotiating a Market, Performing Theory: The Historical Sociology of a Financial Derivatives Exchange" (August 1, 2001). Available at SSRN: http://ssrn.com/abstract=279029 or http://dx.doi.org/10.2139/ssrn.279029.
30. Joris Lammers, Diederik A. Stapel, and Adam D. Galinsky, "Power Increases Hypocrisy: Moralizing in Reasoning, Immorality in Behavior," *Psychological Science* 21, no. 5 (2010): 737–744.
31. Daniel Bergstresser and Thomas Philippon, "CEO Incentives and Earnings Management," *Journal of Financial Economics* 80, no. 3 (2006): 511–529.
32. Rüdiger Fahlenbrach, and René M. Stulz, "Bank CEO Incentives and the Credit Crisis," *Journal of Financial Economics* 99, no. 1 (2011): 11–26.
33. Renée B. Adams, Heitor Almeida, and Daniel Ferreira, "Powerful CEOs and Their Impact on Corporate Performance," *Review of Financial Studies* 18, no. 4 (2005): 1403–1432.
34. Robert F. Bruner, "Does M&A Pay? A Survey of Evidence for the Decision-Maker," *Journal of Applied Finance* 12, no. 1 (2002): 48–68.
35. Jeffrey Wurgler, Xin Pan, and Malcolm Baker, "The Psychology of Pricing in Mergers and Acquisitions, unpublished working paper, Harvard Business School, 2009.
36. Paul A. Griffin and Ning Zhu, "Accounting Rules? Stock Buybacks and Stock Options: Additional Evidence," *Journal of Contemporary Accounting & Economics* 6, no. 1 (2010): 1–17.
37. Jay R. Ritter, "Initial Public Offerings: Underpricing Statistics through 2011" (December 2011). http://bear.warrington.ufl/edu/ritter/IPOs2011Underwriting1912.pdf.
38. Richard A. Booth, "Going Public, Selling Stock, and Buying Liquidity," Villanova University School of Law Working Paper 96, November 2007. http://law.bepress.com/villanovalwps/art96.

39. Tim Loughran and Jay R. Ritter, "Why Has IPO Underpricing Changed Over Time?" (December 3, 2002). AFA 2003 Washington, DC meetings. Available at SSRN: http://ssrn.com/abstract=331780 or http://dx.doi.org/10.2139/ssrn .331780.

40. Brad M. Barber, Yi-Tsung Lee, Yu-Jane Liu, and Terrance Odean, "Just How Much Do Individual Investors Lose by Trading?" *Review of Financial Studies* 22, no. 2 (2009): 609–632.

41. Pete Comley, *Monkey with a Pin: Why You May Be Missing 6% a Year from Your Investment Returns* (Pete Comley, 2012).

42. Max M. Schanzenbach and Robert H. Sitkoff, "The Prudent Investor Rule and Trust Asset Allocation: An Empirical Analysis," *American College of Trust and Estate Counsel Journal* 35 (2010): 314; Harvard Law and Economics Discussion Paper No. 668; Northwestern Law & Econ Research Paper No. 11-05. Available at SSRN: http://ssrn.com/abstract=1611209.

43. John Kay, "The Kay Review of UK Equity Markets and Long-Term Decision Making," Final Report (2012).

CHAPTER 6

Debiasing

By this point, I hope the message has gotten through—we spend our lives immersed in a sea of bias, and like the air we breathe it's so natural we don't even realize it exists—most of the time. Unfortunately, in finance our biases are inclined to lead us into error, penury, and worse.

Having spent most of the book setting up this premise I'd now like to start looking at how you debias yourselves. After all, if the world is full of biased people we probably only need to be a little bit better than them to be reasonably successful.

This, of course, is a nice theory but is unfortunately easier said than done. Nonetheless, there are a few things we can do to ease our way through the minefield.

NUMBERS, NUMBERS, NUMBERS

I'm afraid that the boring answer to debiasing is to spend time sweating the numbers. The brutal fact is that if we're interested in making money from stocks then we need to take the time to understand the finances of the corporations we're thinking of investing in. Moreover, we can't simply take the numbers at face value: company accounts are a snapshot of the viability of the firm at a specific point in time and good finance departments are adept at managing the numbers to give the world the best possible view of the company. And this is perfectly legal.

There's a good reason, for instance, why company reports start with a narrative and end with the numbers. The narratives can be useful but are all too often used to distract investors away from the real issues—and, of course, they're biased as well. Annual reports, as Thomas Keusch and colleagues[1] have shown, are full of self-serving bias: when things go well it's down to the skill of the management, and when things go wrong it's down to the vagaries of the economy or some other unpredictable external factor.

Even better, managers tend to use the personal pronoun when things are going well, but revert to the third person when things have gone wrong. As Feng Li has found,[2] the amount of self-serving bias is predictive—the more executives suffer from the problem the more likely the company is to issue overly positive earnings forecasts. In fact, such firms will tend to have more debt and are more likely to repurchase stock than issue dividends—which, as we've seen, is a potential indicator of a management more concerned about their own remuneration than the welfare of the owners of the company.

Despite all this, actually reading the latest annual report before buying into a corporation is probably more than most investors do. But beyond that it's worth learning how to really dig into the numbers. This book is not about that kind of financial analysis—there are plenty of other books out there that do that (and the accounting rules change regularly, so you need to keep abreast of these)—but taking the time to understand how reports work, what profit and loss accounts and cash flow statements mean, and why accruals are important is well worthwhile.

Personally nothing beats a solid balance sheet for me. All corporations will suffer some kind of setback at some time of another. Just like you and me they need to have reserves to fall back on when the hard times hit. If the firms you invest in have this type of attribute then even if you're the most overoptimistic, self-serving, blindly anchored investor ever seen you will still have a chance of a decent return.

LESSON 1

Annual reports are a combination of a management-inspired narrative and a regulated set of numbers. The former may be heavily biased to an overly positive view of the world. The latter may be legally manipulated. However, understanding the numbers and the way that they can be adjusted to make them look better must be a key plank of any logical investment strategy.

LOSING MOMENTUM

In the real world, running against the herd is often a desperately stupid thing to do: driving the wrong way up one way streets or wagering blindly against the odds at horseracing are not strategies that should be recommended to any even halfway rational person. Yet we're frequently exhorted to be contrarian by pundits, at least those who aren't telling us the exact opposite. So what, exactly, are we supposed to do?

Contrarianism is really a reaction to the idea of the Efficient Markets Hypothesis—the idea that the price of any given stock must be right, because everything that can be known about the stock must be reflected in the price. That's nonsense for many reasons, only some of which are psychological. So being contrarian means going against the market view of a stock or even the market itself.

From this it follows that contrarianism is a form of debiasing: at least a way of avoiding the more extreme forms of herding. Of course, it's not a straightforward process—markets may be imperfect but they are often more or less right. So effective contrarianism involves hard work and analysis and research—but it does, I believe, put you in the right mental frame of mind to address debiasing properly.

Unfortunately, it is not a panacea. Going with the herd is actually an investment approach in its own right—it's known as momentum investing, and has been shown to give extremely good investment returns. Narasimhan Jegadeesh and Sheridan Titman[3] published a famous paper in 2001, which established that a strategy of holding a portfolio of winning stocks and shorting losing stocks yielded outsize returns over periods of up to a year. There are lots of explanations for this, which are highly contradictory and tend to make you go cross-eyed from reading them, but it's not hard to create a psychological explanation for the effect, using herding, anchoring, and normal overconfidence.

Once behavioral bias enters the equation we should generally tread carefully anyway, because any kind of mass psychological effect is open to sudden reversal and, indeed, momentum investing is risky at market turning points. Any approach that assumes tomorrow will be the same as today is going to go wrong at some point.

In any case, momentum investing is potentially another case of the vanishing anomaly, where tried and trusted techniques for so-called guaranteed investment success start to fail just as soon as they become popular enough to be exploited by the billion dollar automated processors of the investment industry. There's evidence that this is happening—M. Scott Wilson[4] has shown that a momentum strategy offered negative returns in U.S. markets (that's a loss to you and me) between 2005 and 2010, a finding replicated by Debarati Bhattacharya and colleagues.[5]

Broadly, momentum investing as a generic strategy is likely to be quite dangerous, although to be fair, that's true of most generic investment strategies. Investing blindly isn't a good option. So if momentum investing is not for us, what about its polar opposite?

> ## LESSON 2
>
> Momentum investing is not a debiased approach: it's based on assumptions about psychology and reliant on markets behaving properly, neither of which is a safe bet. Moreover, momentum investing appears to be subject to the law of the disappearing anomaly.

MEAN REVERSION

If momentum investing isn't contrarianism, then what is? Well, broadly it would be fundamentally based, and generally operating on the basis that what's gone down must, eventually, come back up. This comes down to the assumption that mean reversion operates in markets.

Mean reversion was discovered by Francis Galton, who we've already met in association with the wisdom of crowds. Mean reversion, or regression to the mean, is the idea that any abnormally large value of a variable—let's say the return on the stock market in any given year—is likely to be succeeded by a lower value. Applying the same idea to people (one of Galton's favorite pastimes), he noted that although short people tended to have short children and tall people to have tall children, the short children tended to be slightly taller than their parents and the tall ones slightly shorter.

So if stock markets and stocks tend to mean revert, then buying them when they're down and selling them when they're up—the lifeblood of a contrarian approach—would yield above average returns. Almost by definition this is a debiased approach, because you will be doing the opposite of what most people do—selling when things are cheap and buying when they're expensive.

Unfortunately there's a problem with this, because markets and stocks don't exactly follow the distribution you'd expect if they really did mean revert. Bad years in markets are quite often followed by worse ones and sometimes stocks keep on going down, or up, virtually forever. Again, it's easy enough to construct a psychological explanation for this—it's our tendency to extrapolate current conditions into the future. The behavioral psychologists Werner de Bondt and Richard Thaler[6] show that this tendency to overweight recent information and underweight base-rate data—a combination of recency and base-rate neglect—is sufficient to explain overreaction in stock prices.

What this leads to is a hypothesis that good news can lead to stocks being overpriced and bad news to them being underpriced—and that a contrarian strategy of selling the winners and buying the losers would be successful. Certainly the research backs up the idea that buying past losers will generally be successful.

However, if this strategy is well-known we should expect people to exploit it, and if people start exploiting it then the risk of it starting to fail under the weight of expectation will once again raise its ugly head. Kevin Wang[7] has come up with a theory that people do adopt such a strategy, despite the intuitively obvious suggestion that if a company produces good results you might reasonably expect it to continue doing so. And this is exactly what he found—rather than analyzing the fundamentals to decide whether a firm that's doing well is likely to carry on doing well or that one that's doing badly is likely to carry on failing, investors can get carried away with a mean reversion strategy that sees them selling and buying exactly the wrong thing at the wrong time.

So following an automated mean regression strategy is letting our biases in by the back door—it's no more a debiased approach than momentum investing. It is contrarian, it's just not very sensible. We have to go back to the numbers, I'm afraid, to find stocks that have been marked down unfairly. It's the iron law of the markets: no free lunches.

LESSON 3

Stock prices do seem to overreact on both the upside and the downside, such that some element of mean reversion really does exist. Unfortunately, simply following a strategy of selling winners and buying losers is no more free from psychological bias than any other blind, mindless technique.

SHORT SHIFT

A little earlier I mentioned the idea of shorting stocks. Shorting or short-selling is the ability to sell stocks you don't own. Of course, in the real world this is a bit of a peculiar idea—if I were to sell my next door neighbor's car I would find myself incarcerated in no time at all. But stock markets are not the real world and selling short is perfectly legal and frequently done.

What shorting is doing is effectively betting that a stock will fall in price. In theory when the stock falls you can buy it at the lower price and then pocket the difference between the price you originally sold it at and the new lower price. In practice it's a bit more complicated than this, but not a lot. And in complex portfolios managed by experienced investors it's not always an unreasonable thing to do—you can effectively insure your portfolio against it falling in price by going short on stocks or markets.

However, if I discover any of you have gone short on a stock I will come around to your house with a megaphone and shout abuse at you all night. Short selling is very dangerous for the unwary because it exposes you to unlimited losses. If I buy a stock, the maximum I can lose is the amount I paid—the firm can go bust and I can lose all the money I invested in it. This happens from time to time, even with large corporations and it's very painful, but the loss is fixed.

If you go short, however, there is no limit. If I short a stock for $100 and it goes up I am losing money. Simplistically at $200 I have losses of $100 per share. At $1,000 I stand to lose $900 per share. And so on, indefinitely. Your losses are unlimited.

On top of this, people—especially politicians—seem to have an irrational hatred of short-sellers. As James Meeker[8] has recorded, leaders from Napoleon to George W. Bush have sought to blame the shorters when markets fall dramatically. Invariably, when there's a stock market crash governments will attempt to ban short-selling, arguing that the shorters are driving down the markets and making things worse, which they may be to a certain extent, but you don't see the same reaction when markets are booming—no one has ever been prevented from buying shares even when they're wildly overpriced.

One nasty effect of all of this antishorting nonsense is that sometimes markets don't function properly. If markets are overpriced then the theory argues that people will sell them and drive them down. Unfortunately, due to a combination of fear of unlimited liability and the tendency of governments to intervene this often doesn't happen.[9] And that's not really good in the long term, because it helps leads to market bubbles.

Given all of this negativity it's not surprising that short-selling isn't popular. However, when it's done properly it's extremely valuable for the debiasing investor. This reflects the fact that most short-side investors need to be pretty damn sure of their investment logic before taking on the risk of unlimited liability. From this, it follows that stocks that are being very heavily shorted by the market are probably ones to avoid.

The point is that institutional short-sellers really do need to do their analysis properly: typically they're not exploiting momentum effects or any kind of psychological bias, but are identifying mispricing in the firms' fundamentals.[10] After all, they're up against waves of emotionally biased investors and automated momentum trading algorithms. To make money in that kind of environment you need to be sure of your numbers.

Of course, this is not an invitation to short. But it is always worth checking if a particular stock is being heavily shorted before buying in—because if it is then it suggests that there's some underlying uncertainty that the short sellers are looking to exploit. They do make mistakes, but they make less than most.

LESSON 4

Short-sellers are less biased and more focused on fundamentals than the run-of-the-mill investor and it's worth checking whether a stock is being heavily shorted before you purchase it—and if it is you need to figure out why. But do not, under any circumstances, try shorting yourself: you will lose your house, honor, and probably all of your shirts.

DIWORSIFICATION

One of the great ideas in stock investing was the concept of the portfolio. By holding an array of stocks, instead of just a couple, you diversify away some of your risk. So, if one of your companies goes bust then you have only lost a small percentage of your money. Conversely, of course, if one of your companies does really well you only benefit to the proportion of your portfolio that you hold.

Portfolio Theory was invented back in the 1950s by a young economist, Harry Markowitz,[11] and became really popular in the 1970s, after a long period of stock market underperformance revealed that most investment experts hadn't had much of a clue what they were doing. Portfolio Theory automatically figures out which stocks to buy and sell, and supposedly removes the human factor.

Unfortunately it does no such thing, because Portfolio Theory relies on heaps of information about the investor's risk profile and is essentially based on the Efficient Markets Hypothesis. It's darn complex to use as well, so much so that its inventor basically ignored it when it came time to figure out how to allocate his own retirement savings.[12]

Out of Portfolio Theory has come a great myth, however, and one that investors need to be very careful of. This states, roughly, that in order to diversify away most risk you don't need to hold more than 15 stocks: any more leads to so-called diworsification, and a lowering of returns without a reduction in risk. Unfortunately, many investors firstly misinterpret this statement and secondly, and even worse, believe it. It's not true and it's important to understand why.

Firstly, though, diversification across both stocks and asset classes is just about the closest thing to a free lunch you'll ever get in investment. Even if you're the most biased investor who's ever gone near the markets, diversification can save you from a lot of potential problems. Lives have been ruined by insufficient diversification, but have never been destroyed by too much.

However, it's important to understand that diversification can only protect you from so-called unsystematic risk. This is the risk that one particular firm will fail. In the worst case, if you hold 20 stocks in equal proportions and one fails you lose 5 percent of your portfolio value. If you hold two stocks and one fails you lose 50 percent. Simple math.

A properly constructed portfolio can also help limit correlations between stocks. So, if you hold two firms who are in the same line of business and one fails because of poor business conditions it's possible that the other may also face the same problems (although when competition fails sometimes this has the opposite effect). Highly correlated stocks tend to move up and down in price together, so people with portfolios comprising only IT stocks didn't do very well in the wake of the dot-com bubble: their diversification was illusory.

Calculating these correlations and figuring out the optimal portfolio is what Portfolio Theory does and is very complicated, but many people get around this by simply buying companies operating in different sectors—such as defense companies and pharmaceuticals or restaurants chains and oil companies. Avoiding too many companies in the same sector is a form of diversification. None of this prevents your exposure to systematic risk, though, which is what happen when markets collapse—all stocks of all kinds fall. In this kind of situation you need to have diversified into other sorts of asset classes—government bonds, foreign stocks, property, and so on. Even this isn't always safe, but it's just about the best you can do.

There's another problem, which is the idea that 15 stocks is enough for sufficient diversification: in general it's not, as Meir Statman has shown.[13] In fact, 30, 50, or even 100 stocks may not always be enough. The problem is that the perfect portfolio is a statistical construct and what it means is that if you are unfortunate enough to not pick the one or two great performing stocks you will underperform the average: William Bernstein[14] has demonstrated this by looking at the range of possible 15 stock portfolios formed out of the S&P 500 in terms of terminal wealth—the value you have to retire on when you liquidate your fund. Fully 75 percent of them didn't even beat the market.

Edward O'Neal[15] made a similar discovery with mutual funds—one fund is not enough to diversify away the risk of a low final value—and Andrew Clare and Nick Motson[16] found the same sort of result with diversification across asset classes. Overall, the general theme is clear—diversifying more is not diworsifying.

LESSON 5

Investors should diversify heavily across asset classes and stocks. Diworsification is actually a debiasing technique as it prevents you from becoming too focused on one particular sector.

DISCONFIRM, DISCONFIRM

Perhaps one of the nastiest behavioral issues is confirmation bias. This causes people to seek evidence to confirm their existing views, rather than looking for that which might disconfirm it: we touched on this in our discussion around the Barnum effect, our tendency to read insightful information in random rubbish, but confirmation bias is quite general and when you reread this book (and you will reread it, won't you?), you'll find lots of examples dotted around.

The psychologist Raymond Nickerson[17] has written an excellent review of the topic, which I encourage you all to read out of general interest. He finds confirmation bias popping up in all sorts of places—ancient number mysticism, witch hunting, government policymaking, medicine, judicial decisions, and scientific investigations to name but a few. Given how reason is often ignored in investing it should be no surprise to find it prevalent in the subject.

The classic test of confirmation bias is something called the Wason Rule Discovery Test.[18] Subjects are presented with a series of numbers, told they follow a rule, and are asked to figure the rule out by choosing further sequences of numbers. The sequence given is 2, 4, 6—so what's the rule? Go on, have a guess.

Invariably, people come up with some hypothesis and then generate sequences to confirm it. So 8, 10, 12 is quite popular and generates the answer "going up by two each time." The sequence does meet the rule, but the rule suggested is wrong. The problem is that people are going about the question the wrong way, asking questions to confirm their hypothesis rather than trying to disconfirm it.

So, if I now tell you that the further sequence 11, 12, 13 also meets the rule, can you guess what it is? So does 100, 217, 1,000,009. Any idea?

The answer is "any three numbers in ascending order." It's easy to disconfirm this once you start looking for alternative sequences, but most people never
do. And this is a generalizable problem that's exacerbated by human psychology: we don't look for evidence that disconfirms our theories. So what do you
think we do *after* we buy a stock that our theorizing says is a great investment?

Yep, of course: we become resistant to any ideas that suggest our favorite stock pick may be less wise than we reckon. Bulletin boards are a particularly enjoyable source of rampantly irrational behavior: JaeHong Park
and colleagues[19] have shown that people actively seek confirming evidence
from such sources, seemingly caring little that the positivity is coming from
anonymous sources of unknown providence. It's quite likely we're seeing
group polarization as well, so the virtual communities are not clever places
to look for useful investment advice.

To counter this there are a few important debiasing techniques. Firstly,
always try and imagine that your investment has gone broke, and try and
think why this might happen. This tends to inject reality into any investment
situation. Secondly, avoid time-critical investment decisions—these situations accentuate confirmation bias.

Thirdly, try and find an investing buddy and agree, randomly, to act on
different sides of the investing equation. One of you tries to find reasons to
invest and the other to divest: this forces you into thinking through the full
range of possible outcomes.

Fighting confirmation bias and debiasing yourself by actively seeking disconfirming evidence is really, really hard. But if you get into the habit of doing so, and start to view your investments as money rather than extensions
of your personality then it may well be the most valuable thing you ever do.

LESSON 6

Confirmation bias is an accumulation of lots of different biases, and
is insidiously present in many situations. Learn to fight it: look for the
evidence that your theory is wrong, it's the best debiasing technique
you'll ever learn.

REVERSE POLARIZATION

Closely associated with confirmation bias is group polarization, the tendency of groups to adopt more extreme positions than the individuals comprising the group. Group polarization is made more problematic by the way

that the mass media delight in taking extreme positions—after all, a middle of the road attitude doesn't really make for interesting reading—and the way in which we're attracted to salient stories, which we tend to remember and are highly available.

In general, adopting an extreme position isn't sensible for any logical investor, but we all have our own pet likes and hates, and the average investor is usually going to have strong views about the advantages of free market style capitalism over the alternatives. All in all it's quite easy to get swept along in the spirit of the moment, whether that's some newfangled investment trend, a stampede for the market exit, or some wonder invention that's going to revolutionize the way we live. Finding a way of debiasing this type of polarized, salient effect is a valuable tool in the never-ending fight against psychological bias.

One simple way of doing this is to use a decision tree: that is, to identify as many options as we can and then try to assign probabilities to each of them. So, for instance, if we're looking at investing in a particular stock we should create a set of options around how well we think the firm will perform. This can be as simple as you like but goes something like:

1. Firm goes bust.
2. Firm produces below market performance.
3. Firm performs in line with the market average.
4. Firm produces above average performance.
5. Firm shoots the lights out.

Now, the first key thing here is that you're not allowed to assign a zero probability to any of these. I admit, obviously, that the chances of (say) Apple going bust are very low but it's worth remembering that times change. As the economic historian Leslie Hannah has recorded,[20] back in 1900 over 40 percent of the world's stock market capitalization was accounted for by railroad companies and the largest non railroad company was the Suez Canal. Times change and as the demise of the Bethlehem Steel Company shows, in finance nothing is forever.

So you need to assign a probability to each of these options. Then you need to try and find reasons to back each of them up. Now frankly, unless the probability assigned to (4) + (5) outweighs the combined probability of the other options you shouldn't invest—you can get a market average result investing in an index tracker, so why take the downside risks of an individual stock?

To come up with high values of (4) or (5) you also need to do better than to argue that the firm is the next big thing. If you can see that, then so can other people: and if the valuation is already sky-high you're not likely to see outsize returns (which is not to say this can't happen, but it's unlikely). In general, to outperform the market the firm either has to be in a sector that is itself making above average profits or have a niche that competitors can't touch.

The general law of the market is that if some firm is making lots of money then other firms will try to grab some of the pie, and in doing so will reduce the profitability of the area. This is one of the reasons why mean reversion in stocks is real—corporations currently doing well are likely to do less well in future. It's also one of the reasons momentum investing works reasonably well over short periods, because it takes time for competitors to build up their positions.

The ideal investment is one that's cheap, or at least on a market average rating, with some anti-competitive moat—basically a firm that can defend its market leading position. Moats can come in many forms—Coca-Cola's brand is one, for instance, no one can replicate it—but tend to be associated with firms that are expensive to buy. Occasionally they strike trouble and that is often the time to purchase them—but when a company is in trouble and the media is full of negative stories most people are psychologically averse to investing.

It's actually quite easy to see how and why investment trends occur, viewed through the prism of behavioral bias. What we need to remember is that valuation matters: if you buy a good firm making above market average returns at a fair price and hold it for long enough you will make money. If you buy a great company at a high price you may also make money—but you'll probably make less than you expect. And if you buy speculative firms at any price you'll probably end up working till you drop.

LESSON 7

Simple decision trees are a great way of forcing us to think through all of the options associated with buying or selling a stock. Remember that we should have no interest in buying market average firms—we can match that kind of performance with virtually no risk by purchasing low-cost index trackers.

EXPECTED VALUE

We hate losing. Absolutely detest it. That's the lesson of loss aversion—we simply cannot stand the thought of having an investment that fails. There may well be a good physiological reason for this—the pain researcher Dale

Langford[21] has shown that social empathy in mice can trigger pain reactions, so how much more likely is it that mental anguish over our stocks will make us feel physically sick?

So, as we've seen, we'll grimly hold on to our loser stocks even as they decline while we'll celebrate selling great firms at a profit, even if they then go on to outperform for years to come. Even worse, sometimes we'll get so excited by our profitable stocks that we will hold onto them, even though the numbers clearly indicate that the chances of them outperforming in the future are negligible. But herding and polarization will serve to convince us to hold onto these bum deals because they "can't lose."

However, a bit of careful thought about these situations serves to demonstrate that selling likely winners and holding likely losers is never going to be a successful strategy. Actually, let me rephrase that: any thought whatsoever will show that this is the case. So rather than worrying about whether a stock has gained or lost a lot we need to think about what the *potential* is for a gain or a loss. The critical thing is that we should try to evaluate each and every stock in our portfolio—both before and during (and possibly after) we hold it to figure out the expected gain. This is a decision tree approach to investing, which forces us to consider both the probability of an expected gain and also the potential magnitude.

Consider a great blue sky story stock where the potential (at least according to the market) is infinite. Now look at the current market capitalization of the stock compared to its earnings and try to figure out what will drive the stock in the future to gain enormous amounts. Now try and figure out what might happen to ensure it loses an enormous amount.

Consider a down in the dumps, old fashioned, out of favor stock. Make the same analysis—perhaps this is a firm backed by lots of assets so maybe the likelihood of it shooting the lights out is low, but the chances of losing everything is also low.

So with BlueSky Inc., the chances of winning big are small (let's say 10 percent) and the chances of losing everything are large (let's say 50 percent). With OldFirm Inc., the chances of winning big are also small (let's say 5 percent) and the chances of losing everything are small (let's say 5 percent). Both stocks are trading at $1,000 a share.

Let's assume winning big is the share price doubling to $2,000. So we get the expected value of winning big for BlueSky is 5 % * $2,000, the chance of losing everything is 50 * $0, and the chances of the status quo are 40% * $1,000. Adding these up you get an expected value of $100 + 0 + $400 = $500.

For OldFirm we have 5% * $2,000 + 90% * $1,000 + 0 = $100 + $900 + 0 = $1,000.

On this basis you wouldn't invest in either of them, but you'd certainly never go near BlueSky.

Now let's look at QualCo. The chance of the share price doubling is 30 percent, of losing everything is 1 percent, and of staying the same is 69 percent: an expected value of $1,290. Depending on your timescale that's a good investment.

Okay, now this is rough and ready, but the point is clear, I hope—you need to try to reduce your thoughts, aspirations, and hopes to numbers and probability. To estimate the true potential value of BlueSky you need, if possible, to find something that's been around a while to compare it with. But if not, be cautious.

One of the really tricky issues is that we can often only analyze the true value of a firm after we've invested in it. This is because we need to get to know the firm before we can really figure out the true value. So it's important to continually reevaluate the expected value of your investments, because if you don't you will be led astray. I'd suggest you do this twice a year, after major earnings announcements, when you can compare your expectations to reality.

It's imperfect, but it's better than nothing. And remember that the really good investors want the odds heavily in their favor, so they'll reject what might look like good investments to you and I.

LESSON 8

Expanding decision trees into the realm of expected value moves us into proper ways of considering the future. You will be wrong, but for the right reasons. You'll be getting feedback about how you're wrong. And gradually, you'll improve.

INVESTING IN THE REARVIEW MIRROR

As we've seen, hindsight bias, our tendency to believe we can predict the future because we think (incorrectly) that we predicted the present in the past, is virtually ineradicable. It's a pervasive human bias that is seemingly impossible to eliminate. And from hindsight bias comes overconfidence, and nothing hurts an investor more than an unwarranted belief in their own abilities, because when we invest in stock markets we are playing with uncertainty, and uncertainty is unpredictable, at least in the short term.

If hindsight and overconfidence are so damn difficult to prevent, perhaps we have no choice but to live with them, but I still believe that it's at least worth the effort to try to reduce their effects as much as possible. And there are a few areas of human expertise where the so-called experts actually do make a decent shot at prediction, even in the face of rampant uncertainty—weather forecasters, for instance, are surprisingly accurate.

One of the best papers on this subject is "Managing Overconfidence," by the strategic management experts J. Edward Russo and Paul Schoemaker,[22] and includes a Confidence Test, which has a nasty tendency to reveal to us exactly how biased we are. We are all generally far more confident than we have any right to be: as the research paper points out, we really ought to know how much we don't know. Unfortunately, as copious amounts of research continue to reveal, we often have very little appreciation of how foolish we really are.

As Russo and Schoemaker showed, and as lots of other research I've mentioned confirms, experience does go some way toward reducing overconfidence and the effects of hindsight, but only a little, and levels of overconfidence, even in areas in which we are supposedly experts, are still dangerously high.

Addressing this isn't easy, but one surefire way of reducing the effects is to force people to face up to their errors. Three groups of professionals have been shown to be reasonably good forecasters—geologists, accountants, and weather forecasters. In each case these groups get constant, unrelenting feedback about their forecasts. This may be because of the business area or because of corporate policies, but either way it's clear that the feedback is effective at improving accuracy—although it should also be noted that the visibility of this feedback means that people who aren't able to adapt to the demands of the situation are likely to find themselves investigating alternative career opportunities fairly quickly: this is evolutionary style self-selection at work.

The fact is, feedback works, if you can tolerate it. Unfortunately most people can't, because it's too painful. We'll look at the form this should take in the next chapter but here's a very simple rule for you:

LESSON 9

If you can't tolerate feedback on your investing success (or failure) then stop investing for yourself. Good feedback will result in improved performance far more quickly (and less expensively) than experience.

LIVING WITH UNCERTAINTY

The very nature of uncertainty is something we hate and have done for time immemorial. Rather than glumly accepting the inevitability of life we have done dumb things like inventing volcano gods and trusting economists to understand and predict the future. Neither are much good, but we at least have someone to blame when things go wrong.

Although uncertainty is all around us always, most of the time we choose to ignore this and modern life in first world countries is almost designed to insulate us from it. We demand a safety first culture that rips the joy of surprise out of the heart of our existence. We sue when things go wrong because someone must be to blame, when the reality is that not every risk can be predicted and not every event can be foretold. So when we start investing, an area in which uncertainty lies at its core, we are exposed to a type of environment that we're firstly not suited to and secondly have little experience in. It's a recipe for irrational behavior.

The outward sign of uncertainty in stock markets is the extent to which stock prices fluctuate. This, as we've seen, is known as volatility and volatility is often equated with risk, which is predictable, rather than uncertainty, which isn't. Risk tells us that a stock will usually rise or fall 10 percent for no apparent reason, uncertainty is what happens when it doubles or halves overnight—the volcano god has struck.

Volatility is yet another stock market anomaly: research by Yale economist and author Robert Shiller[23] has shown that stocks jump about far more than the theories suggest they should. This isn't a minor effect either—he shows that the unexpected volatility is 13 times greater than it should be.

However, sizable rises or falls in stocks are quite common and are neither a reason to get excited or depressed, as long as you've done your homework. Imagine if you could jump on a website any time you chose and discover the up-to-date value of your home. Imagine further that this price fluctuates based on the value assigned to it by a bunch of people you've never heard of making apparently random bets based on intuition, government statistics created by anonymous economists, a set of automated trading computers in a faraway city and, a couple of times a year, the real price achieved by one of your neighbors actually selling.

So the price of your home will fluctuate wildly, along with your emotions. Even worse, because prices tend to go down a little bit more often than they go up (although when they go up, they go up more), if you constantly check your web-based house price monitor throughout the day you will get more disappointments than you do happy moments. And the share price of even very large, extremely stable, companies can vary enormously in any one year—falls (or rises) of 20 or 30 percent are not at all uncommon, even if the firms haven't fundamentally changed.

Unfortunately, people tend to use share price as a signal of corporate health, rather than looking at the underlying economics of the firms, so you will get herding and anchoring effects. Debiasing these effects is difficult. Firstly, you will need to learn to live with a certain amount of volatility. Secondly, you need to make darn sure you do not need to liberate cash from your stocks in the short-term, because you cannot guarantee the value of them over that period. This has to be a long-term program, not about short-term gain.

But whatever you do, turn off the portfolio tracker, and do not have the business news on in the background. Markets are full of short-term noise, corrections are common, life goes on. Knee-jerk reactions are not going to help you make money, they'll just lose you more.

LESSON 10

Don't track your stocks on a regular basis, and do try to ignore the latest and greatest in media noise. And never, ever invest with money you may need in the short-term: volatility is your enemy and will strike just when you can't afford it.

SUNK BY THE *TITANIC* EFFECT

You would think that the introduction of safety measures would reduce the possibility of accidents but, human nature being the wonderful thing that it is, this ain't necessarily so. Sometimes, in fact, introducing safety measures can increase the risks, and this is never truer than when it comes to investing.

The classic example is that of the *Titanic*, the unsinkable ship that sank on its maiden voyage, with huge loss of life. The theory goes that the ship was inadequately equipped with lifeboats because it was assumed to be unsinkable—but have you ever wondered why it was assumed to be unsinkable? Or why it had any lifeboats at all?

Well, the ship had 16 water-tight compartments below the waterline, separated by bulkheads, and was built to stay afloat if four or fewer than these filled with water. No accident had ever occurred that had caused such an accident but when the *Titanic* hit the iceberg it opened up five of these and the ship promptly sank. The suspicion is that the crew was less careful and vigilant than they otherwise would have been, because of the belief that they were safe.

This, of course, is human reflexivity in action once more. We are, I believe, inherently lazy when it comes to doing our own thinking—we prefer to automate our processing whenever possible—so if we're presented with a situation in which we believe things can't go wrong we'll tend to take this as gospel, and stop worrying.

What's true in the real world is also true in the financial world. At various times over the last half-century, various ideas have flourished that have suggested that risk has been abolished. Most recently this was one of the problems behind the sub prime crash when risk management was devolved to computer models. When things went wrong many managements revealed themselves to be sunning themselves on the decks of the *Titanic*—the CFO of Goldman Sachs blithely explained that the crash was a one in 100,000-year occurrence. Kevin Dowd and colleagues[24] rather dryly pointed out that this would be equivalent to winning the UK lottery more than 20 times in a row.

Our tendency to rely overly on safety mechanisms that we don't understand is understandable but hugely dangerous. In our technologically complex world we are increasingly comfortable with this approach—in fact, we have very little choice in the matter, because we're cosseted and protected by manufacturers and suppliers that are petrified of being sued. But in stock markets, in investment, in finance, we can't afford to take this approach. Only we can protect ourselves—so we need to assume that things that have never happened can, and make sure we take enough lifeboats with us to get everyone to safety.

In fact, the best cure for the *Titanic* effect, the best way of maintaining a decent commitment to debiasing, is to have regular small accidents. Odd though this sounds it ensures that people stay attentive, rather than simply falling asleep at the wheel. This is yet another reason we need to keep track of our failures, because if we don't regularly reevaluate our investing approach we may miss the fact that calm seas are becoming increasingly choppy.

LESSON 11

Never assume that markets are safe or that investing methods are foolproof. Celebrate your errors, and make sure you constantly learn from them—and remember, as soon as you think you are safe you are most at risk.

CHANGING YOUR MIND

The economist John Maynard Keynes is famously said to have responded to a critic who accused him of being inconsistent by stating "when the facts change, I change my mind." Unfortunately changing our mind is something we're particularly bad at doing, especially after we've made a commitment, such as getting engaged, invading the Middle East, or buying a stock. Admittedly, those decisions may be on a different scale, but the principle is the same—it's commitment bias in action.

This was first noted by organizational behavior expert Barry Staw,[25] who showed that negative consequences of decisions would often cause people to invest more time, money, and effort in them. This is related to something called the sunk-cost fallacy, where people justify continued investment in an approach on the basis of the prior expenditure. This, of course, is wrong—the past can't be recovered, we need to make decisions based on the future likelihood of success.

The classic experiment on sunk costs was carried out by psychologists Hal Arkes and Catherine Blumer,[26] who showed that people who paid more for theater tickets were more likely to attend the show. There's a bit of a debate about what is actually going on in people's minds when they exhibit this kind of behavior, but we mainly need to try and figure out how to deal with the problem.

The psychologists Winston Sieck, Jennifer Smith, and Louise Rasmussen[27] have studied how people make sense out of living in different cultures, where their usual rules don't apply. They've identified a number of useful ideas for how such sojourners think about their thought processes in order to make sense of what's going on—a process known as metacognition:

1. Notice when something is odd. This, so-called anomaly detection is the early warning sign that something isn't right with your mental model. Sadly, it's all too easy to explain these away, but try to avoid this—if something is odd it needs explanation.
2. Ask what's going on. Basically, try and come up with questions that will allow a new hypothesis to be formed. Remember to try to disconfirm your theory, rather than confirm it.
3. Try and come up with alternative explanations. Brainstorm, bounce ideas around, but above all look for some different way of understanding the events.
4. Use all your knowledge. We all have experience in multiple walks of life, we need to draw on all of our knowledge, not just the limited subset that we might describe as having to do with investing.
5. Do not come to a conclusion, especially before you start. Suspending judgment until you have more data is a perfectly valid thing to do.

Using this as part of a checklist is a key element of the investing toolkit, and this is especially true *after* you've invested. Perhaps the critical thing is to remember why we're investing, which, surprisingly, may not be as obvious as you might think.

LESSON 12
_____

The sunk cost fallacy and commitment bias are liable to induce you to stay with an investment that is failing. Loss aversion will tend to keep us in loser stocks anyway, but this can apply to runaway winners as well. Don't ignore events that don't fit your prior expectations, and always try to explain them.

LOVE YOUR KIDS, NOT YOUR STOCKS

Rationally there's only one good reason to own a stock: you think you're going to make money from it. If you think you can make more money by owning a different stock then you should sell the one you own and buy the one you don't. Obviously this is complicated by the fact that we don't know for sure what will happen in the future, but the general idea is, you'd have thought, quite simple.

Yet as anyone who has spent any time in the company of private investors will know, we can become terribly, terribly attached to our stocks. Even sensible people can sometimes develop crushes on the most unsuitable investments, where logic flies out of the window. There are times you might even think that we end up in love with our stocks.

Well, guess what? We do.

The underlying metaphor is love, but the psychological bias is one we've met previously—affect, the faint whisper of emotion that guides us through life. Research by Meir Statman, Kenneth Fisher, and Deniz Anginer[28] suggests that people seem to treat stocks they think will have high returns—the stocks they like—as though they are also low risk. In fact, the opposite tends to be true, and unloved stocks tend to perform better than loved ones.

When Jaakko Aspara and Henrikki Tikkanen[29] dug into this problem, they came up with some quite startling findings. Firstly, and not so unsurprisingly, they found that when an investor has a choice between two stocks with the same expected return they will favor the one they like the most. However, they also found that the feeling of affection for a company could override financial analysis—in effect, people will invest in a firm with a lower expected return because they like it.

Even more startlingly, they also discovered that where an individual identified with the stock, feeling that they shared core values, they were more likely to be motivated to invest in the company. This suggests that we gain some form of emotional benefit from investing in companies that we believe are aligned with our views, over and above any potential financial benefit.

Well, it's not for me to argue that this is entirely wrong. Clearly people who feel strongly about smoking or weapons or the environment may be very strongly motivated to avoid investing in firms that deal in these areas. If this is the case, then you need to set your filters appropriately. However, otherwise I would strongly argue that whether you like a company or not should have no influence on your investment decisions.

It's quite likely that affect has a role to play in both the overpricing and underpricing of certain stocks. Corporations that have shocked on the downside may well be punished by the double whammy of a financial downgrade and negative affect—this is one area where we may find bargains. On the flip side, the glamour stocks that are in the public eye, with wonderful products and fantastic marketing, may require us to pay premiums in order to be associated with the buzz. This will often translate into wonder stories of how a company can grow its earnings exponentially forever—it's the halo effect.

My advice is simple—whenever you feel the need to associate yourself with a halo go analyze a few numbers and try and figure out what a firm needs to do to maintain its rating. Often, when you do some analysis and start listing the assumptions that are necessary to make the numbers add up you very rapidly come to the obvious conclusion: love your wife, your kids, and the family dog, but not your stocks.

LESSON 13

The corporate affect heuristic leads us into investing in corporations we like, and paying a premium for firms exhibiting positive halos. Usually this is not a sensible proposition, and can fairly easily be demonstrated by analyzing the future earnings potential—and by listing out the assumptions needed to justify the rating. Stocks with negative affect, on average, produce better returns.

COGNITIVE REPAIRS

By now you will, I hope, have reached the point where you're thinking that if all of this psychological mayhem is so well understood then there really ought to be some way of improving our investing behavior. The grab bag of ideas presented in this chapter are obviously useful tools, but surely there's some overarching method of dealing with the issues?

Well, sadly, the general answer to this is that there isn't. Behavioral bias is fiendishly difficult to eradicate, because it's built into our general patterns of operation for good reasons. I've worked in organizations where the psychological flaws in the makeup of the managers were easy to discern, but getting them to do something about them was almost impossible; this is just blind spot bias and the fundamental attribution error in operation.

Yet people can point to the fact that while the laboratory evidence appears to suggest that we're hopelessly compromised we are still able, as a species, to achieve great things. The behavioral psychologist Gerd Gigerenzer[30] has argued—persuasively in my opinion—that many of the findings of the behavioral finance school are illusions caused by narrow framing. We'll look at this in the final section of this chapter.

However, human history is a vast and exponentially growing directory of inventions and achievements—somehow, despite our individual ineptness, we are able to make progress and overcome our biases. Personally I believe that it's bias that makes us so amazing. People will single-mindedly pursue ideas through to remarkable conclusions in the face of the evidence and the logic. However, we all need to remember that what we're seeing is survivorship bias in operation: we only ever see the Warren Buffetts, the Richard Bransons, the Bill Gateses of the world. All the Toms, Dicks, and Sallys who tried and failed are lost to history.

So the rest of us, who aspire to moderate wealth and general happiness, need to avoid the extremes of psychological incompetence and seek a middle ground. One way of attempting this is through an idea known as Cognitive Repairs, developed by Chip Heath, Richard Larrick, and Joshua Klayman.[31] Their focus is on organizations rather than individuals, but I believe that a key part of successful investing is developing your own network of associates who you can interact with.

They identify a range of significant behavioral biases and then draw on examples to show the kinds of things that can be done to resist them. The important thing, though, is to institutionalize them; it's simply not enough to recognize problems, you need to develop a process to deal with them. Let's take a couple of examples.

One example given is that people prefer explanations that make themselves feel better. We know this is true, it's simple self-serving bias. However, what we need to recognize is that it's not success or failure that matters in any given situation but our ability to cogently explain our results. If you can't really explain what happened then you don't have any ability to repeat the result—or to avoid repeating it. To do this effectively you need to have people you can trust to force you to explain yourself.

Another example is that we tend to only consider a part of the relevant information when it comes to making decisions. This is a feature of availability—we recall the information that is accessible to us. The cognitive repair for this is simple—by introducing processes that require people to examine the widest possible range of information.

The trick is to base these cognitive repairs on our own faults. Biases are so wide-ranging and difficult to keep track of that if we try to cover all of them we'll end up mired in an impossible quagmire of rules and cross-checks. But this can only be developed out of personal experience, and we don't want to be making big mistakes in the meantime.

LESSON 14

Some corporations have learned to manage the behavioral biases of their employees by introducing cognitive repair strategies that accept the inevitability of the underlying biases, but attempt to repair the damage, wherever possible. This is a strategy we'll look at in the next chapter, but at an individual level.

SATISFICING

I want to end this extended discussion of our various failings in a slightly odd way—by discussing the failings of the researchers whose findings we're attempting to overcome, because not everyone agrees that the findings of behavioral research are clear-cut and straightforward.

One of the most effective critics of the standard theories about why we're biased is the German psychologist Gerd Gigerenzer, who has argued that many of these explanations are simply too complex to be believable. Instead, he suggests that many of our peculiar habits can be explained by something called satisficing.

Satisficing is an idea created by the polymathic American Herb Simon,[32] who argued that we don't have the cognitive bandwidth to optimize our decisions—we simply can't think through all of the possible options. So when we satisfice we're basically finding a solution that's satisfactory and satisfying—a good enough solution.

Gigerenzer[33] has taken this idea and developed some satisficing algorithms to see if the idea works—and the results have been surprising. For instance, he shows that the classical idea that the more knowledge you have the better your decision will be is probably wrong. In fact, it argues—and is supported by some evidence—that sometimes the more data you have the worse your results will be.

This idea, that many—if not all—of our biases are generated because the human brain is using "fast and frugal" heuristics to make snap judgments under conditions of uncertainty is very attractive. It certainly explains a lot of human behavior that otherwise doesn't make a lot of sense.

A second problem is that of so-called ecological validity. This argues that sticking humans in laboratories and subjecting them to strange tests that have no relevance to their real-world activities is bound to produce odd results. And, again, I'd have to agree that there's plenty to concern the scientists in this regard.

Nonetheless, I think most of the findings we've discussed so far are quite robust. Unfortunately, stock markets are laboratories—laboratories on a grand scale, maybe, but they're not to be confused with real life. If this is true, it's a grand irony—behavioral finance is good for finance, but not so useful for the rest of our lives.

LESSON 15

Behavioral finance has a lot to teach us about how we should and shouldn't invest, but it doesn't necessarily tell us about how we should behave the rest of the time. Our biases are with us for good reasons and in everyday life they don't often guide us wrongly. The trick is to understand when to trust our intuitions and when to stand back and think them through—and when it comes to investing it never hurts to delay a decision in order to think it through.

THE SEVEN KEY TAKEAWAYS

This chapter has looked at a raft of things we can do to debias ourselves, to help remove the worst excessive of behavioral bias.

Let's draw together a few key ideas from this chapter before we move on. The main takeaways are:

1. Try to learn to focus on numbers rather than feelings. The way markets work if we avoid big losses we'll tend to make decent gains.
2. Focus on value investing rather than momentum-based strategies; it tends to be more resilient to changes in the way the herd moves. Stocks tend to mean revert, so buying against the herd, as long as there's a margin of safety, is usually the safer option.
3. Short sellers tend to do a lot of fundamental analysis—don't ignore their findings, but a well-diversified portfolio will save you from a heap of confusion and misery.
4. Develop methods for debiasing, not just intuition. A best guess at future earnings, which can then be analyzed to see where it went wrong, is better than no guess at all.
5. Feedback is essential to debiasing—experience will help, but constant feedback, regularly analyzed, will improve your investing.
6. Don't pay too much attention to media stories; they're designed to be salient, but don't allow yourself to be convinced that there is any model that can save you from your own biases—there isn't, you have to figure this out for yourself.
7. Don't believe you can ever overcome bias. You can't, it's an accidental outcome of our brains' attempts to make fast decisions in a data rich world. If you ever think you've got it cracked you're in big trouble.

So, all well and good, but how do we pull all of this knowledge together to help us overcome the issues of bias? That's the challenge we look at in the next chapter.

NOTES

1. Thomas Keusch, Laury H. H. Bollen, and Harold F. D. Hassink, "Self-Serving Bias in Annual Report Narratives: An Empirical Analysis of the Impact of Economic Crises," *European Accounting Review* 21, no. 3 (2012): 623–648.
2. Feng Li, "Managers' Self-Serving Attribution Bias and Corporate Financial Policies" (July 12, 2010). Available at http://ssrn.com/abstract=1639005 or http://dx.doi.org/10.2139/ssrn.1639005.
3. Narasimhan Jegadeesh and Sheridan Titman, "Returns to Buying Winners and Selling Losers: Implications for Stock Market Efficiency," *Journal of Finance* 48, no. 1 (1993): 65–91.
4. M. Scott Wilson, "Are Momentum Strategies Still Profitable for U.S. Equity?" (October 14, 2010). Available at http://ssrn.com/abstract=1951137 or http://dx.doi.org/10.2139/ssrn.1951137.
5. Debarati Bhattacharya, Raman Kumar, and Gokhan Sonaer, "Momentum Loses Its Momentum: Implications for Market Efficiency," Midwest Finance

Association 2012 Annual Meetings Paper, November 7, 2012. Available at http://ssrn.com/abstract=1928764 or http://dx.doi.org/10.2139/ssrn.1928764.

6. Werner F. M. de Bondt and Richard H. Thaler, "Further Evidence on Investor Overreaction and Stock Market Seasonality," *Journal of Finance* 42, no. 3 (1987): 557–581.

7. Keven Q. Wang, "Mean-Reversion and Momentum" (working paper 2006).

8. James Edward Meeker, *Short Selling* (New York and London: Harper & Bros., 1932).

9. Edward M. Miller, "Risk, Uncertainty, and Divergence of Opinion," *Journal of Finance* 32, no. 4 (1977): 1151–1168.

10. Jennifer Francis, Mohan Venkatachalam, and Yun Zhang, "Do Short Sellers Convey Information About Changes in Fundamentals or Risk?" (2005). SSRN 815668.

11. Harry Markowitz, "Portfolio Selection," *Journal of Finance* 7, no. 1 (1952): 77–91.

12. Jason Zweig, "Your Money and Your Brain," *Money Magazine* (2007): 104–109.

13. Meir Statman, "How Many Stocks Make a Diversified Portfolio?" *Journal of Financial and Quantitative Analysis* 22, no. 3 (1987): 353–363.

14. www.efficientfrontier.com/ef/900/15st.htm.

15. Edward S. O'Neal, "How Many Mutual Funds Constitute a Diversified Mutual Fund Portfolio?" *Financial Analysts Journal* 53 (1997): 37–46.

16. Andrew Clare and Nick Motson, "How Many Alternative Eggs Should You Put in Your Investment Basket?" (July 10, 2008). Available at http://ssrn.com/abstract=1157884 or http://dx.doi.org/10.2139/ssrn.1157884.

17. Raymond S. Nickerson, "Confirmation Bias: A Ubiquitous Phenomenon in Many Guises," *Review of General Psychology* 2, no. 2 (1998): 175.

18. Peter C. Wason and Diana Shapiro, "Natural and Contrived Experience in a Reasoning Problem," *Quarterly Journal of Experimental Psychology* 23, no. 1 (1971): 63–71.

19. JaeHong Park, Prabhudev Konana, Bin Gu, Alok Kumar, and Rajagopal Raghunathan, "Confirmation Bias, Overconfidence, and Investment Performance: Evidence from Stock Message Boards," McCombs Research Paper Series No. IROM-07-10 (July 12, 2010). Available at http://ssrn.com/abstract=1639470 or http://dx.doi.org/10.2139/ssrn.1639470.

20. Leslie Hannah, "The 'Divorce' of Ownership from Control from 1900 Onwards: Re-calibrating Imagined Global Trends," *Business History* 49, no. 4 (2007): 404–438.

21. Dale J. Langford et al., "Social Modulation of Pain as Evidence for Empathy in Mice," *Science* 312, no. 5782 (2006): 1967–1970.

22. J. Edward Russo and Paul J. H. Schoemaker, "Managing Overconfidence," *Sloan Management Review* 33, no. 2 (1992): 7–17.

23. Robert J. Shiller, "Do Stock Prices Move Too Much to Be Justified by Subsequent Changes in Dividends?" *American Economic Review* 71 (1981): 421–436.

24. Kevin Dowd, John Cotter, Chris Humphrey, and Margaret Woods, "How Unlucky Is 25-Sigma?" (2011). arXiv preprint arXiv:1103.5672.

25. Barry M. Staw, "Knee-Deep in the Big Muddy: A Study of Escalating Commitment to a Chosen Course of Action," *Organizational Behavior and Human Performance* 16, no. 1 (1976): 27–44.

26. Hal R. Arkes and Catherine Blumer, "The Psychology of Sunk Cost," *Organizational Behavior and Human Decision Processes* 35, no. 1 (1985): 124–140.

27. Winston R. Sieck, Jennifer L. Smith, and Louise J. Rasmussen, "Metacognitive Strategies for Making Sense of Cross-Cultural Encounters," *Journal of Cross-Cultural Psychology* 44, no. 6 (2013): 1007–1023.

28. Meir Statman, Kenneth L. Fisher, and Deniz Anginer, "Affect in a Behavioral Asset-Pricing Model," *Financial Analysts Journal* (2008): 20–29.

29. Jaakko Aspara and Henrikki Tikkanen, "Individuals' Affect-Based Motivations to Invest in Stocks: Beyond Expected Financial Returns and Risks," *Journal of Behavioral Finance* 12, no. 2 (2011): 78–89.

30. Gerd Gigerenzer, "On Narrow Norms and Vague Heuristics: A Reply to Kahneman and Tversky," *Psychological Review* 103 (1996): 592–596.

31. Chip Heath, Richard P. Larrick, and Joshua Klayman, "Cognitive Repairs: How Organizational Practices Can Compensate for Individual Shortcomings," *Research in Organizational Behavior* 20 (1998): 1–37.

32. Herbert A. Simon, "Rational Choice and the Structure of the Environment," *Psychological Review* 63, no. 2 (1956): 129–138.

33. Gerd Gigerenzer, Peter M. Todd, and ABC Research Group, *Simple Heuristics That Make Us Smart* (New York: Oxford University Press, 1999), 563–607.

CHAPTER 7

Good Enough Investing

So, I hope we're all prepared to face up to the nasty fact that we're all biased, all confused, and all self-deluded. But in the land of the blind the one-eyed are monarchs, and we don't need to improve ourselves very much in order to make a difference, relative to everyone else. This chapter will bring together the research I've presented and some of the methods I've only so far mentioned, to come up with a good enough process for investors when they come to make investing decisions.

But I want to be clear: this is just the start of a journey. The process of becoming a better, less biased investor can't be summarized in one short chapter. In fact, as we'll see, my aim is to teach you to fish because if you buy a man a fish he eats for a day but if you teach a man to fish then he eats forever. Only we have to deal with the fact that sometimes the fish disappear, and then the lake. And then the volcano goes off and nothing looks the same again.

Remember: markets are adaptive, people are reflexive, and the ground underneath our feet is unstable. But if we understand where that instability comes from we can, at least, start to build earthquake proof homes.

I want to start this chapter with seven simple takeaways from the vast amount of research we've covered in this book. These are my guiding principles, and I try to revisit them every so often to see if I'm still honoring them.

#1: THE RULE OF SEVEN

We can only deal with a limited set of ideas before we lose focus—this is the issue of information overload. This is probably best known from Sheena Iyengar and Mark Lepper's work, who showed that if a shopper was presented with a few jams to choose from they were far more likely to make a purchase than if they were presented with dozens and dozens.[1] People are overwhelmed by too much choice, procrastinate, and fail to make a choice.

So, the idea that we can gather vast amounts of information and distill it down to a single decision is nonsense. The research on horse handicappers shows that once they get more than a few pieces of data their ability to make effective decisions declines. We know why this is—it's called the Rule of Seven and George Miller showed back in the 1950s that it's related to a physiological restriction in our short-term memories—we can only hold seven, plus or minus two, chunks of information for processing at any one time.[2]

Remember: we satisfice, we do a good enough job to get by in everyday life. And the same is true in investing: we need to do a good enough job, with the tools we have available to us. Gathering vast amounts of data and then trying to make sense of it won't lead to better outcomes, and will probably lead to worse ones.

LESSON 1

We can only deal with a limited subset of information—about seven chunks. So our investing decision-making process needs to be built around this limitation, otherwise we'll start procrastinating and making worse decisions.

#2: HOMO SAPIENS, TOOL MAKER

One of the defining characteristics of our species is the way that we use tools. Tools are wonderful things and they vastly extend our natural abilities. And in this instance we need to use tools to extend our limited satisficing capabilities. I've already discussed a couple of simple tools that can help you, decision trees and checklists, and we'll look at these again later in the chapter.

However, I have to stress that these tools are not a substitute for thinking for yourself. Used correctly they can extend our ability to process data beyond the Rule of Seven, but used incorrectly they become a crutch which will fail just as soon as market conditions fail. It's critical—absolutely essential—that you use these tools as a support mechanism rather than as the primary decision-making method.

Remember that the world's greatest financial organizations went up in flames in 2008 because their leaders were, all too often, relying on models rather than looking at what was really going on. They'd replaced proper analysis with an unthinking reliance on methods they didn't really understand. And you need to understand what you're doing it you're going to consistently succeed across different times and markets.

LESSON 2

We can augment our decision making with tools, but we need to understand these. This is why you're going to have to develop your own process, rather than relying on me to create one for you.

#3: META-METHODS

The very flexibility of humanity means that no method I can give you will work for all time. I could produce something that works really well now, and would beguile people into thinking I've found a miracle investing technique but it would simply be another application of the Sharpshooter Effect.

This is another key point—*nothing works forever*. This means we don't just need a method that works for us now but one that we can constantly adjust as conditions change. We need a meta-method, and to work, I believe, this method needs to help us adjust our approach just as much as we need to adjust it.

RULE 3

In investing, nothing works forever. Our tools need to be adaptive, because that's what markets are.

#4: BE SKEPTICAL

Easy to say, hard to do. Confirmation bias is one of the worst offenders in the universe of behavioral biases, but is one that can be overcome with the proper attitude toward stocks and other investments. It is, I believe, an issue of satisficing—we simply don't want to put the extra effort in to disconfirm our beliefs, but it simply has to be done.

Running a few simple tools can help us deal with confirmation bias, because they can identify issues we will otherwise gloss over. But really this is an attitude issue; if you approach the topic of investing in the right way then confirmation bias can be controlled. But it can never be defeated.

RULE 4

Confirmation bias is one of the keystone behavioral biases, which we need to directly target if we're going to avoid the worst pitfalls. Always be skeptical, because everyone wants a piece of you.

#5: DON'T TRUST YOURSELF

If you've learned one thing in this book it ought to be this: we are unreliable witnesses to our own lives. We need to recognize that our beliefs and memories are temporary facets of a whole range of environmental, temperamental, and behavioral conditions and that we can't simply rely on our own unadorned judgments.

Whether this is our rampant overconfidence, or issues around availability or salience of information, or our issues of emotional control, we're subject to forces we often barely comprehend. In this environment we have to learn to rely less on subjective opinion and more on hard facts. And sometimes we have to take the long view. In particular you must avoid mental accounting. All of your capital is in the same pot, there is only one exception.

The exception is that everyone should start with a rainy day fund. This is the money you would need in the event you suffer a crisis in your life. Most of us will at some point—whether we lose our jobs, a loved one falls ill, we find ourselves unexpectedly single, or some other situation we cannot possibly anticipate.

So you should have a rainy day fund set to one side. If possible, this should be sufficient to last at least three months. The critical thing is that you should try to avoid, at all costs, being forced to liquidate parts of your portfolio in a desperate hurry. This exposes you to temporary downturns in the market and, worse still, likely means you're making investment decisions in a state of high emotion.

Remember, emotionless investing is ideal. And whatever you do, do not borrow to invest. Really experienced investors can do this because they understand the risks, but most people I know who do this end up losing.

> ## RULE 5
>
> We can't rely on our own judgment, without calling on other sources. We are biased and we often don't realize it, so thinking we can be successful without some form of outside help is generally wishful thinking. But avoid mental accounting at all costs; it will destroy your returns if you don't.

#6: SELF-CONTROL IS KEY

In a famous experiment, the psychologist Walter Mischel showed that one-third of four-year-olds will wait an undefined period of time in a room alone with a piece of candy in order to get a second piece. The other two-thirds simply ate the candy they were presented with. Remarkably, Mischel and other researchers went on to show that the kids with self-control had markedly better life outcomes—and they were much better with money.[3]

Self-control is critical to successful investing. This may mean putting yourself out of the reach of temptation by using passive index trackers and regular investing or it may mean learning to be calm in the face of huge tides of emotion. But if you are the sort of person who regularly buys stuff on impulse and likes to run up credit card bills without worrying about how you're going to pay for them you're probably going to struggle over the long term.

This is important: if you can't delay the impulse for immediate gratification you're going to be a poor investor. It's far better to hand the task over to a third party.

> ## RULE 6
>
> Self-control is key to managing behavioral bias. If you can't manage this then don't invest yourself. But you'll probably be a nightmare for your adviser as well.

#7: GET FEEDBACK

I've said it before and I'll say it again (honest, I will). The best way to become a better investor is to get feedback. I'm skeptical, to say the least, that individuals can do this for themselves. We find it all too easy to gloss over the errors, to engage in mental accounting and move the losses somewhere else, to avoid taking losses in the hope that everything will work out alright, and to perform a myriad of other things that don't help us in the slightest.

The techniques in the rest of this chapter deal with two things: helping you debias yourself in making decisions and helping you build up a system of proper feedback. In the end, however, nothing beats an independent pair of eyes scrutinizing your performance and behavior.

RULE 7

Get feedback, as often as possible.

A BEHAVIORAL INVESTING FRAMEWORK

The most important lesson in this book is the need for you to figure out how to adapt your own behavior to the market. This can't really be taught, and is something you have to work through for yourself. But I do think that we can put some structure around this process, using the simple rules we've covered, in order to provide a framework.

The framework here is a simple one, and it's one that's used across a whole variety of industries. The aim is to ensure that we follow a process and that the process naturally adapts to our learnings. At the heart of this method are two artifacts—documents if you like—the personal investing mission statement and the investment checklist. These must, ultimately, be yours, but I'm going to explain how to create them and to adapt them.

We've already touched on the mission statement, but this is your cornerstone, it's the statement of principles that you will rely on when things become uncertain; as they're bound to do at some point. The investment checklist is a way of bundling up all of the individual things we have to think about into a set of checks: it's a tool, and it allows us to overcome the Rule of Seven, because tools are designed to overcome our mental and physical limitations.

That said, the devil is in the details. People can come up with elaborate and complex justifications for all sorts of exceptional behavior. The aim here, though, is to make sure we write down what we do, and why we're doing it, so we can review it later on. The seven stages of the framework are set out in Figure 7.1.

1. Make it personal. Write down your personal investing mission statement.
2. Build a checklist. This needs to cover your investing criteria, and also your behavioral ones.

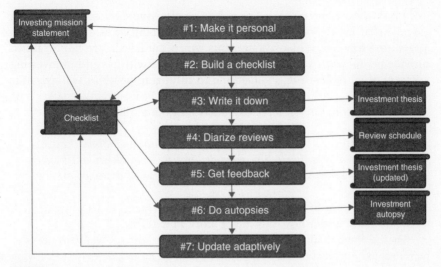

FIGURE 7.1   Seven Stages of Behavioral Investing Framework

3. Write it down. Write down your investment thesis for any given investment decision.
4. Diarize reviews of your decisions. Make sure you do them.
5. Review your decisions and get some real feedback.
6. When you finally sell a stock, do an autopsy, and make sure you learn
   the lessons. It's all too easy to let this slide, especially if you're licking
   your wounds.
7. Update your mission statement and checklist with the learnings from
   reviews and autopsies.

Follow this framework and you'll discover one of two things. Either you
will improve as an investor or you will find that you simply can't control
your instinctive urges. If you're in the latter group you need a damn fine
adviser, and you need to stop investing for yourself.

STEP #1: MAKING IT PERSONAL

Although I'd love to be able to provide you with simple advice on how to
conquer your investment biases, the truth is that if I could do that I would be
a very rich man already. The issue is that what will work for me won't always
work for you, so you need to start by making your approach to the problem
personal. This starts with your personal investing mission statement.

I know, we've probably all been subjected to some ridiculous branding exercise that led to some meaningless statement that we're all supposed to attach to. However, mission statements, when done well, are important to provide people with a sense of purpose. When we're lost—and in investing you will often be lost—it is something to turn to in order to reassert your sense of values.

So my personal mission statement, as I set out earlier, is:

My mission is to invest in high quality corporations when they are undervalued relative to the market, and to hold them until such time they become extremely overvalued relative to the market.

There are a lot of complex things in this statement, so let's just unpack them and think about how this might work in real life.

Firstly: "high quality corporations." What's that about? Well, this needs to be translated into real financial metrics. I'm not going to suddenly start diving down into the details of financial analysis, but broadly I'm looking for corporations that have a track record of delivering above average returns (which suggests a defensible moat) and that have clear and transparent accounts.

Secondly: "undervalued relative to the market." This is a statement about intrinsic value—that I believe the company will produce superior returns to that of the market, which in turn suggests that at a given moment in time the firm is undervalued relative to the market. To be blunt, I hunt for possible investments in firms that have suffered recent bad news and bad publicity—remember that markets overreact to news in both directions.

Thirdly: "extremely overvalued relative to the market." This indicates, I hope, that I will tend to hold investments for a relatively long time and will do so beyond the point at which the corporation is no longer fairly valued. There are a number of reasons for this:

1. It's hard to find quality stocks at decent prices; once you have one that can deliver superior returns then trading away those returns for a temporary, one-off benefit rarely makes any sense.
2. The research on overconfidence clearly states that most times I try and trade I will likely get it wrong, and reduce my overall returns. All things being equal I prefer to sit on my hands, as long as the original investment thesis continues to hold.
3. I will sell when the overvaluation becomes extreme—when a firm starts to trade on massive multiples of its earnings then I start to get concerned, because this either indicates the presence of herding behavior, where people are following each other, halo effects in operation or, most likely, a combination of such effects.

- I will also sell if my original investment thesis turns out to be wrong. It's inevitable that I will make mistakes, so it's important to write down exactly why you're investing in a stock and then regularly review this. If the stock is performing badly and it's clear that the original idea was wrong then I will sell. This perhaps is the hardest thing of all to do, because loss aversion is a killer. But the more you do it, the easier it gets.

This approach also explains why, as I mentioned in the section on anchoring, many of my investments will initially fall below the purchase price. If you're buying on bad news then the market will tend to keep on pushing the price down, well below any level you might think reasonable. If I were to sell every time I see a loss in my portfolio I'd not have much left. Tricky stuff, this behavioral investing.

So, start with a mission statement, revise it regularly until you're happy with it, and return to it frequently when you're reviewing your results. Because you are going to review your results, aren't you?

LESSON 1

Commit yourself with a personal investing mission statement. This is your anchor, don't let it drift without making a conscious decision.

STEP #2: BUILD AN INVESTING CHECKLIST

The evidence that checklists improve any behavior that is based on repeatable steps is very, very strong. The original results came out of Peter Pronovost's simple checklist to prevent an infection issue in hospitals—and the results were astonishing.[4] There was nothing new presented, it was just the practice of making sure people followed all the steps that made the difference.

Checklists force people to go through the process of actually considering every step that's listed. With a checklist we can make the Rule of Seven redundant.

There are two issues with this. First, that the checklist is only as good as the effort you put into it and your willingness to obey it. Pronovost's checklist is still often not enforced and he suggests this is a combination of ego, a dislike of bureaucracy, and an industry that's focused on exciting new research rather than fixing mundane problems. And, of course, this is about overconfidence—and checklists help us deal with this.

The second issue is what do you do with the results of the checklist—
because you'll likely find that there are multiple issues with any investment.
It's not as straightforward as making sure someone doesn't die of a simple
infection. Well, my sneaky response is that I don't care about the mechanics
of investing: there are a lot of resources out there to help you run investing
metrics in order to determine whether or not a given stock makes a good
investment. What my checklist is going to do for you is force you to address
your own issues—it's not so much whether or not a stock is a good investment for you, it's more whether or not you are in the right frame of mind to
make the correct decision.

This is behavioral investing: get the person right and you're halfway to
getting the investing decisions right.

LESSON 2
_____

Build a checklist. But this one's personal.

STEP #3: WRITE IT DOWN

When you make an investment write down your investment thesis. Try to
come up with a statement of why you are making the investment, what you
expect to get out of it. Perform an expected value analysis and use decision
trees. It's not hard, and if you're wrong so much the better, because it's easy
to go back and play with the numbers until you get the right result, the result that actually happened in real life. Remember, we learn far more from
our mistakes than we do from our successes.

Writing it down allows us to review what we've done. If you rely on
your memory you're exposing yourself to false memory syndrome and hindsight bias. You will _not_ remember correctly.

Again, I encourage you to develop your own system of notes, but the
following is a starting point:

- Write down why you believe this stock meets the requirements of your
  mission statement. If it doesn't (and exceptions do occur) write down
  why you still think it makes sense to invest.
- Get a snapshot of all financial metrics at the point at which you decide
  to invest (everything, including stuff you don't use).
- Write down your investing thesis—why you're investing, what you

expect to get out of the stock in a year, three years, and five years (or whatever timescale you choose to invest over).

- Make sure your analysis is repeatable, whether it's an expected value approach or something else (you will forget to write things down and then find you can't replicate your results—no matter, do it better next time).
- Make a note of environmental factors (the weather, your own disposition, anything else you think is noteworthy). Stupid as this sounds it becomes useful data later on.
- Make a note of where you found the investing idea—whether it was a friend, an Internet forum, a newspaper article, or some financial filtering of your own.

You'll figure out other stuff as you go along. Three points:

1. Do it immediately, for preference start building the information before you invest. As soon as you own a stock commitment bias will kick in.
2. Do not edit your notes after the event. If you remember something relevant add it as an addition. You will be amazed at how often we try to rewrite history to make ourselves feel better.
3. Don't make exceptions. Once you do that you're lost.

LESSON 3

Write down why you're investing, and do it immediately.

STEP #4: DIARIZE REVIEWS

When you make an investment immediately diarize a review of the stock. I don't recommend doing this overly frequently but I'd suggest that you do one after three months, and then go to six-month reviews. Some people will prefer to do this at the point results or earnings updates are released, but I tend to lose sight of these dates, so I prefer to automate the process.

As we've seen, too frequent inspection of your shareholdings and their prices will tend to lead to overtrading, so it's important to get into the habit of not worrying about the daily ups and downs of stock prices. They aren't really relevant in the long term.

A bigger question is whether or not you should take account of actual news flow around the corporations you've invested in. The problem with news flow is that it will tend to be either sensationalized, in order to make a story—and will trigger emotional responses and create salience and availability issues—or it will be managed by PR departments who will tend to massage the information into a more palatable form. But the evidence is that stocks underreact to real news, both on the upside and the downside, so this is a potentially difficult area.

As in so many things in this area it's not simple and will depend upon the personality of the investor. I tend to review corporate announcements, looking for things that don't look or sound right—it's the idea that we should force ourselves to take notice of things that don't really fit our expectations.

The list of things to worry about includes management speak, where the tone of announcements is changing, odd corporate transactions, large gifts of stock options to managements who aren't obviously outperforming, and significant changes to accounting statements—particularly around accruals (I'll talk about accruals and exceptional items on the balance sheet later, but this is one area where accounting and psychology need to collide).

Critically, though, you must set trigger points for reviews. If you don't you almost certainly won't do them. We're all busy, we need all the help we can get.

LESSON 4

Make sure you know ahead of time when you're going to review your investments. Diarize reviews and decide how you want to treat newsflow, although I'd recommend not doing a full review every time something changes, it will drive you mad.

STEP #5: GET FEEDBACK

The purpose of a review is two-fold. Firstly, you should be reviewing the current state of your investment at the current point in time. By using a checklist you can analyze the stock against your original, or even your adapted, investing criteria and see whether it still meets your investing criteria. Usually I'd expect investors to hold stocks at prices they wouldn't normally buy at, because the alternative is to expose yourself to overconfidence and overtrading.

The second purpose is to generate data, by comparing your original expectations against the current status. This is why what you write down when you make the investment is so critical—because it's the baseline against which you can analyze your progress and determine what you've done wrong. This is not simple, and will build over time as you begin to pick out the patterns in your own behavior.

The most important thing is to try to make the review objective rather than subjective. It's all too easy to fall into the trap of arguing that your original investment thesis was right, but it just hasn't happened yet—this is one of the classic arguments used by experts to show that their predictions weren't wrong. Of course, this may be true, but very often it isn't—and when circumstances change we need to be prepared to change our minds.

This assumes, of course, that we're trying to generate our own feedback. If at all possible it would be better if you have a buddy that forces you through the process, and tries to explain your reasoning. If you hold a significant number of stocks, that might not be possible on every occasion—but even a few such external reviews will help to provide a different viewpoint on your investing decisions.

LESSON 5

Make sure your review covers both the current state of an investment—should you buy more, sell, or hold—and also the historical reasoning that got you into it in the first place—does the investment logic still hold, and if not, what went wrong?

STEP #6: DO AUTOPSIES

However an investment works out you need to carry out an autopsy. This can sometimes be the hardest thing of all—because often the last thing you want to do when you've gotten rid of a stock for an enormous loss (and you will, we all have) is start thinking about what an idiot you were.

But autopsies are critical to the feedback process, because it's only when we finally pull the trigger that we can realistically start to think about what went wrong. It's only by going back to the beginning, reviewing our investment thesis, and working our way through the various reviews that we can see how things went wrong and start the long, painful process of trying to make sure that this doesn't happen again.

I also want you to do intermediate autopsies as well. Remember that loss aversion will often stop us from taking a loss when we should abandon ship, so it's important that we should review stocks that have taken a big dip to try and figure out if we should still be holding them. I'd suggest a 30 percent drop is a good point to carry out an intermediate autopsy—you may decide that this is simply the market being fickle and your investment thesis still holds. Stuff happens. But you should at least pull up the floorboards and have a look.

And, annually, I think there needs to be a spring cleaning, when you review the stocks you sold and the stocks you analyzed and didn't buy. Sins of commission—holding losers—are more painful than sins of omission—selling winners (or even failing to buy them)—but forcing yourself to go back and look at these is an important part of the accelerated learning process I want you to go through.

Remember, as well, that just when you think you've got this investment thing cracked the markets will turn all moody on you. Investment markets are fickle beasts, and it pays to be humble in the face of them. Once you get lax on your method you'll pay the price. Believe me, I should know.

LESSON 6

Carry out autopsies on stocks when you sell them, whether they're winners or losers. Carry out annual autopsies on the stocks you sold and the stocks you never bought. Keep learning.

STEP #7: UPDATE ADAPTIVELY

It's one thing to do all of this analysis and review, but it's another thing to effectively learn from it. Remember the Rule of Seven—we can only really keep seven things in mind at any one time. So any lessons we learn need to be reflected back into the methods we're using.

So, if we're using a checklist or some other tool to analyze investment opportunities then we need to be prepared to update the tool in light of new information. We need to address our approach to investing if it's consistently not working. We need to build feedback into the *method* as well as into analysis of individual investments.

This is even more essential because of the adaptive nature of markets. What might work during a long bull market might well start failing in a bear market, when uncertainty increases. Although I can go on indefinitely about value investing methods relying on intrinsic value and long-term stock holding as a way to overcome the ebbs and flows of markets, I also recognize that this will lead to underperformance over extended periods of years before mean regression kicks in. This is not for everyone.

However, the key thing is that whatever your preferred approach to investing you continually review it to make sure it works. All too many people fail to analyze their results and continue to lose money, at least relative to the market, because of this. They continue to overtrade and throw away their gains yet very often they think they're successful investors. Sadly they're not.

The fools will always be with us; but we don't have to be one of them.

LESSON 7

Don't just rely on the method you have—keep improving it. Markets are adaptive, we need to modify our behavior in response.

THE WORST OFFENDERS

To be honest it's almost impossible to identify the worst behavioral biases, but simply to prove a point I'll take a stab at it, describing how the Behavioral Investing Framework helps address each point: the cognitive repairs we're trying to affect by using the method. If you were to think that this is an example of the Texan Sharpshooter Effect in operation I wouldn't be inclined to disagree with you, but we need to start somewhere:

- *Overconfidence.* Checklists are an automatic defense against overconfidence—if you use them correctly. The problem is we're inclined to cut corners.
- *Loss aversion and the disposition effect.* We sell our winners and hold our losers. The cumulative effect of reviews, autopsies, and feedback of all kinds will be to convince you that this is wrong. Selling at a loss is not an assault on your integrity, it's just a commonsense approach to a perfectly normal mistake.
- *Mental accounting.* The process covers everything outside of your checking account and your rainy day funds. You cannot put some stuff aside and treat it differently. This is one pool of capital, manage it properly.

- *Hindsight bias.* Although hindsight bias is ineradicable, in writing down our reasons for what we do and then reviewing them we're forced to face up to the fact that our past selves weren't so smart. And neither are we.

- *Herding and confirmation bias.* If your research and analysis shows you that things are going wrong then you need to listen to it rather than the siren calls of people who don't understand or care. Believe in yourself, because the majority—at least the vocal majority—can be (and often are) wrong. This is one place where you shouldn't rely on other people to guide you right.

- *Blind spot bias.* We may believe that we're always right when everyone else is wrong but the evidence will make us confront the fact that we're not, and we'll be better investors for it. Delude yourself all you want that you're the best lover, greatest basketball player, fastest driver, or smartest shopper in existence—you'll find someone to believe you. But markets are unforgiving, and they can't be fooled.

- *Availability and salience.* If you only attend to the things you can bring to mind then you'll be driven by your memory's quirky interests and the most recently memorable information you can bring to mind. Forcing yourself through a checklist will eliminate most of this, because it will make you attend to other issues.

- *Emotion.* Reacting emotionally to some kind of event is natural, but usually unwise. Force yourself through the method and you will have to take some time to consider your decisions. It's a positive consequence of the approach.

- *Investment superstitions.* It's quite hard to continue to exhibit pigeon level superstitions in the face of data that you've generated yourself. Getting real data is what matters, rather than leaving it up to our brains to find illusory patterns.

- *Halos and narratives.* It's very, very hard to ignore the positive vibe and wonderful stories around some stocks. Sometimes it's not necessary to do so, but generally we need to look at what's underneath the covers. To be frank, it's unlikely that any method can make you ignore a blazingly exciting story to start with—but the results will be instructive.

- *Framing and social biases.* The approach says nothing about where you get your ideas, but it does require you to take a solitary approach to evaluating the results. It can't stop you posting on Facebook, but it can bring you face to face with your errors. Of course, deluded people will avoid this anyway, but there are some people you just can't help.

Whenever I've done something particularly stupid—and I still do, to this day—I retreat back to a single idea, one outlined by Richard Feynman at the end of his paper on the causes of the *Challenger* shuttle failure. He pointed out that logic and simple science had been ignored in targeting the goals of political necessity and public relations. In order to meet the deadlines, NASA's management had ignored the science. Feynman ended his paper:

> *For a successful technology, reality must take precedence over public relations, for nature cannot be fooled.*

In a far less important area, in our personal investing, the same is true today. We can fool ourselves, our friends, and the people whose opinions we value. But in the hard area of nickels and dimes markets will not be fooled. The only people who lose by not accepting this, by putting image before substance, is ourselves. Don't do it.

LESSON 8

Used wisely, the method can reduce the worst excesses of the worst of behavioral bias. Remember that markets can't be fooled where it matters most—in our pockets.

TOOLS

Our meta-method doesn't rely on you using decision trees and checklists, but I strongly advise that you do. The online materials that accompany this book include a tutorial to use decision trees and an extensive checklist to aim to eliminate behavioral error. You'll need to customize this checklist, over time, as you work through the issues that impact you.

You will also need to create summary review forms for your portfolio. I've handily included a few of these. They require you to include buying and selling prices, and market index values, and will automatically calculate your return against the market. If you're consistently making a loss against the market (by which I mean you're making less than the market average) then you will either need to start using index trackers or hand your investments over to a professional adviser.

Summary review forms should be tallied up at the end of each year. No more and no less. Annual reviews are quite sufficient for our needs—we don't want to expose ourselves to the fear and emotion of regular market updates.

LESSON 9

The online materials contain a bunch of stuff to help. You don't have to use them, you can develop your own, as long as they fit within the overall method. But I'd suggest starting here.

THE MECHANICS OF INVESTING

I want to end the chapter by discussing the stuff that we don't discuss: the mechanics of investing. Good investors don't simply rely on gut feel and hope, they do proper analysis and try to figure out what the likely future opportunities are. The problem with nearly all books that try and document this is that they open themselves up to one of two problems.

Firstly, anyone can find a few examples of successful investments that support their approach. This is the Texan Sharpshooter Effect at work again. It's in the failures that we find real evidence of how an approach works.

Secondly, we face the problem that a method that works today may not work tomorrow—it's the adaptive nature of markets. Even tried and tested methods such as value investing, which have worked over long periods, can go through long cycles where they don't work, which will try your patience and your wallet.

But there are a few things we can pick out of the research in this book that can help guide us a bit, and we need to bear these in mind as we roam the world's markets looking for investing opportunities:

- *Diversification.* Diversification is as close to a free lunch on the markets as we'll ever get. When everything goes down then it won't help us much, but diversifying across sectors and stocks can save us from most everything else. Index trackers are a great way of getting diversification, but they bring their own problems and if you use them make sure you have a basket of them, one index tracker is not diversification.
- *Frame broadly.* A similar point to the previous one—but don't have separate portfolios of different stocks—one for index trackers, one for blue chip stocks, one for speculative ones, and so on. This obscures your real performance and allows you to hide from your mistakes.

- *Mean reversion.* Across time and markets mean reversion does seem to work—stocks that have done well do less well and stocks that have done badly will outperform. It's a contrarian strategy and is, therefore, one that will tend to be defensive against behavioral bias. It is not, however, a cure-all: many badly performing stocks do badly because they're rubbish. Make sure you can tell the poor businesses from the good ones.
- *Moats.* Any business that can defend itself from competitive pricing is in a powerful position. I try and identify such stocks just in everyday life—Coca-Cola, Visa, and so on. Usually these businesses are far too expensive to buy but just occasionally something goes wrong and they go on sale. All things being equal a great stock at a good price is always a fantastic investment.
- *Avoid popular stocks and stories.* It's not an absolute rule but typically by the time an idea is popular then it's no longer a safe investment.
- *Fees and overtrading.* Fees destroy returns, overtrading generates fees. Overtrading is usually a sign of overconfidence anyway, so it's a warning sign that you're not doing your analysis very well or you're being fooled by your blind spot bias.
- *Always challenge advice.* Never, ever blindly accept advice even when it concurs with your own thinking. It's a good habit to get into to always challenge any idea because it forces you to confront your own confirmation bias. Better still, join a debating society, and make yourself argue for things you don't believe in.
- *Watch out for accruals.* Earnings that are not real earnings are always a danger. Corporations use all sorts of tricks to inflate their real earnings and do so quite legally. Look out for exceptional items which aren't exceptional and should be treated as normal operation costs. Look at financial results from multiple years—do these "exceptional" items recur? Above all, crosscheck the cash flow statement—it's harder to obscure this, because cash is cash not possible future revenue. Oh, and always cross-check cash in the bank against the interest earned—if the interest level looks low then the company is probably manipulating its year end to have maximum cash on hand.
- *Avoid IPOs.* Nearly all IPOs are being sold from a position of strength and we are on the wrong side of the equation, the wrong side of Akerlof's lemons. We may miss a few great investments but mainly it's safer not to go near these.
- *Don't fight the industry.* As private investors our edge over the institutions with their supercomputers, fabulously clever analysts, and fabulous riches is patience. We don't need to make our return this month or this quarter. We have an investing lifetime.

LESSON 10

No investing method will work all the time, but even so there are lessons which are constant. Make sure you include them in your investing checklist.

THE SEVEN KEY TAKEAWAYS

This chapter has looked at tools we can use to debias ourselves and a few simple reminders of things good investors should do.

Let's draw together a few key ideas from this chapter before we move on. The main takeaways are:

1. Don't try and gather too much information. Focus on key things and use tools to summarize data.
2. Do use tools to support your investing process, they will help with cognitive repairs and defend you against your own worst biases.
3. Always use a method that demands you analyze your actions—feedback is the best learning tool.
4. Continually revise your method. Markets adapt to their environment and the market is your environment, so you must adapt too.
5. Learn broad lessons, not specific ones. Some things are true over all times and all market conditions.
6. Maintain your self-control. Markets will go mad, you will make bad investment decisions, things will go wrong. Changing strategy without knowing why is the worst thing you can do.
7. Always question your advisers, personal or professional, and do so regardless of whether you agree with them or not. In fact, do so especially if you agree with them.

So, finally, I now want to look at the broader picture. Making money is great, but it shouldn't be an end in itself. To achieve happiness we need more than money. So what's the point of all this?

NOTES

1. Sheena S. Iyengar and Mark R. Lepper, "When Choice Is Demotivating: Can One Desire Too Much of a Good Thing?" *Journal of Personality and Social Psychology* 79, no. 6 (2000): 995–1006.

2. George A. Miller, "The Magical Number Seven, Plus or Minus Two: Some Limits on Our Capacity for Processing Information," *Psychological Review* 63, no. 2 (1956): 81.

3. Walter Mischel, Yuichi Shoda, and Monica L. Rodriguez, "Delay of Gratification," In *Choice Over Time*, ed. George Loewenstein and Jon Elste (New York: Russell Sage Foundation, 1992), 147.

4. Atul Gawande, "The Checklist," *The New Yorker* 83, no. 39 (2007): 86–95.

CHAPTER 8

A Few Myths More

It would be easy to end this ramble through the slightly dodgy outer limits of our inner lives with a summary of the main ideas and research, but I'd like to do something a little more ambitious. I want to try to identify some of the outcomes of the research, rather than just replaying it. For instance, do you know why you invest? If you think it's solely to make more money you're probably wrong.

In fact, the findings of behavioral psychology can illuminate all sorts of interesting areas of our psyches, and can help us dispel a whole range of silly myths that actually get in the way of us becoming better investors. For instance, here's an extraordinary finding. If you want a favorable decision from a judge, do everything you can to get a hearing early in the day or straight after lunch.

As it turns out, justice may be blind but she also gets hungry. Researchers Shai Danziger, Jonathan Levav, and Liora Avnaim-Pesso showed that the percentage of favorable hearings in a parole session drops from 65 percent to nearly zero as the morning unfolds, but jumps back to 65 percent straight after lunch.[1] The issue is known as ego depletion, but it really comes down to the fact that there's a cost to self-control in terms of our internal resources.

The psychologists have named this issue resource depletion and Anastasiya Pocheptsova, On Amir, Ravi Dhar, and Roy Baumeister's research suggests that it increases our tendency to use anchors and triggers our loss aversion anxieties, makes us more likely to procrastinate, and causes us to get confused by extraneous options.[2] This latter problem is also known as the decoy effect, and is a clever technique used by marketers, who use decoy options that no one would ever want to buy to deflect purchasers toward more expensive products.[3]

This is a right mish-mash of behavioral psychology, but the broad point is that the lessons in this book are not irrelevant outside of finance. In fact, they're central to the way we operate on a daily basis, and the way that we're manipulated by all sorts of people and organizations. The most critical

thing of all is self-control—and anything we can do to improve it will improve our life chances and our financial decision making. And these two
things are entwined. Money can't make us happy, but poverty is unlikely
to improve our state of mind. It's just that money shouldn't be the point of
all this.

So let's start this chapter by considering why we want to become better
investors. Oh, and don't invest on an empty stomach.

MYTH 1: MONEY MAKES US HAPPY

The common answer to why we want more money is "happiness." In fact,
it seems that money has only a tangential connection to happiness. It's quite
literally true that money can't buy it. Daniel Kahneman (yep, him again) and
colleagues asked people a couple of questions:[4]

1. How happy are you with your life in general?
2. How many dates did you go on last month?

Depending on the order you ask these questions you get different results. If you ask someone the first question first then there's absolutely no
link with the second one. Ask them the other way around, however, and
suddenly a person's happiness becomes inextricably linked with their dating
success.

This issue is known as the focusing illusion and it's a framing problem—putting people in different frames of mind will cause them to behave
differently. Of course, when studies are conducted about the links between
happiness and money this will tend to draw people's attention to the positive benefits that money may bring and triggers the illusion, which means
that they fail to attend to the negative side of things—longer working hours,
greater stress, the misery associated with seeing your stocks falling, and
so on.

The point is, of course, that money is not the be all and end all of everything. If the only reason you're investing is to make more money this will
expose you to all of the issues associated with the behavioral biases that
money triggers. I've come to believe that we should focus instead on the
benefits that money brings—security, more time to do the things we want
to, less stress.

So part of the purpose of all this investing psychology is to be able to
stand back and take the broader view. After all, we only get one life, and we
really ought to make the most of it.

LESSON 1

We should invest to make money in order to do the things that we really value. If all we do is invest to make money we're missing the point. Money is the means to an end, not an end in itself.

MYTH 2: EVERYONE CAN BE A GOOD INVESTOR

Regardless of all of the research on methods of combating behavioral bias there's one thing that stands out when you take a broad view—people who exhibit better self-control tend to be better investors. They're less inclined to react to events, more inclined to stick with their strategy, more disciplined, less emotional, and ultimately more wealthy.

Consider the following bargain: if you give up your favorite treat for a month you can double your monthly salary—forever. Would you make this deal? Of course you would, or so you'd think, but research by Bindu Ananth, Dean Karlan, and Sendhil Mullainathan on fruit sellers in India shows that they are unable to make this particular choice—instead of giving up the equivalent of two cups a tea a day for a month they borrow money to finance their working capital.[5]

This problem isn't exclusive to poor people, because the issue is with us all: we're all bad at resisting so-called temptation goods, only what those goods are varies from place to place. Unfortunately it seems that some of us never become any good at it—and the ability to resist temptation, to exert self-control, and to manage our lives better is critical if we want to be good investors. If you can't control your urges then you'd be better off letting someone else manage your money.

So think of this book as one long argument in favor of self-control. Virtually every problem I've mentioned can be ameliorated to some extent if you can control your urges and keep your emotions in check, while being unable to do so at all will simply mean I've been wasting my breath.

LESSON 2

The key to investing success and, indeed, to success in most walks of life is self-control. Without some, nothing I can do or say will make you a successful investor because you'll always be falling prey to temptation.

MYTH 3: NUMBERS DON'T MATTER

I haven't dwelled on this much, but unfortunately one way of saving your-self from a world of bias-inflicted pain is to ensure you can do the basic math needed to do financial analysis. One piece of research discovered that only 11% of British people could figure out how much money they'd have at the end of two years if they were earning 10 percent interest a year.[6] Other nationalities weren't much better.

With such basic knowledge missing it's hardly surprising that many investors rely on gut feel and following other people in order to make their financial decisions. The truth is that very often they don't do the basic analysis because they can't do it, and are therefore more likely to be exposed to behavioral failings as a result.

Annamaria Lusardi has argued powerfully in favor of improving general math skills. We are increasingly left to fend for ourselves with defined con-tribution plans and Individual Retirement Accounts and financial numeracy is a key tool in making wise decisions.[7] So is an understanding of behavioral psychology, mind you, but I don't see many people arguing we should all become psychologists.

There is a corollary to this, however, which is that doing more analysis is likely to expose you to choice overload issues. Barry Schwartz argues that people who do lots of financial analysis tend to be trying to maximize, to make the best decision possible, rather than satisficing, and taking the best im-mediate deal on offer.[8] On the other hand, Schwartz also thinks that maximiz-ers make better decisions, but unfortunately they feel less good about them.

And, from personal observation, I think this is right and it's one reason why the methodology I suggest is focused on feedback—it's important to learn what matters and what doesn't. Although I've argued that the best way of learning is from the experience of others the truth is that it's the lessons we experience ourselves from which we learn best.

What I want, however, is to drain every single drop of knowledge from those experiences. All too often investors hide away from their errors rather than embracing them. So yes, you need to be sufficiently numerate to be able to do the basic analysis that's necessary—but you also need to be sufficiently self-aware and self-controlled to ensure that you don't try and take on too much detail.

LESSON 3

You cannot be a good investor without being financially numerate. How-ever, it's not enough on its own, because it can drive you into horrendous levels of detail. Learning what works and what doesn't is critical.

MYTH 4: FINANCIAL EDUCATION CAN MAKE YOU A GOOD INVESTOR

This is a simple idea: surely, as suggested in the previous section, a financial education would be a good thing, especially given the terrible levels of numeracy in our society. Well, in a democratic capitalist society it's generally believed that individuals should have the right to make their own decisions, unconstrained by rules and laws where they're not needed. But what if people are manifestly unable to make the right decisions? What if the range of behavioral biases we've identified are exploited by rapacious institutions eager to lay their hands on our dollars?

Well, of course, this is exactly what happens. Most Americans can't answer simple questions about finance such as whether buying a single stock is more or less risky than buying a single mutual fund.[9] Lauren Willis has researched this area extensively and she argues that most people stand very little chance of understanding financial products regardless of financial education because institutions are very, very good at exploiting their decision-making biases.[10]

The four main problems seem to be:

1. Information asymmetries—basically institutions exploit issues of choice overload and deliberately keep on creating ever more niche products, making it difficult for your average investor to keep up.
2. Lack of knowledge and skills—most people don't have the math or basic financial literacy required to do any kind of analysis on financial products.
3. An inability to debias—markets are by their nature places where behavioral bias runs rife and, even worse, financial education can lull people into a false sense of security—and overconfidence.
4. Inability to reach people at teachable moments—a teachable moment is a critical point in a person's financial development, like buying a house or a first stock, a point in time when they're likely to be especially receptive to education—these moments are when lifetime preferences are set and they're likely to be controlled by financial service firms.

While you can go out and learn the basic math skills needed for financial analysis it's rather harder to learn how to deal with these other kinds of issues. But the fact that you're reading this book is evidence that you're at a teachable moment, and there will be others ahead, moments when you need to revisit bits of it. Remember that every failure is an opportunity to get better. Just make sure you can recognize them when they happen.

LESSON 4

Don't fall prey to the problems exposed by the limitations of your basic financial education. Take steps to address each of the four possible issues, and be prepared to revisit the lessons from time to time. Getting the basics right is a lifetime's work.

MYTH 5: I WON'T PANIC

One of the books I'd recommend you read is *Manias, Panics, and Crashes*, by Charles Kindleberger, which discusses the history of financial panics.[11] Kindleberger was one of the first economic historians to point out that the lessons of history suggest that the theory of economics might be a bit wrong and that this might be, just possibly, because people don't behave entirely rationally.

Some more academic research reveals that Kindleberger's list is just the tip of the iceberg. Carmen Reinhart and Kenneth Rogoff have analyzed data from 800 years of financial records and have concluded that there's a banking crisis somewhere in the world every couple of years or so.[12] They argue that technology certainly hasn't improved this record and may even have made it worse—but that the delusional behavior of governments and investors is pretty stable over time.

The lesson from this is that there's a panic of some kind just around the corner. At the time of writing we're still recovering from the monster crisis of 2007 and 2008 and it's possible that the next few years will be a period of unusual stability as regulators and governments are unusually careful—although don't ever fool yourself about the myopia of investors, we're perfectly capable of forgetting about the last crisis almost as soon as a recovery is under way.

So, if you invest for more than a few years you will eventually find yourself adrift in a financial panic, all anchors lost, and with all advice obviously worthless. Until this has happened to you, you won't understand the feelings and emotions that will drive you—and if you're not prepared you will make some terrible decisions. You will panic, along with the rest of the herd.

These are the times when you need to understand what you're doing and to understand your history. Crises pass, but the human behavior in response to them doesn't—we hang on grimly until the pain is too great, we sell at the bottom, and then we sit on the sidelines as the market recovers.

If you're not ready for a crisis then when it hits you'll be in huge trouble. Read widely and think carefully, and always consider what the impact on your life would be if the value of your investment portfolio dropped by 20 percent. And then consider what the effect would be if it dropped by 50 percent. Invest long enough and you'll see the former happen a few times and you'll experience the latter at least once.

As an investor I want to sleep at night—I certainly don't want to spend my life worrying about some massive drawdown in the value of my portfolio. So be prepared: it will happen.

LESSON 5

No matter how much you think otherwise, when a mass market panic sets in—and it will, if you invest for long enough—you will panic unless you're prepared.

MYTH 6: DEBT DOESN'T MATTER

A big part of being prepared for the next panic, or indeed for pretty much any kind of market fluctuation, is avoiding debt. This is not an injunction to avoid taking out a mortgage, but I would strongly recommend against borrowing to invest in stocks. This is technically known as "gearing" and when it works in your favor it's great, but when it goes against you it can render you penniless very, very quickly.

It's a common issue for inexperienced investors in bull market conditions to use debt to buy stocks. While this works it's great, because it magnifies your gains but the problem is that when the markets drop suddenly you find yourself having to sell stocks to fund your debts. You're a forced seller in a falling market, so even if you've bought good firms you're still in a terrible position. Never get yourself in a situation where you have to react to the market's short-term madness: it exposes you to everyone else's psychological weaknesses, regardless of your own mental strengths.

Warren Buffett has compared loading up a company with debt to making someone drive with a dagger mounted on the steering wheel of their car.[13] You drive very carefully but any accident, even if it's not your fault, will be fatal. The same is true for us as individuals.

The point of investing is, surely, to sleep soundly at night. Exposing yourself to the slightest of potholes, and the maddest of our fellow drivers is sheer folly.

LESSON 6

Don't borrow money to invest.

MYTH 7: I CAN GET 7 PERCENT A YEAR FROM MARKETS

A lot of investors have unrealistic expectations about what kind of return they should expect. In part this is because it's a common belief that if you hold stocks for the long turn you will always make more money than if you invest in other types of assets. In fact, this seems to be true, and is a puzzle, because it suggests that shares are generally cheap, and we'd expect their price to rise until it cancels out this so-called equity premium.

The usual explanations for the equity premium puzzle center around the idea that stocks are riskier than bonds or other assets. All things being equal a riskier asset should offer you a greater return for taking the risk. But it isn't really clear that a portfolio of proper stocks is any riskier than bonds or gold or anything else.

The behavioral explanation for this puzzle is based on myopic loss aversion—many people are unwilling to accept losses for even very short periods, so sell too soon and give up the premium to other investors with longer horizons.[14] David Fielding and Livio Stracca go further and point the finger of suspicion at disappointment aversion, the feeling aroused when an outcome is less good than expected, regardless of buying price.[15]

Your expectation about how much money you can make is important because it should drive how much you invest in order to fund your retirement, or whatever it is you're saving for. So the common idea that shares return about 7 percent a year in total and about 5 percent a year more than bonds is an important one when it comes to shaping our plans.[16] Seven percent a year adds up to a considerable amount of money for just investing in stocks rather than bonds.

However, Robert Arnott and Peter Bernstein have recalculated these values and reckon the real premium for equities is about 2 percent.[17] The economists Elroy Dimson, Paul Marsh, and Mike Staunton reckon that it's a bit higher but nowhere near the previous estimates.[18] So, you should probably ignore the historical data and plan for an above inflation return of about 3 or 4 percent, which means you should also plan to invest a great deal more than advisers have historically suggested.

LESSON 7

Stocks do yield more than other investments, but not much and only over very long periods. Plan for about 3.5 percent a year, all things being equal.

MYTH 8: INFLATION DOESN'T MATTER

Money illusion is the behavioral trait that causes people to focus on how much money they have or earn rather than what they can buy with it. If you get a 2 percent pay raise and inflation is running at 1 percent, then you're better off. If you get a 10% pay raise and inflation is running at 12 percent, then you're worse off. Yet most people prefer the latter situation to the former.

Money illusion also explains why house prices are apparently more stable than stock prices—because people won't sell when prices fall unless they're absolutely forced to.[19] The point is that when we calculate returns we need to ensure that they're adjusted for inflation. If we're making 5 percent when inflation is running at 1 percent, that's a real 4 percent return (and a so-called nominal 5 percent).

This could also explain the equity premium puzzle: people usually think that increases in share prices include the excess returns that stocks offer over other types of investments—and systematically undervalue them. This is another form of money illusion, but one that we can use to our advantage if we treat stocks as long-term investments, rather than for the short term.

As always, price is what you pay, value is what you get. Buying a stock should be a long-term commitment, although only as long as the stock continues to meet its side of the bargain.

LESSON 8

Always adjust for inflation, but remember people don't always do this properly with stocks.

MYTH 9: EVERYONE HAS SOME GOOD INVESTING IDEAS, SOMETIME

The idea in this book is to try to improve your investing skills by giving you the knowledge to handle your behavioral biases. There are few of us who can't get better acquiring a bit more self-knowledge. However, it turns out that there are some people who simply never get better, no matter how much information you impart or how many hard lessons they experience. These people are too stupid to understand that they're stupid.

Justin Kruger and David Dunning's research has shown that there are a subset of people who are especially poor at assessing their own abilities.[20] These people aren't just normally overconfident: most of us overestimate our abilities by about 6 percent, people who suffer from the Dunning-Kruger effect do so by an extraordinary 60 percent.

This all has to do with the ability to assess people's competence. Unsurprisingly, given that people who suffer from Dunning-Kruger can't assess their own competence it's no shock that they can't identify people who are good at what they do. But, beware, in the investment arena these people are possessed of truly magnificent delusions about how good they are at picking stocks.

Unfortunately, as we've seen, we are particularly attracted to overconfident pundits. So remember that someone who is confident about their abilities but can't offer a public and verifiable record is probably unreliable, possibly delusional, and, quite likely, should be sitting in the stupid corner.

LESSON 9

Some people will never become better investors, but they don't understand this and come across as superconfident. Don't take people at face value, trust them only when they've established a track record and then only with great care.

MYTH 10: I DON'T NEED TO TRACK MY RESULTS

If there's one idea I hope I've gotten across it's that we need to track our results in order to know whether we're doing well or not. Over and above the actual research that shows that a lot of investors don't actually have a clue about whether they're making money relative to the markets or not, there's research that indicates our brains are hard-wired to ignore negative information.

As we saw earlier, the cognitive scientists Tali Sharot, Christoph Korn, and Raymond Dolan have demonstrated that we tend to ignore information that ought to reduce our optimism and take notice of that which reinforces it,[21] which basically is confirmation bias, our preference for evidence that supports our preexisting ideas and our tendency to discount equally valid disconfirming ideas.

The researchers suspect that favorimg of good news conveys some kind of evolutionary advantage—certainly a bias to pessimism seems to be linked with depression—which means its effect on investors is an accidental side effect. Of course, this doesn't matter—it just reinforces the point that none of us are smart enough to escape the legacy of our own brains.

In fact, there is a simple rule we can take from this. Always look for reasons to sell, because our brains will always find reasons to buy.

LESSON 10

Our brains are designed to make it impossible for us to analyze our results unaided. You must track your results; otherwise, you'll have no idea how well you're doing.

THE SEVEN KEY TAKEAWAYS

This chapter has looked at a few of the myths we tell ourselves about investing.

Let's just draw together a few key ideas from this chapter before we move on. The main takeaways are:

1. Know why you're investing: set goals, don't judge yourself against other people.
2. Money does not make us happy. We can do things with money that make us happy. Don't confuse these.
3. Make sure you have the math skills needed to analyze investments, but don't let yourself believe this is enough to become a good investor.
4. Markets crash all the time. Just because you haven't experienced a crash doesn't mean one won't happen. Prepare yourself.
5. When a crash happens debt is disastrous. Don't use it.
6. Make sure you take inflation into account when you plan your investment strategy. Don't expect to make much more than 3.5 percent without having excess skill. Most of us don't.
7. Track your results. Come on. Do it.

So, finally, let's summarize the findings.

NOTES

1. Shai Danziger, Jonathan Levav, and Liora Avnaim-Pesso, "Extraneous Factors in Judicial Decisions," *Proceedings of the National Academy of Sciences* 108, no. 17 (2011): 6889–6892.

2. Anastasiya Pocheptsova, On Amir, Ravi Dhar, and Roy Baumeister, "Deciding without Resources: Psychological Depletion and Choice in Context" (January 1, 2007). Available at http://ssrn.com/abstract=955427 or http://dx.doi.org/10.2139/ssrn.955427.

3. Joel Huber, John W. Payne, and Christopher Puto, "Adding Asymmetrically Dominated Alternatives: Violations of Regularity and the Similarity Hypothesis," *Journal of Consumer Research* (1982): 90–98.

4. Daniel Kahneman, Alan B. Krueger, David Schkade, Norbert Schwarz, and Arthur A. Stone, "Would You Be Happier if You Were Richer? A Focusing Illusion," *Science* 312, no. 5782 (2006): 1908–1910.

5. Bindu Ananth, Dean Karlan, and Sendhil Mullainathan, "Microentrepreneurs and Their Money: Three Anomalies," unpublished draft, 2007.

6. Annamaria Lusardi, "Numeracy, Financial Literacy, and Financial Decision-Making," NBER Working Paper No. 17821, 2012.

7. Ibid.

8. Barry Schwartz, "The Tyranny of Choice," *Scientific American Mind* (2004).

9. Annamaria Lusardi and Olivia S. Mitchell, "Financial Literacy and Planning: Implications for Retirement Wellbeing," NBER Working Paper No. 17078, 2011.

10. Lauren A. Willis, "Against Financial Literacy Education," *Iowa Law Review* 94 (2008); University of Pennsylvania Law School, Public Law Research Paper No. 08-10; Loyola-LA Legal Studies Paper No. 2008-13. Available at http://ssrn .com/abstract=1105384.

11. Charles P. Kindleberger and Robert Z. Aliber, *Manias, Panics, and Crashes: A History of Financial Crises* (New York: Palgrave Macmillan, 2011).

12. Carmen M. Reinhart and Kenneth S. Rogoff, "This Time is Different: A Panoramic View of Eight Centuries of Financial Crises," NBER Working Paper No. 13882, 2008.

13. www.tilsonfunds.com/BuffettNotreDame.pdf.

14. Shlomo Benartzi and Richard H. Thaler, "Myopic Loss Aversion and the Equity Premium Puzzle," *Quarterly Journal of Economics* 110, no. 1 (1995): 73–92.

15. David Fielding and Livio Stracca, "Myopic Loss Aversion, Disappointment Aversion, and the Equity Premium Puzzle," *Journal of Economic Behavior & Organization* 64, no. 2 (2007): 250–268.

16. Ibbotson Associates, "Stocks, Bonds, Bills, and Inflation," 2000 Yearbook. Chicago: Ibbotson Associates.

17. Robert D. Arnott and Peter L. Bernstein, "What Risk Premium Is 'Normal'?" (January 10, 2002). Available at http://ssrn.com/abstract=296854 or http:// dx.doi.org/10.2139/ssrn.296854.

18. Elroy Dimson, Paul Marsh, and Mike Staunton, "Global Evidence on the Equity Risk Premium," *Journal of Applied Corporate Finance* 15, no. 4 (2003): 27–38.

19. Markus K. Brunnermeier and Christian Julliard, "Money Illusion and Housing Frenzies," *Review of Financial Studies* 21, no. 1 (2008): 135–180.

20. Justin Kruger and David Dunning, "Unskilled and Unaware of It: How Difficulties in Recognizing One's Own Incompetence Lead to Inflated Self-Assessments," *Journal of Personality and Social Psychology* 77, no. 6 (1999): 1121.

21. Tali Sharot, Christoph W. Korn, and Raymond J. Dolan, "How Unrealistic Optimism Is Maintained in the Face of Reality," *Nature Neuroscience* 14, no. 11 (2011): 1475–1479.

CHAPTER 9

The Final Roundup

When you go to see a top-class conjuror at work, pulling rabbits from hats and silk handkerchiefs out of the ears and other parts of their scantily clad assistants, hopefully you don't believe that what you're looking at is really magic. You know that what you're watching is a highly skilled act of misdirection, which you're happy to pay for in order to get the privilege of seeing a professional entertainer at the top of his or her game, deliberately setting out to fool your brain, for your own amusement.

Often the magicians are using something called joint attention to fool us. Joint attention is essential to human society because it causes us to focus our attention on the same thing, which is a useful attribute for a social creature if you want to hold a conversation about an object or engage in joint activities. You can demonstrate joint attention simply by standing on the sidewalk and staring up in the air at a random point on a building: if people aren't too busy and distracted by other things they'll start looking in the same direction, trying to figure out what you're looking at. Don't try this in New York, though; you'll probably get flattened.

Magicians use both their gaze and their body language to direct our attention to one aspect of their performance, while the actual trick is going on somewhere else. And even though I know this I still find it incredibly hard to not look where they want me to. Joint attention is automatic and incredibly powerful, for the very good reason that without it human society would fall apart. It's one of a vast range of similar, largely unconscious, behaviors, some of which we've discussed and most of which are far, far harder to demonstrate, but no less easy to overcome.

Well, as we've seen, the same tricks that magicians use to puzzle and delight us are often used for more malicious purposes; to part us from our hard earned cash against our will. It's a nasty fact of life that almost the entirety of the inaptly named investment industry is a gigantic machine designed to separate us from our money, while keeping us in a state of vague happiness about the entire embezzlement.

The really cruel twist is that the perpetrators of this crime do so perfectly legally, because they're particularly clever practitioners of the art of compliance. They use our own brains against us, to make us willing participants in a process that sees billions of dollars transferred from the pockets of hard-working people to the coffers of some of the wealthiest corporations and individuals in the world. Accurate estimates of the value of this transfer are hard to come by, but almost certainly run into billions of dollars each year: as we discussed earlier, maybe as much as $170 billion[1] per year in the United States alone.

What's quite remarkable about this is that even people who fully understand these issues, and exactly how difficult they are to overcome, appear to ignore their own knowledge when it comes to investing. One study of finance professors found that their beliefs about the way that stock markets worked were "almost entirely unrelated to their trading behavior."[2] And these are the experts who tell the rest of us how to behave.

This book has been about how this happens, why we accept it, and what we can do to stop it. It is an investing self-help book, but I hope you agree that it's one of a rather unusual kind. I don't promise to make you rich—I have a much lower but much more realistic aim: to help you avoid making yourself poor. All things being equal, if you can avoid impoverishing yourself you'll end up reasonably wealthy.

Our journey has shown you things about yourself that you've probably found hard to believe. This is one of the cruel tricks our brains play on us—it leads us to believe that when we're unsuccessful we're unlucky, but when others fail it's because they're stupid. In fact they're not stupid, but neither are you unlucky—we're all victims of the unusual suspect at the heart of this conspiracy—our own brains.

Of course, if what I've told you was believable to start with then we wouldn't make the mistakes we do, and I've made most of the mistakes in this book, at one time or another. More frighteningly, despite knowing about all the stuff I write about I still make the same mistakes from time to time. We're dealing with the complexities of human nature, and it's hard to change.

Of course, if I was any good at investing I wouldn't be writing a book about it, would I? No, I would be practicing my ideas in secret, making money by exploiting my unique insights. If you think about this rationally, no one who has a working method of investing would ever write about it.

Fortunately, I don't have to deal with that question, because I don't have a great new way of investing to peddle. What I actually have is a very long list of things that I wouldn't do again. I've discovered that there's science behind my list, the emerging science of behavioral finance. Virtually every stupid thing I've ever done can be traced back to a behavioral bias, an unconscious psychological trait that makes me—and you—do highly irrational things that cost us money without even realizing it. And a whole industry has grown up to exploit these biases, and us.

Behavioral finance is the study of human psychology in the sphere of finance and its findings are telling us remarkable things about the ways in which you and I behave—and misbehave—when money is involved. We think we behave rationally and calmly and make objective judgments but what the evidence shows is that we don't. In fact, we behave like the social creatures we are, driven by forces about which we have little understanding and over which we have little control.

So, even though we ought to know that investing self-help books are a scam we still buy them by the millions. I have a bunch of them on one of my bookshelves, glowering at me as I write. And they're extremely convincing, advancing clever ideas and backing them up with powerful evidence to show that they're correct. Unfortunately they're nearly all based on that clever little piece of magical misdirection—the Texan Sharpshooter Effect. This, unfortunately, is what most investment gurus do—they find evidence that supports whatever point they want to make and then present it to "prove" their ideas.

The Texan Sharphooter Effect, like many such behaviors, is based on the underlying preference of our brains to look only at the information we can easily bring to mind, to that which is readily available. When you see a target with a bunch of closely grouped bullet holes we assume that someone who is a really good shot has been practicing their skill, and we find it very, very difficult to imagine an alternative situation.

It's quite easy to find a few good examples of any idea and then present them as though they're strong evidence. By and large, anecdotes aren't evidence, yet we're very attracted by stories, by individual examples, and so we find it difficult to disregard them. All too often we're swayed by our own personal experience—so we invest in things we're aware of, even though this is often exactly the wrong thing to do. This is due to the problem of availability, where what we decide to do comes down to whatever we can bring to mind.

What I've tried to demonstrate is that the truth is usually revealed by careful studies and by lots of statistical analysis rather than by plausible narratives. We're badly designed when it comes to understanding stats, so we generally prefer to rely on experts who feed us stories; usually the ones that they think we want to hear. Of course, I've tried not to bore you with all the stats, you can read data tables in your own time if you want, but I hope you'll at least check a couple of the better and more readable studies I've mentioned because otherwise you're just relying on my expertise.

I've also tried, in the jargon, to make this book actionable—to provide you with a set of rules and takeaways that you can use to put the ideas in the book into effect. And here, for the last time, I want to summarize the major points. If you take nothing else away from this book take these. Print them and stick them above your computer and read them before you trade:

1. We **all** suffer from behavioral bias. Believing that you don't is a manifestation of blind spot bias, but even knowing this won't help. Work on the assumption you're biased and try and recalibrate—aim a little higher than you think you need to.
2. Don't trade when you're emotional, tired, or hungry. Whether it's because of panic in a market downturn, a long day at the office, or another screaming match with the teenagers all of these things affect our propensity for risk taking.
3. Don't compete with institutions. They have deep pockets and clever people and will exploit your short-term biases. But they are incentivized to the short-term and we don't need to be—although they'll try to encourage you to take them on in their own backyard.
4. Don't trust expert or inexpert opinion without evidence. Whether it's a talking head on CNN or a confident tweeter the only money you put at risk is your own. Seek out evidence, either that their ideas are right or that they have an above average record. Very few people do, and the ones that do usually don't advertise.
5. Always seek to disconfirm any idea you might have. We tend to fall in love with our ideas and try to find people who agree with us. Always invert any investing idea you might have and try and see the possible downsides. If you can't see any you aren't looking hard enough.
6. Force yourself to generate feedback regularly. Unless you suffer from Dunning-Kruger this will improve your investing results markedly over a couple of years. Just remember that today's market conditions and tomorrow's may be different and what works today won't always work tomorrow. You need a meta-method, not a Texan and a rifle and a pot of paint.
7. Track your results. Do it. It makes sense.

Good luck, and let me know how you do on my website, www.psyfitec .com. This is not the end, but the beginning of a journey that will last as long as you invest. Together, we can better figure out how we can overcome the enemy within—our own brains.

NOTES

1. One study in Taiwan suggests that overtrading cost individual investors $6.4 billion a year during 1995 to 1999, equivalent to about 3.8 percent a year

and a staggering 2.2 percent of Taiwanese GDP. The same researchers suggest that U.S. investors have lower costs of about 2 percent a year, which, if we (inaccurately) extrapolate from the U.S. Census data of individual U.S. household equity holdings of $8,514 billion (www.census.gov/compendia/statab/cats/banking_finance_insurance/stocks_and_bonds_equity_ownership.html), would imply a stunning $170 billion in excess costs in 2012 *alone*, equivalent to about 1.1 percent of U.S GDP. It's not possible to say whether this is an overestimate or an underestimate, but it indicates the sheer scale of the potential bezzle. See Brad M. Barber, Yi-Tsung Lee, Yu-Jane Liu, and Terrance Odean, "Just How Much Do Individual Investors Lose By Trading?" *Review of Financial Studies* 22, no. 2 (2009): 609–632.

2. James S. Doran, David R. Peterson, and Colbrin Wright, "Confidence, Opinions of Market Efficiency, and Investment Behavior of Finance Professors," *Journal of Financial Markets* 13, no. 1 (2010): 174–195.

About the Companion Website

This book includes a companion website, which can be found at www .wiley.com/go/investpsych. The website includes a set of worksheets and guidance for the following toolkits:

Behavioral Investing Toolkit 1: Mission Statement
Behavioral Investing Toolkit 2: Investment Thesis
Behavioral Investing Toolkit 3: Investing Checklist
Behavioral Investing Toolkit 4: Feedback
Behavioral Investing Toolkit 5: Diarize Reviews
Behavioral Investing Toolkit 6: Autopsy
Behavioral Investing Toolkit 7: Update

The website also includes a spreadsheet that extracts the main lessons from the book. To access the site, go to www.wiley.com/go/investpsych (password: behavioral).

About the Author

TIM RICHARDS is a polymathic student of the investing sciences; originally a physicist, later a computer system designer involved in technology that will be in most readers' pockets and purses (mobile phones and chip-based credit cards), then a psychologist and always an investor, Tim has spent years analyzing the weird and wonderful behavior of investors, fund managers, securities analysts, and all of the associated members of the global investing community.

Tim is the creator of the behavioral finance-based website, The Psy-Fi Blog, where he brings his wide-ranging experience and wryly cynical world view to bear on the weird and wonderful world of finance. The Psy-Fi Blog offers a unique insight into the application of behavioral finance, through reference to a growing body of research that shows conclusively that we are not as smart as we think we are. By linking behavioral finance research to real-world events and showing their connections to other areas of knowledge, Tim constantly aims to remind us that the only proper way of living is to seek knowledge beyond our comfort zones.

Tim lives in the United Kingdom with a scruffy dog and a rotating group of daughters, who take turns attempting to look after him. He's still alive, so he reckons they're doing a pretty good job under the circumstances.

Index

Abductions, child, 20, 34–35
Accruals, 89–90, 91, 205
Adaptive Markets Hypothesis, 80, 90
Adverse selection, 120
Advice, challenging, 205, 224
Affect heuristic, 56–58, 101–102, 178–179
Age, 82–83
Airely, Dan, 47, 107
Akerlof, George, 105, 120, 149, 150
Aknin, Lara, 125
Alter, Adam, 74
Altruism, 141–142
Amabile, Teresa, 44
Amir, On, 209
Ananth, Bindu, 211
Anchoring, 46–48, 147
Anecdotal evidence, 19, 58, 223
Anginer, Deniz, 178
Annual autopsies, 200
Annual reports, 159–160
Anomalies, 89–92, 177
Arkes, Hal, 177
Armstrong, J. Scott, 139
Arnott, Rob, 216
Asch, Solomon, 99–100
ASOS (Internet retailer), 64
Aspara, Jaakko, 178–179
Asymmetric, differential price discovery, 135
Asymmetry, information, 120, 121, 213
Attention, 27–28, 221
Authority, deferral to, 39–40, 44, 51–52
Autism, 58, 116
Automated trading, 89, 93–94, 134–135, 174
Autopsies, 199–200
Availability:
  anchoring and, 48
  cognitive repair for, 181, 202
  hot-hands effect and, 24–25
  noise traders and, 79

  problems caused by, 223
  recency effect and, 21–23
  representative heuristic and, 31–32
  salience and, 19–21
Avnaim-Pesso, Liora, 209

Babe Ruth effect, 54, 81
Backfill bias, 132
Backfire effect, 49, 102
Baker, Michael, 143
Balance sheet, 160
Bandura, Albert, 107
Bangladeshi butter production, 91
Barber, Brad, 41, 55–56, 78, 140, 151
Bargh, John, 30
Barnum, P.T., 11
Barnum effect, 10–12
Baron-Cohen, Simon, 116
Base rate neglect, 31–32, 162
Baumeister, Roy F., 209
Beauty contest investing, 117, 123
Beauty effect, 44
Beauty premium, 70–71
Behavioral Investing Framework, 192–201
  about, 192–193
  autopsies, 199–200
  checklist, 195–196
  feedback, 198–199
  investment thesis, 196–197
  personal investing mission statement, 193–195
  reviews, scheduling, 197–198
  updating adaptively, 200–201
Behavioral portfolios, 110–112
Bénabou, Roland, 101
Bergstresser, Daniel, 107, 146
Bernstein, Peter, 216
Bernstein, William, 166
Beunz, Daniel, 115
Bhattacharya, Debarati, 161

231